Since studying journalism at RMIT in Melbourne, Kathryn Bonella has worked as a journalist in television and print. She moved to London eighteen months after graduating and freelanced for *60 Minutes* and various English and American TV shows, newspapers and magazines. Kathryn returned to Sydney in 2000 to work as a full-time producer for *60 Minutes*. In 2005 she moved to Bali to co-write with Schapelle Corby the number-one bestseller, *Schapelle Corby – My Story*. Kathryn followed up with her two international bestsellers: *Hotel K* and, most recently, *Snowing in Bali*.

www.kathrynbonella.com

Also by Kathryn Bonella

Schapelle Corby – My Story
Hotel K
Snowing in Bali

OPERATION PLAYBOY

KATHRYN BONELLA

Quercus

First published in 2017 by Pan Macmillan Australia.
This edition published in the United Kingdom in 2018 by

Quercus Editions Ltd
Carmelite House
50 Victoria Embankment
London EC4Y 0DZ

An Hachette UK company

UK PB ISBN 978 1 78747 696 7
Export PB ISBN 978 1 78747 823 7
Ebook ISBN 978 1 78747 695 0

10 9 8 7 6 5 4 3 2 1

Typeset in 12.5/16 Janson MT by Midland Typesetters, Australia

Printed and bound in Great Britain by Clays Ltd, Elcograf S.p.A.

To anyone who ever takes an international flight . . .
you just never know who is sitting next to you.

CONTENTS

AUTHOR'S NOTE

Because of the nature of the revelations contained in this book, some names have been changed in order to protect the identities of the people involved. This includes instances when they are referred to in quoted media articles. All phone numbers and email addresses have also been changed.

FOREWORD

There is something compelling about the story of a good-looking, smart, educated and sophisticated guy with gorgeous girlfriends, who speaks several languages, reads philosophy, is incredibly articulate – and chooses to become a drug lord. I'm describing one of the main 'characters', Jorge, but the portrait fits most of those in *Operation Playboy*. They are far from the cliché mafia bosses or South American gangsters, although they have to constantly deal with those types to run their drugs business.

These playboys created a vast network in Brazil and became a major drugs link between Indonesia, South America and Holland. They moved cocaine from Colombia, Bolivia, Peru and Paraguay through Brazil and across to Amsterdam, the Wall Street of drugs, sold it, and reinvested in top quality marijuana and ecstasy pills to send back to South America or Bali. Or they sent cocaine directly to Bali. Either way, they became very rich.

After writing *Snowing in Bali*, where some playboys were featured, I felt there was more to tell, a deeper and broader look at this drugs business. By telling the story of Operation Playboy, I could trace this network's reach across the globe. This expansive geography is one major point of difference to *Snowing in Bali* – the other is that this story is told from both sides of the law, following the police hunt for a specific group of playboys.

The police I interviewed are just as impassioned as the playboys, particularly Chief Fernando Caieron, a federal cop based on the

1

little island of Florianópolis in south Brazil. He was introduced briefly in *Snowing in Bali*, but he had his own story to tell. He dedicated literally dozens and dozens of hours to interviews with me during my trips to Brazil. We talked everywhere, from Florianópolis police headquarters, to coffee shops, and even while he was getting a haircut. He is a busy cop, but he found time because this story is just as much his as it is the playboys'. Operation Playboy was Chief Caieron's baby: he set his sights on catching these playboys and wanted to make his mark on the world.

He outlined the way it worked. It started with surfers carrying top quality weed – skunk – and ecstasy from Amsterdam back home to Brazil. Those carrying the drugs would promote themselves to bosses, and then hire others to carry the drugs. They were multiplying, more and more and more people were trafficking drugs. Soon, it was both ways – cocaine out and grass and pills back. Caieron called it a cancer and had a master plan to cure it or, at the very least, put it in remission.

As a journalist, I've always had a passion for human stories, and one of the questions that endlessly intrigues me is why do these people do it when they could do virtually anything with their lives? They take this risk, gamble life and limb, literally in Indonesia, when they don't need to.

There's the blatantly obvious lure of cash, a lottery win every couple of weeks. It's not hard to understand that drawcard and the lavish and glamorous lifestyle it affords, or the freedom to indulge any whim – the ability to jump on a plane and go where you want, when you want. One of the bosses described it like this:

It's like, 'Hey, let's go to Courchevel in France to snowboard,' or 'Let's go skiing at Lake Tahoe, or Mentawai to surf.' 'Okay, let's go.' I surf, snowboard, surf, snowboard, surf, party. We have a lot of fun.

They do not want to live ordinary lives. They find the ball and chain of routine terrifying, being stuck in a humdrum job and tied to a desk, going around on a hamster wheel, is their idea of sheer hell.

I was interviewing one of the playboys in a jail courtyard when he looked up at a tall office block visible over the jail wall. 'That's prison,' he said. He felt sure he was freer than the people who slogged at jobs they probably hated to pay the rent or mortgage.

But it's more than just the cash, and the subsequent freedom, glamour and hedonistic whims. The thrill of the game gets into their blood. Most of these playboys are thrill seekers anyway. They love to surf monster waves and fly across the skies in hang-gliders or paragliders. Living on the edge, but not tipping over it, is soon as addictive as the drugs they deal. Trafficking is their ultimate rush.

One described it as 'better than an orgasm'. Another said the sensation of getting through an airport with a bag of drugs was '. . . like making a score in a stadium full of people calling your name'. And another said, 'It's a gamble, and when you gamble, you know you can lose or you can win, but you can't stop.'

Fernando Caieron spent years watching these guys and came to understand their motivation:

> There is a danger in this kind of activity, they are always on the edge, always at the limit trying to be aware of everything because one mistake and it's all gone, everything can be lost in one second: it's heaven to hell in one second. There's always adrenalin, always a rush, and this makes you feel more alive, like they are truly living their life. And if you don't take any risk, you don't balance anything, it's like, you see, plateau. So, these guys really push to the limit.

Fernando Caieron understood first-hand that sense of rush. During our interviews, he often got goose bumps reliving arrests or telling of a moment a snitch spilled a crucial bit of information. This was how he felt after one big bust: 'It's insane, it's insane the things you feel, it's hard to put in words how excited, the kind of emotion, you are 200 percent satisfied. I mean, you are completely satisfied, completely. It's an overdose of excitement.'

Fernando Caieron put his heart and soul into Operation Playboy and is proud of what was achieved.

In talking about specific playboys, he opened up the playing field and the players to me. Some of those people he talked about, I knew already, while others I decided to try to track down and interview. I wanted to hear their side of the story.

I found playboys through my contacts from *Snowing in Bali* and *Hotel Kerobokan* and by investigation. I tracked down one of the main players to Europe, where he was facing a drugs charge. I had a single day to ask for an interview, as the jails do not allow visits unless the prisoner agrees. It was unlikely he'd accept a visit from a complete stranger, so I decided to take a gamble. I flew to Europe and went to his one day in court. He was a major player in Operation Playboy, and someone Chief Caieron talked about a lot. I knew he could help bring the story to life.

The day of the court case, I went with a translator and sat near some local journalists at the back. A court reporter saw me using my phone to record, which she was doing too, but I hadn't got permission. She had a message passed to the judge and I was called up to the front of the court. The judge told me not to record. When I turned back around, all eyes were on me. As I walked towards my seat, I looked straight at the playboy sitting in the dock and smiled. He instinctively smiled back, but I saw his confusion. The snitching local reporter had done me a big favour. We were all sitting behind the dock and I'd been wondering how to catch his attention. Suddenly, that wasn't a problem anymore.

At the end of the short hearing, between the court and the cell, I was able to grab a very quick word with him. Fortunately, he'd read *Hotel Kerobokan*. He agreed to see me. If I put in the requisite written request for a visit to the jail, he'd approve it. Then he was gone, whisked off by police.

It typically took three weeks for the request to pass through all the red tape. I waited, hoping he didn't change his mind. He didn't. It was granted. I started going to the jail and speaking through the glass on an intercom phone to this guy. It was amazing. He was more than happy to talk. I also gave him a copy of *Snowing in Bali* to read. Since then, we've been in close contact. He was one of the most fascinating playboys, and became one of my best sources.

All the main players I approached agreed to talk to me for this book. It's a secretive world and it was only thanks to their interviews that I was able to piece together the full narrative of Operation Playboy from both sides.

People often asked me after *Snowing in Bali* why the drug dealers talk on the record. I think sometimes they're not even sure why they're telling their story. For some, there is no doubt it's a cathartic process. It's a secret world and they harbour incredible stories of intrigue and excitement that they've never told anyone before. So as they start talking, it comes out with passion, their eyes sparkle with excitement or flash with pain as emotions overcome them. I've always felt it is a privilege being a journalist and able to ask questions not even their closest family ask. For some, there's also guilt. As I got to know these playboys over several years and during the series of rolling interviews, they each opened up more and more. One of the main characters teared up several times as he told his story for the first time.

> *Every time we talk about this, my heart rate goes higher; excitement, regret, all the things I went through. It brings me some emotion, every time it brings me a different energy – every time I leave here, there is a weird energy around me.*
>
> *I remember when I had that conversation with you last year. When you left, I ask, dude why am I doing this? I don't know – for some reason, I feel that I have to tell you this.*

It was also helpful that I'd written *Snowing in Bali*. Some of those I interviewed for that book, like Rafael, I re-interviewed for this one. For another main playboy, he read *Snowing in Bali*, knew the 'characters', intimately knew the game, and felt the book was a very accurate portrayal. It helped him to trust me with his story.

> *I'm telling you, that's a brilliant book. It's like wow, the story, the context, it's incredible how you can put it all together and make the story so real – even for me. I mean, I'm inside the story and know the details and stuff – and well, you really live that, you really observed the energy, it's incredible, I really, really, like it. For me, was very important for me to read this book.*

He shared it around the jail.

> *People really like the book. They got into the story and they come to me and talk, and you can see that they get very excited. The stories that for me seem quite normal, for other people it's like wow, something amazing. They accept and they really like the book . . . cos I have a*

friend of mine, a Jewish guy, he is a serious gangster, and he really
likes the book. Every day, he wants to talk to me about the book and
the stories.

Getting stories for this book and putting all the pieces of the
jigsaw puzzle together has been a fascinating ride, from finding
the playboys and introducing myself, and flying several times
across the globe and back, to Brazil, Europe and Bali.

I spent hours and hours talking on the phone to the guy in
the European jail. He was so committed to our interviews that
he got a phone, about half the size of a cigarette lighter, and
hired a guy to hide it for him – up his butt.

I hired an arse. I'm renting an arse every week to hold it for me.
Two days a week we cannot even take it out of his arse because there's
a shift with two guards who are completely obsessed to catch us. They
know we have a phone but they can't really figure it out. Every week
when they come, they search us, strip us naked. So, when they are in
charge, we can't touch this phone. We keep two days really low profile.
He even goes to the gym with this thing in his arse. He plays football
with it. I was joking with him that he seems even happier – I think he
likes it. I told him, when you get this, you smile more and more happy.
It stinks a little bit sometimes ... but what can I do?

Some days when we spoke, the guards suddenly opened his cell
door, and he'd cut the call, then phone back, telling me what
happened.

They just opened the door by mistake. I think, 'Whoa, what the fuck!'
It's a big crime in this country to have a telephone in jail, so it's a bit
of adrenalin when they open my fucking door. It's never 100 percent safe,

I'm taking a risk, but I think it's for a good cause – good reason, so I don't give a fuck if they put me in isolation for 30 days – I don't give a fuck really. But yeah, just a bit of adrenalin. Kathryn, listen, just to let you know I'm on this project.

Sometimes the calls were brief because the phone wasn't properly charged, due to diligent guards on duty or, one night, because the guy in the next cell had overdosed. It was a reminder of exactly where this person was talking from: speaking about his dazzling jet-set former life from a hell.

And I guess that's also the point. I don't condone what drug traffickers do. I paint a picture of the hedonistic, fascinating lives, but also of how it can all end so tragically, so dark and so far from what had inspired it.

I find this story intriguing. Drug trafficking is not a niche business, it's pervasive and all around us, but invisible. Unless there's a bust – or a book.

CHAPTER ONE
SNOWING IN IBIZA

Jorge stepped out of his shiny black Hummer looking like a rock star, in black Prada boots, a white Gucci shirt, gold Bulgari rings dazzling on his fingers, and a Rolex strapped to his wrist.

A string of sexy girls slipped out behind him, his birthday party guests, with more hopping out of his Porsche Cayenne. Taking his Finnish go-go dancer girl by the hand, he walked towards the front door of Amnesia – Ibiza's hottest club. Tonight, Jorge had hired a VIP area. With bottles of French champagne and bags of blow, he was ready to party until sunrise.

Once settled, he unclasped a gold chain from around his neck and slipped off a bronze fingernail, as long as a witch's talon. He dug it into the bag he'd pulled from his pocket. He sniffed. Then, again and again, he scooped a pile onto it and put it under the girls' noses, giving them all a sniff of the shimmering Bolivian blow. It was expensive on the Spanish party island, but not for Jorge. He had kilos of it at his nearby penthouse.

With his long blond hair loosely tied back in a ponytail, his casual charisma, intelligence and wit, Jorge was hot, and the girls loved him all the more for what was in his pocket.

From his exclusive balcony seats, he could look across the pulsating sea of people dancing to electronic music, with lights strobing, and lasers scissoring high through floating dry-ice clouds.

More go-go dancing babes, who Jorge knew from Italy and France, as well as some guys, drifted into the VIP area. Despite blatant displays of cocaine and cash, he never admitted to being a drug dealer. So when a guy started hassling him for blow, Jorge handled him.

We were sniffing and drinking champagne, and then this guy starts pissing me off. He wanted to get some blow, and so I put this bag in front of him and say, 'You want to sniff?' 'No, I want to buy.' 'No, I'm not selling drugs. But you wanna sniff?' He says, 'Yeah,' so I take this nail, like a spoon, and put a mountain of blow on it, and put it under his nose and say, 'You wanna have a line – now sniff, man?', and he says, 'Nooo, it's too much.' We're sitting at the table with all these girls watching this scene. So, I stand up and say, 'You don't want it . . . ffffffffff . . .' and I blow – it's snowing, snowing . . . I was literally blowing thousands of euros into the air.

Sometimes at parties in a circle of girls dancing, everyone was asking me for blow to sniff. Many had it, but mine was the best. And I get so crazy on champagne and blow, that I just start to put mounds of blow on this nail, and ffffffff . . . 'Want to sniff, girls?' I just enjoy the faces of the people looking, they have open mouths, like shock, then look at each other – 'What is this fucking guy doing, this is not happening.'

Some people get down on the floor to try to get it . . . and I was so high that I was blowing fffff 500 euros each time, and people come

and say, 'Hey, can you sell me five grams or ten grams?', and I always
say, 'What the fuck are you talking about, I don't sell drugs, man, I just
use.' But everyone knew I was a dealer. I was going crazy; I was
playing very arrogant. All these pretty girls by my side all the time –
I was on top of the world in Ibiza.

– Jorge

Jorge was complex; an avid reader of philosophy books, funny, with a smile that lit up his face and one arm covered in tattoos. He was the son of a top Brazilian prosecutor, and an adoring mother who was a school principal and philosophy teacher on a little island, Florianópolis, in south Brazil. Jorge grew up there, surfing, smoking spliffs, and doing his homework at the back of his dad's law offices. He was tough, but gentle natured. A pacifist with loads of empathy, and as magnetic to women as the endless blow he showered on them.

Days after his birthday, Jorge flew to Amsterdam, his second home, a city as symbiotic to drug dealers as Vegas is to gamblers. After a deal he could party in prostitute paradise. He'd spent many long nights indulging his insatiable libido in the Red Light District.

It's like a paradise. I think there's no place on earth that I walk the
same blocks, the square metres so many times, and spend so much
money in one place.

– Jorge

As always, he was dressed like a catwalk model, draped in thousands of dollars' worth of designer clothes, exquisite bling and a spritz of Hermès cologne. Riding his Vespa into hooker heaven, he had no thoughts of his Finnish go-go dancer in Ibiza. He'd never been faithful. Being shackled to one woman, or a nine-to-five life, was his idea of hell.

'Fifty euros, suck and fuck,' the girls cooed from their windows.

Long ago, Jorge had learnt their tricks; tourists got nothing for their €50.

They don't fuck you, they fool you. The Red Light District is a game, if you don't know how to play, they rob you.

– Jorge

The hookers often procrastinated for the full 20 minutes, leaving an aroused client fumbling frantically for their wallets to get a happy ending.

Jorge started his Red Light ritual with a recce along the canals, over little bridges, eyeing off the girls, window shopping for colour, body shape, nationality, making a mental map of those cabins he'd be working his way through tonight. With an eye for beauty, he didn't miss the pretty moonlit reflections of ornate Dutch houses on the canals. Then he went to the Excalibur Pub to fire up his fantasies with cognac and coke.

At the Excalibur, I play games with my imagination. My plan tonight is to fuck one blonde, one brunette and a beautiful oriental girl I saw at the end of my first tour. I always have a line of coke because I want to get high to give wings to my imagination.

– Jorge

He loved this place; no chat-up lines, just open your wallet to open their legs. 'This place is like magic.' It was after 10 pm, when the top girls all worked, as that's when the window rents were the most expensive. Jorge's pockets were full of what he needed to cast the spell of sustained sex: a bag of cocaine, thousands of euros, and Viagra.

He started with a German. Her cabin was roomy, with a double bed, a mirror on the ceiling and sex toys scattered about. 'Fifty euros, suck and fuck,' she said, as he slipped her €150. She smiled; he got what he came for, then went into another cabin, and another, and another.

I've never had a problem with women, I've always got very beautiful women by my side, but there is something in prostitution, this power to just point your finger and say you, you, and you . . . I was free, I was in control of my life – at least in that fraction of time. I was happy.

– Jorge

After ten windows, he was sated.

I tipped the last girl another €100. I always wanted to be nice with these girls, I wanted to share with them my dirty money; they're brave, tough, and beautiful and live a quite different life as well. It's part of the chain of illegal business, split a slice of cake on the streets. I left the windows about 5.30 am, crazy out of my brain, but satisfied. I felt great.

Soon I would be back to the same ritual. I think my record there is 12 windows in one night, maybe more – I lost count. But now I needed a shower and my beautiful bed.

– Jorge

*

Jorge, like most of the cocaine bosses he knew, was in the game for the freedom and wild abandon it afforded. But his passion for hedonism was matched by the zeal of a police chief in Flori-anópolis – to bust the playboys.

Chief Fernando Caieron was the federal cop in charge of narcotics in the south of Brazil. He was smart and arrogant, with a ripped body from daily gym workouts and a pretty-boy face that masked brutal cunning. He would become Jorge's nemesis and the cop the playboys feared.

Caieron called his pursuit of them 'Operation Playboy'.

CHAPTER TWO

WALK IN THE PARK

YEARS EARLIER

'Thanks for calling Domino's Pizza, this is Jorge, how may I help you?'

Jorge's blue and red Domino's t-shirt, cap and shorts were a far cry from Gucci. 'Was a fucking ugly uniform.' As he shovelled salami onto pizzas, washed dishes, and zipped around San Diego in an old black Volvo, he sensed the world was his oyster. He worked hard, doing more hours than most despite being a Brazilian kid on a US tourist visa.

On his days off, he drove up to Las Vegas, or down to Mexico's border city Tijuana to party and surf; on weeks off he flew to Hawaii. After two years in San Diego, he transferred to Domino's in Waikiki to be close to some of the world's best waves. He took with him 1000 LSD tabs and some Mexican grass, to use and sell. He then twice smuggled grass between islands for a Brazilian surfer. He kept hearing the name Curumim, supposedly a charismatic guy from Rio, famous for his quality Dutch weed.

Jorge didn't meet him, or have any vague sense he would soon influence his entire life.

The waves were too tantalisingly close, rolling in as Jorge was stuck rolling out pizza dough.

> *I couldn't handle it. I was working in Waikiki, going back home to the north shore, and the guys would say, 'Ah, today you missed Pipeline.' I say, 'You know what, fuck delivering pizza, I'm going to surf and sell weed.' So, I quit Domino's.*

> – Jorge

But Hawaii was expensive, and selling grass wasn't lucrative for him, so he moved home to Brazil's surfing mecca island, Florianópolis. Dubbed the 'magic island', it was kissed with the exquisite natural beauty of 42 velvety beaches stretching along 53 kilometres of coast. Its bays sparkled like diamonds, scattered with the colourful sails of the boats on the water and gliders in the sky. Glossy travel magazines described it as a cross between Saint-Tropez and Ibiza. At night, it came to life with the world's top DJs playing at rave parties.

The picturesque little island was the capital of Santa Catarina, luring the richest from Brazil and Argentina to chopper in for the summer, and park their spare Ferraris and Lamborghinis outside their holiday mansions. With its wealth and Brazil's lowest crime rate – a very low bar given the country's massive murder figures – Florianópolis was considered a first-world part of Brazil, despite the slums – *favelas* – sprawling across the hills. Shacks were haphazardly banged up on steep, unstable land, as well as on prime real estate, hijacking some of the most majestic water views; glamour and abject poverty nestled side by side, a signature of Brazil.

Jorge grew up as one of the rich city kids who piled their boards into cars driven by parents or chauffeurs for the 30-minute daily ride to Joaquina, a beach they claimed as theirs. The water was full of these young city surfers, mostly from the island's top school, Colégio Catarinense. Surfers from other beaches were unwelcome. Localism was strong and fights for the waves could get nasty. Jorge had surfed across South America, and planned many more trips, so he wasn't into ocean ownership. But Joaquina uncovered his appetite for slamming down waves, and for danger, making adrenalin his oxygen.

It nicely nurtured him for a career that started so naturally.

While he'd been delivering pizza in America, some of his best friends had begun carrying Dutch weed to Brazil and Bali for Curumim – a name that instantly rang a bell for Jorge. His friends had met some of Curumim's friends from Rio on a beach in south Brazil. They'd shared some grass, chatted, and soon agreed to run drugs for him.

Jorge was enjoying life. After months back home, he was living with a gorgeous new girlfriend, Jéssica, studying business administration and surfing. But he was running up debts. Watching his friends blithely coming and going and making wads of cash, he was tempted to join them.

'How does it feel when you pass through customs?' he asked close friend Salami, one morning after a surf. 'Do you think it's possible for me to do it?'

'Yeah, bro, of course you can do it. You're perfect for that job. It'll be a walk in the park.'

But Jorge was conflicted. 'I had to choose, black or white. To stay or to embrace the world and carry bags.' It was against his upbringing. Jorge's father, a district attorney, was a straight man working in the endemically bent Brazilian judiciary who wanted his son to follow him into law. But Jorge was not a fan of nine-to-five conservatism, or close to his dad. 'He was a good father to me, but he was the authority, very straight, very cold, I didn't have this intimacy with him; I never said, "I love you Daddy".'

As a kid, Jorge had watched his parents fall out of love, and then acrimoniously divorce when he was 18. He didn't want their life. Instead, he chose to slash the shackles of expectation and chase his dreams.

Since I was a kid I was obsessed with adventure. When I discovered the perfect waves I could surf if I had money, I began to dream high. I started to feel that I would be very rich, and surf all the best spots on the planet; that life was much more than the reality I had.

So, I think that surfing was a bridge to get into this drug trafficking story . . . because surfing gave me the desire to go around the world, and smuggling was the bridge to get there. And, it was right then I chose to become a drug dealer.

– Jorge

He put the word out: he was for hire.

Was like boom, suddenly I was going to Amsterdam to get the bag.

– Jorge

'Smile!' Under falling snowflakes, Jorge stood smiling for a photo outside the tourist-filled pot café, The Bulldog, where he'd just smoked a joint. He was fresh-faced and happy, wearing a dark-blue overcoat he'd just bought at a Dutch market. He had been unprepared for such icy cold. Big House, also a trafficker from Florianópolis, had met him at Amsterdam's Schiphol airport, taken him on the train to The Bulldog and snapped his photo. Now, he was escorting Jorge to a cheap hotel, before taking him to meet the bosses.

Traipsing across Leidseplein, they left footprints in the snow. The hotel was behind the Marriott, a five-star establishment that would one day become one of Jorge's favourites. Today, he was ecstatic with three stars. Just being here was enough. After checking in and dumping his bags, they walked two blocks to the bosses' eighteenth-century attic headquarters.

Big House buzzed, then Jorge shadowed him up the four flights of grimy blue carpeted stairs. The three bosses, Curumim, Andre and Ryan, all looked over their new 'horse' – a term Curumim had coined for intelligent mules.

'Who the fuck is this? You hired a horse or a rock star, Andre?' Curumim rasped, drinking scotch, creating a baptism of fire for the new guy. 'Fuck, this is Axl Rose, he's not a horse.' Jorge was unfazed. Andre, who had to admit he did resemble Axl Rose, explained to Jorge that he'd be running in three days' time. Curumim settled down, especially when Jorge mentioned they had mutual friends in Hawaii, and that he spoke fluent English – a great asset for a horse.

For the next two days, Jorge played tourist. Despite niggling pre-run nerves, he soaked up the beautiful city, awed by its eclectic richness, dazzled by everything from the Gothic architecture to its Red Light windows where hookers sat waiting for customers. Just as alluring to him were the other windows, along P.C. Hooftstraat, Amsterdam's Rodeo Drive, full of designer clothes. Jorge was dreaming of the day he could afford to satisfy his lust for what was on display in both types of windows. 'I knew from this time that Amsterdam would be the city I most love in all the world.'

Then it was time to do what he'd come for. Leave.

Andre cycled from the attic to Jorge's three-star hotel with eight kilos of Dutch grass hidden inside a paraglider sail squashed into a backpack. He gave it to Jorge with some advice. 'Always stay in the airport shops until last call on your flight and if the police stop you –'

'They won't,' Jorge snapped. Andre just nodded. His new horse was a bit cocky, but confidence was key.

It served Jorge well. He breezed into São Paulo with no trace of angst before taking a domestic flight to Florianópolis. A friend, also a horse for Andre, picked him up and drove 90 minutes south to Garopaba, a fishing and surfing town.

Andre was waiting, having arrived home the day before. He congratulated Jorge then got to work unfurling the sail on the lawn, extracting the vacuum-sealed bags of grass. Sharing a celebratory joint on the balcony afterwards, Jorge soaked up the view, impressed. Andre's Bali-inspired beach house was surrounded by lush bush, with a swimming pool and top surf beach, Silveira, out front. This was expensive real estate, and just one part of Andre's empire, all built from drugs. Jorge couldn't wipe the smile from his face.

> *I was feeling this buzz, this energy around me that was the beginning of a new life, where money comes so easy and so fast. When I meet these people on my first visit to Amsterdam, and see they have the world in their hands – they live in Amsterdam, have this apartment, go to Hawaii, to Bali, they have money – I thought that's what I'm going to do, I'm going to be exactly like them. I realised that this was my destiny.*
>
> *– Jorge*

With cash in his pockets and a grin on his face, Jorge was excited about the future as he was driven back to Florianópolis. 'It was like a drug, I wanted to do it again, I needed to do it again.'

And, he did. He was quickly in a revolving door to Europe. Again and again, he flew to Amsterdam, met Curumim, and flew out with a bloated backpack. The heavier, the better. More weight equalled more money – and more risk. 'It was kind of suicide because you get paid by the kilos you carry. I was going to Holland and praying; "Oh my god, I hope they're going to put ten kilos on me, so I can get $10k." One time when Curumim put only four kilos in my bag I was devastated. Like, "Oh fucking hell, just $4000."'

Jorge strutted through airports with insouciant confidence. He always experienced the same pattern of emotions; pre-run days were jittery, but the second his hands clasped the bag, his fears magically vaporised.

It's like some spell comes over me, making me completely calm and sure of myself, as soon as I grab the bag. I just put myself in the character of the travel guy – I'm on holiday, I have money, I forget about the drugs. It's a weird feeling. But I always succeed, always pass through, never shaking, never sweating, completely calm. I was untouchable. I had attitude. I had this strange feeling of being protected.

– Jorge

Jorge thinks he is the image of Jesus; long hair and beard – like a Jesus but with tattoos – he loved his crazy visual. He thought, 'Nothing will happen with me, I have my shiny star over me.' That's his idea.

– Timi, fellow horse

Jorge became Curumim's rock-star horse, a prolific runner, always set to jet off to Amsterdam at a moment's notice. His perfect English and sharp brain made it easy to talk his way out of any hot spots. Just as Salami had predicted, drug trafficking was a 'walk in the park' for Jorge. Right up until it wasn't.

After flying into São Paulo airport, he stood waiting at the baggage carousel. Within minutes, the crowd vanished with their bags, and he stood there alone, empty-handed. He was still hoping to see his bag roll out when the luggage belt abruptly stopped. His mind started racing; where was his bag, did the cops find the drugs, were they watching him? He glanced around, trying to stay cool, then took a deep breath and walked across to the airline desk.

'My bag hasn't arrived,' he told the girl. She slid a form across the counter, and advised him to fill it in. They'd deliver it to him when it turned up. These were critical seconds; fight or flight, stay to get the bag or get the hell out fast. The grass was rolled up in a sleeping bag in his suitcase, an unsubtle style dubbed the 'anaconda'. Giving an address was a big risk. But he grabbed the pen, and wrote Mercure Hotel, near the airport. He had to. He couldn't let Curumim down.

That night he didn't sleep, and in the morning the airline called; they'd found his bag, but could he come to the airport for a customs check?

It was like fuck, fuck, fuck, fucking hell. I can't believe I have to go back to face that. But I was on a mission, I thought I have to at least try to get my bag, I can't give up in the middle. What are the bosses going to do – kill me? My mission is to bring the bag safe, so I have to keep on it. So, I went.

– Jorge

Jorge was taken through to meet a federal police officer airside, past customs and passport control, not feeling so cocky now.

'Come with me,' the cop commanded. Jorge followed, unsure whether he was walking into a trap, but it was too late to lose his nerve.

Even if I noticed that he was up to something, I was inside the international airport. You can't run, you can't go anywhere. So I have to act, pretend I just want my bags and see what's going to happen. I was really taking a big gamble.

– Jorge

The cop unlocked a door to a luggage room. 'You recognise yours?' he asked. Jorge spotted his suitcase among a chaotic collection of bags. He didn't know what to do. If he pointed to it, would that be it? Handcuffs, the end, before it had even really begun? He took a breath – had no choice, had to do it – pointed, 'Ah yeah, that one.'

I'm thinking, ah fucking hell, I'm fucked. I was shitting my pants. Then he says, 'Okay, you can pick it up and go.' He let me go. Can you believe that? I got in a taxi and I was like, 'Wow, I don't know how I passed that.' At the hotel, I went to the lobby and asked for a whisky to relax and enjoy the feeling. I was in the skies actually. After a finish like that, you just want to do it again. It's this feeling of being powerful, untouchable, I can fool even the federal police.

– Jorge

On his next run to Amsterdam, Curumim upped the ante. Jorge was offered a new game – Bali.

CHAPTER THREE

BALI

Jorge was strapped in for paradise with four kilos of grass and 15,000 ecstasy pills rolled up in a sleeping bag, anaconda style, inside his checked-in luggage.

After landing in Jakarta, he cleared customs and flew on to surfing mecca Bali, excited about hitting the waves. As he walked through Denpasar airport, the bags in his hands suddenly felt heavier. His mind was trying to absorb the words on the sign: 'death penalty to drug traffickers'. This was news to him.

> *Curumim pitched Bali to me like a heaven. I was like, 'Wow, it's one of my meccas, my dream places, it can't be more perfect. He never told me 'If they catch you, you're going to get the death penalty.'*
>
> – Jorge

He glanced around looking for cops, telling himself that his bags didn't contain enough drugs for the death penalty. Throwing off the unfamiliar sense of paranoia, he strode across the terminal and out into Bali's blinding sunlight, squinting as he looked for the scantily clad dream babe to emerge from the silhouettes of waiting people – just as Curumim had promised. But his only welcome party was a swarm of eager taxi drivers. One took him to the hotel where the 'dream babe' was waiting. The fantasy image in his head imploded.

> *She was this ugly fucking bitch – sorry to be so honest but she was a monster, horrible, a bad-looking girl. The kind of woman I don't like; very vulgar, behaves like a man, talks like a man.*
>
> – Jorge

'You are fucking crazy, bringing drugs here. You risked your life. This place is not a joke,' the woman, Barbara, belatedly warned him, despite regularly bringing bra-fuls of blow to Bali herself.

> *I was shocked that she was ugly, but she was nice to me. She showed me the island, and we became friends.*
>
> – Jorge

She seemed to know everyone and soon introduced Jorge to some of the drug dealers. Dimitrius the Greek from Rio, who Jorge had once met in the attic, was on the island and invited him to a casual lunch, where he met Bali blow boss Rafael. He was a guy from Rio with long blond hair, a beautiful face and six-pack abs visible through his tight white t-shirt. Seeing the diamond sparkling in his tooth and a Rolex on his wrist, Jorge sensed a kindred spirit. The feeling was mutual.

Rafael invited him for a surf the next day, and to lunch afterwards with his Swedish wife and kids at their new Canggu ocean front house, built on cash from a blow run to Sydney. Jorge's charisma and casual charm won them all over, helping to propel him into the inner circle.

One day I came back from the surf, and Rafael was having a BBQ at his house – was a lot of gangster guys and his wife. He took me to nice restaurants, like Ku De Ta. He opened himself up to me and we talked business right away, even though I was just a horse. I was accepted very fast, and it was the time Rafael was exploding, making a lot of money.

– Jorge

Jorge was staying at Bali Village in the tourist area, Legian, on Curumim's tab. The cluster of bungalows set in rustic gardens was dubbed 'Curumim's stables' because of the constant rotation of his horses. On this first trip, Jorge actually believed the place was Curumim's as he was always calling it 'my hotel', and kept a room permanently booked, full of surfboards and paragliders for trafficking.

Jorge's ten-day sojourn gave him a glimpse into the glamorous lives of Bali's drug bosses, the waves, babes and blow. It had also opened the door for him to work with Rafael, and help keep it snowing in Bali. Jorge now had stars in his eyes – the magical island had cast its spell.

I didn't want to leave Bali. I fell in love with the island. I saw the glamour and this was pushing me. I saw the way these people were controlling the island, how everyone wants to lick the balls of Rafael. It was the perfect trip.

– Jorge

Jorge flew out, with Bali silver chains draped around his neck and chunky silver rings on his fingers. He was sure he'd be back, not to carry drugs but to send horses. For now though, he was on his way to Amsterdam to grab a bag of skunk and pills to take back to Brazil for Curumim. On arrival that night, he sat in the attic smoking a joint with Curumim, and confronted him on airbrushing out that dark detail in his picture-perfect pitch.

'What the fuck, man? You sent me to a place with the death penalty. Are you crazy?'

Curumim, who often called himself Max – short for Maximum, a word he felt personified his personality – assured his rock-star horse that he had connections in Bali to resolve any problem. 'Axl, it's Max's island. Max would have arranged a deal for you. You'd only get four years, not the death penalty. You need to have lots of drugs, and cocaine, to be sentenced to death.'

'Yeah, whatever, man. I've done it now anyway,' Jorge shrugged.

I later figured out he was lying because the amount of drugs I was carrying was absolutely enough to be sentenced to death.

– Jorge

Neither of them had a clue how darkly ironic this conversation would one day become.

Days later, Jorge flew to Brazil with eight kilos of grass. He was looking forward to seeing Jéssica, unaware that she hadn't exactly been lonely in the weeks he was away.

Four weeks later, he was back in Amsterdam.

CHAPTER FOUR

THE ATTIC

For the playboys, the drugs game was the elixir of dreams, a dazzling lure to a fantasy life.

> *It becomes like a kind of a fashion in Florianópolis, to go to Holland or Bali, bringing drugs.*
> *Everyone wants to be a horse. And there were all these girls, like the girls who like musicians or football players, there was this group who like horses.*
>
> – Jorge

More Joaquina surfers were jumping on planes for the prizes – globetrotting, hot babes, hookers and cash: just carry a bag and your bounties will be boundless. Many ran for Curumim, who promised dreams, masterfully using his charismatic spiels to paint fantasies so horses could see, feel and taste the spoils of success. It was all theirs to grasp just by clasping one of his bags. It looked easy. It was easy, most of the time. And no one was making a secret of it. At Joaquina beach, it was flash and splash. Jorge, Salami and others wore European clothes and t-shirts emblazoned with marijuana leaves, or logos for The Bulldog. They brazenly smoked stinky Dutch grass in the car park. And they were constantly flying to Amsterdam.

Amsterdam is so crazy because everyone does business there.

– Andre

The city was the Wall Street of drugs, its laws lax and attitudes soft. People from across the globe flew in to buy and sell.

Thanks to its famously frenetic drug trade, trafficking in and out of the city's Schiphol airport was riskier than other European cities, but sentences were light. Sometimes customs simply confiscated the drugs and sent the trafficker back home with a note for the boss explaining the missing drugs. It wasn't by chance the Dutch were closing down their underpopulated jails, or renting them out to other European countries. And it wasn't a mystery why the playboys loved the little city.

They rode around on bicycles, often stoned from hours in the pot cafés, or with bags of grass swinging from the handlebars. Curumim loved whizzing past Dutch police, shouting out, 'Hey, we have lemon juice!', confident they wouldn't understand Portuguese or have any clue that lemon juice was his code-name for Dutch weed. They'd ride over canals on quaint little bridges, along tree-lined streets, often parking their pushbikes outside the eighteenth-century building crowned by Curumim's attic.

The attic was tiny, with one bedroom, one bathroom, an open-plan living and kitchen space and a big round window overlooking the street. There was an old red couch set against one wall and a collage of photos of horses surfing in Bali on the other. Curumim often pointed to it during his pitches: 'You want to surf like that in Bali? Just carry this bag. A beautiful girl will meet you . . .'

This tiny attic was the drug hub for Brazilians in Amsterdam, although the worldly bosses welcomed friends from all over the globe. Andre, Curumim, Dimitrius and Ryan regularly met here to discuss business. It was also a party palace, especially for Curumim. They put up their more trusted horses here to save on hotels, and he loved holding court and regaling them with stories of how he started his champagne lifestyle.

MANY YEARS EARLIER

Curumim had blazed the trafficking routes from Amsterdam to Brazil and Bali. It had all started when he was 16 years old, and went to Colombia to compete in a hang-gliding championship. He flew back with a gold trophy in his hand and white powder in his underpants.

Marco Archer Cardoso Moreira was born in the Amazon in northern Brazil with a silver spoon in his mouth, but it quickly tarnished. After a move to Rio, his mother, whose family owned a media empire, fled her abusive, alcoholic husband, leaving behind her two toddler sons.

So, Marco grew up poor in the rich Rio neighbourhood of Ipanema beach. To compensate, he honed his sharp wit to win a spot among the cool rich kids. They nicknamed him Curumim, meaning little Indian boy, and his names were used interchangeably.

He became best friends with Beto, a gorgeous, blond-haired guy who was two years older. His father was so rich from real estate deals he was dubbed Rio's Donald Trump. The witty Marco grew up as part of their family, always going along on their ski trips to Italy or hang-gliding in the Swiss Alps. Curumim idolised Beto, dutifully doing anything he asked, including running up into the dangerous Rio favelas to buy blow. 'You want black or white?' the drug dealers would ask the plucky schoolboy.

'White,' he'd reply, handing over cash before getting his lunch box filled with cocaine.

In their teens, Beto had organised Marco's first fateful blow run, setting up the meeting in Colombia. With his precocious talent for gliding, Marco soon flew to competitions across the globe and never missed a chance to carry kilos of cocaine in his glider frame, well camouflaged among the rest of the team's gliders.

> *I take cocaine to America, to Italy, to Spain, to Portugal, Switzerland, Germany, Australia, everywhere. I'm a Brazilian champion, so when I come they check but they don't really check.*
>
> – Marco

When his travels took him to Amsterdam, he quickly got a taste for the strong Dutch grass, particularly the citrusy smelling White Widow, inspiring the name lemon juice. At first he carried grams of it to smoke, but then started taking kilos hidden inside brand-new stereo speakers for a growing client list. He was soon such a regular guest at the Schmidt Hotel in Amsterdam that the manager offered to rent him a nearby apartment – the attic. It was five minutes' walk to the designer shops, the museums, the concert halls, in an exclusive area backing onto the sprawling Vondelpark and fronting a busy road with trams to anywhere. For only €1000 a month, it was perfect.

From the early days, he let other bosses use the attic too, usually asking for a payment of space in their horses' bags.

It fast became a networking hub in Amsterdam. Andre and Dimitrius had first met there, awkwardly. They'd both been expecting it to be empty.

Andre was cooking up some shrimps when he heard keys turning in the lock. Seconds later, a baby-faced guy with straight, jet black hair styled in a bowl cut – earning him the nickname Prince Hair – walked in. Both were a bit wary, but Andre broke the ice.

'Hi, I'm Andre,' he said offering his hand.

'Oh hi, I'm Dimi.' Each had heard of the other from Curumim.

They shared the shrimp and a joint, chatting about business. Dimitrius told Andre he was in town to buy three kilos of grass to take back to São Paulo in three days' time. Andre told him which supplier had the best stuff at the moment, and that afternoon they jumped on bikes and rode there together.

The coffee shop was warm and smoky, with people toking on joints around tables or as they played the pinball machine. Standing behind the bar was a short, bald guy with big blue eyes and a huge smile – a Dutch Danny DeVito. 'Hello, what can I do for you today, my friends?'

He knew and trusted them both – crucial given it was a crime for coffee shops to sell more than five grams per customer. Today, Dimitrius wanted four kilos – three for his client and now one for Andre after agreeing to add it to his load on the ride over.

DeVito grabbed his coat and led them back outside, along the familiar snowy path, past fish and food markets, to an apartment around the corner. Once inside, the smell of skunk hit their nostrils. Mounds of it were piled across a large table, with three guys busily cutting, weighing and packing it into small zip-lock bags to sell in the coffee shops.

DeVito walked over to a wall lined with ten blue plastic barrels and started unscrewing the lids. 'You're in luck today, my friends. I have the best in town,' he said, plucking a little bit from one barrel, and putting it near Andre's nose.

Andre inhaled. 'Mmm. A sweet bouquet.'

'So, this is €3000 a kilo. This,' DeVito said, teasing some from another barrel, 'is €3600. But look at the quality.'

'Oh, it smells so good,' Andre said, then pushed his palm down onto the skunk in a blue barrel to see if it stuck. Unless it was oily, it wouldn't survive a long haul flight without disintegrating.

Andre went from barrel to barrel, filling his nose with the scents of Super Skunk, Orange Bud, Godzilla, the citrusy fragrance of White Widow. He was in heaven – this was his drug of choice. He inhaled with the same reverence of a wine connoisseur sniffing a fine French vintage.

For me, the scent is so sweet, so good, because I love it. You have low quality marijuana, like in Indonesia or Paraguay; it's so cheap, people take big chunks with their hands. But when you go to Europe, it's skunk, it's expensive, it's €20 a gram, it's more expensive than gold. So you take a little bit, you hold it up to the light . . . ah, you feel it, smell it, you can compare it like wine. You take scissors and cut just enough to smoke, you smoke, you feel ahhhhh . . . more relaxed and happy, just like champagne.

– Andre

Skunk was the Cristal of weed, up to five times stronger than ordinary grass, and the only kind Andre's rich, powerful clients, including a TV network boss and a global surf-wear brand owner, wished to smoke. They wanted the best, and Andre delivered.

After sniffing all ten blue barrels, Dimitrius and Andre chose their kilos, paid cash, stashed it in their backpacks and pedalled off. They zipped past The Bulldog and Holland Casino, where Andre liked to play blackjack, and along the canals, happy, free and at home in the beautiful city.

I ride the bike smiling. Ah, no problem. Amsterdam is a free world – free drugs. Smiling, fucking smiling.

– Dimitrius

Back in the attic, they shared some joints and chatted about their drug businesses, world travels and surfing. They were kindred spirits, both smart and educated, lured by the dazzle of fast cash.

*

Andre's career as a trafficker had kickstarted after winning the weed lottery when he was 21.

'Andre, do you smoke marijuana?' his father's fishing manager had asked him late one night at his family beach house on São Paulo's coast.

'Yes, Master Antonio,' he answered, wondering why he was asking.

'Well the beach is full of these,' he said, showing Andre an opened Australian Berri pineapple juice can, still with the label on it. 'Is it marijuana?' Master Antonio asked. Andre sniffed. It smelled nothing like the cheap Paraguayan stuff he smoked, but it was definitely grass.

'Are there more on the beach?' he asked.

'Yes, the sand is full of cans,' Master Antonio replied. Andre instantly told a friend staying with him to bring the car, then sprinted off to the beach, blown away by what he saw when he got there. 'It was surreal, I couldn't believe my eyes. There were hundreds of cans.'

In the moonlight, they dashed about collecting cans and stacking them into the car. More and more washed up, lolling back and forth in the white water. Andre only stopped after hearing sirens wailing in the distance.

I couldn't sleep with the noise of sirens, my house full of marijuana cans, the excitement, everything bubbling in my head. The next morning, I went straight to the beach to talk to the fishermen and try to figure out what had happened, but nobody knew.

– Andre

Then it hit the news. Twenty-two tonnes of marijuana, stashed in a variety of Berri juice cans, had been jettisoned from the *Solana Star*, a ship en route from Australia via Singapore to Miami. Brazil's navy had been preparing to raid it after a tip-off by America's Drug Enforcement Administration (DEA). All crew, except the chef, fled Brazil before the cans started washing up along the coast. Each can, packed with up to one and a half kilos of quality Thai stick, was worth around US $1000. For weeks, anything glinting in the water caused a frenzy of people to dive in and swim like crazy towards the shiny object. Many Brazilians won a share in the weed lottery and the term 'the summer of the can' was coined.

Andre cashed in. Despite army road blocks, he made many two and a half hour trips into the city in his rickety car, hiding the Thai stick in a secret compartment in the bottom of one of the buckets of shrimps that he sold to city restaurants.

When I arrived in São Paulo, everybody, everywhere was talking about just one thing: the cans of marijuana. It was the main topic of conversation at university, parties, in bars. I had 250 cans – the 'firm' was open.

– Andre

He quickly made US $100,000, but kept his weed windfall secret from his wealthy parents. Weeks passed, life was amazing. Then one night he drove home in a brand-new car, and his father gave him an ultimatum: 'Son, either stop selling drugs and keep your family, or keep selling the drugs and lose us.' Andre quit his tourism degree at São Paulo university and moved to LA.

Soon, he was carrying drugs as casually as a toothbrush. A passionate surfer with plenty of cash, he naturally flew to Bali, carrying skunk and LSD. There he met Peruvians selling blow, and Marco, who by now was calling himself the Lemon Juice King. Andre fitted right in, and the little island was soon his playground, and Marco a regular partner.

Dimitrius the Greek's kick-off was less storybook.

My friend says to me, 'Fuck, Dimi, you work too much and make small money, I have a better way to make money. It's very easy. You go to Amsterdam and bring skunk to Rio for Curumim and for me. Want to try?' So, I start.

– Dimitrius

Dimi was a boy from Rio who spoke fluent English after studying in the US and was living in Hawaii to surf, paying his way by working odd jobs, cleaning restaurant grease-traps and selling used cars. Carrying a bit of grass to Brazil was a dream job.

But Dimi's start coincided with Curumim's nightmare, wiping out in a near-fatal paragliding crash in Bali. Lying broken on the ground, blood trickling from his nose, he was barely alive. When Bali doctors wanted to amputate his mangled leg, friends frantically raised funds to fly him on a private plane to Singapore. It was touch and go; his heart stopped and started mid-flight. His mum flew in to Singapore and, in her despair, paid a priest to read him the last rites.

Then Marco woke up, cheating death against all odds. Perilously, it instilled in him a sense of invincibility. And an obsession with death.

While Marco convalesced in hospital for months, Dimitrius took over his São Paulo clients.

I was supposed to be just a worker, but as Marco fell down, his customers have no supplier. They asked me to do the job he was supposed to do. So I jumped from worker to little boss. I go, I buy, I pack, I carry, I do everything, every month carrying four kilos of skunk to sell to Marco's partner in São Paulo.

– Dimitrius

Marco flew to Amsterdam months later with a wheelchair, a walking stick and his old blood-splattered paraglider sail. Dimitrius was in the attic to help him.

He was very sick. Walks with a stick; very weak, very skinny. They had to put a net inside the body to hold all the organs. He broke the foot, the hip bone. I pushed the wheelchair, I helped him. He's all fucked up but laughing, making jokes all the time, 'fuck my leg hurts', but laughing. We had a lot of fun, Marco always screaming out of the window of his apartment, 'Drugs, drugs, I love Amsterdam, free drugs.' Screaming . . . ahhh we laughed a lot.

– Dimitrius

Marco needed cash. He wanted to be re-crowned Lemon Juice King. He asked Dimitrius to give him a kick-start by adding three kilos of weed to his monthly four-kilo load. But the speakers Dimitrius was using to carry grass were already full.

Marco says, 'Fuck, we need to carry seven kilos, what you gonna do – gonna carry two stereos . . . won't work.' He looks at me: 'Bring the paraglider.' I bring it to him; 'Let's see the blood, oh look at the blood.' I say, 'Marco, maybe we can put the grass inside here, what do you think?' He says, 'Yes, yes, let's try.' I roll two and a half kilos of the grass in plastic, like a banana, do it again – then, roll up the sail. We put five kilos inside in 30 minutes.

I make it, I tell Marco, 'It's much easier than the stereo, man, because nobody looks at my backpack.' He says, 'Incredible.' Then, I start to put more and more. One day I put eight kilos inside and no problem.

– Dimitrius

Dimitrius and Andre were now both enjoying the high life – two free spirits in a game that gave them the means to live their dreams.

It's like, 'Hey, let's go to Courchevel in France to snowboard,' or 'Let's go skiing at Lake Tahoe, or to Mentawai to surf.' 'Okay, let's go.' I surf, snowboard, surf, snowboard, surf, party. We have a lot of fun.

– Dimitrius

*

The morning after they met in the attic, Andre rode to Leidse-plein to meet a horse who'd just flown in, and Dimitrius went out to buy carbon paper. He was packing the skunk when Andre returned and instantly spotted a problem. 'Ah. You put the carbon paper back to front.'

'Oh shit, I don't believe it.' Both knew that even a small mistake could spell jail.

Dimitrius had already stomped on the skunk to flatten it, wearing socks to avoid crushing the buds, using only slightly more sophisticated packing than the first time with Marco's bloody sail. Four kilos were split in two, wrapped like bananas in plastic and carbon paper, sprayed with anti-dog spray, and then inserted into the sail pockets, known as cells. They reached their arms deep inside the cells to place the bags halfway in and attach them using double-sided tape. Then they folded the swathes of soft fabric over and over, ensuring the skunk was nestled womb-like in the middle of the sail. Lastly, they squeezed it into the backpack, always a tight fit, creating a very bloated bag. Shielded by the carbon paper, the drugs were now set to pass through X-rays.

Dimitrius carried it himself this time but, like Andre, would soon keep his own hands free from drugs at airports. He too would become one of the faceless ghosts Fernando Caieron would be coming after.

CHAPTER FIVE

ULTIMATE SIN

'Fuck off, you little piece of shit! Don't come back inside my apartment, leave my country!' Marco was yelling and flinging clothes out the attic window onto a horse below. He finished his rant by hurling out an empty suitcase and slamming the window shut. The horse knew what he'd done – he'd gone rogue, and the boss didn't like it.

Marco's volatility was legendary; older friends had seen it worsen. Andre had watched his attacks on horses escalate after his fall from the Bali sky.

Marco all the time treats the mules like animals.

– Andre

Marco enjoyed using his power, ordering his horses to neigh, or shouting at them for minor mistakes like bringing the wrong brand of cheese from the supermarket. Jorge was no longer shocked by the outbursts.

He was out of his mind. He liked to scream and make scandals.

One day in the street markets in Amsterdam I saw him yelling at a horse; 'Fuck you, you piece of shit, you donkey, you aren't going back to Brazil with any drugs, get lost.' He was surrounded by Dutch people, but he didn't care. These horses were depending on him for everything and would beg him to stop. I saw him do this a few times, just for small things. In the end Marco always forgave because he needs these people to carry his bags.

– Jorge

So far, Jorge had escaped the tirades but he knew he wasn't immune. It would come when he committed what Marco considered to be the ultimate sin: swiping his game board. Horses that he'd taught then using his contacts and techniques to start their own little games. Cutting loose was a natural step for most but it sent him wild.

I've never seen one mule who says, 'I want to do this for my whole life; this is a fucking good job.'

– Andre

The flames of Jorge's ambitions were being fanned on every trip, whether by glimpsing Rafael's life in Bali, or strolling along the Champs-Élysées. On his first transit stop in Paris, he ogled the towering windows of the designer stores, like the five-storey Louis Vuitton. These glorious flagships diminished those in Amsterdam to minnows. He entered Gucci in awe, splurging on a €200 shirt. He couldn't afford the crushed blue velvet top in Versace, so promised it to himself 'next trip'.

The magnificence of the Champs-Élysées, those giant windows, the shops; it all had a big impact on me. I saw all this silk, you can feel the quality, the smell of the leather boots. It was like everything changed on that trip. I thought, 'Wow, this is the way that I want to dress from now on.'

But I couldn't afford €700 boots or €400 shirts yet. I was dressing really nice, but it was not so fancy, not black label clothes, was red labels, like Diesel, Donna Karan, middle, not high fashion, not like Fendi, Jean-Paul Gaultier, Dior – not yet, it was a progress, little by little, evolution.

– Jorge

He started calculating how many runs he'd have to do to fulfil just his sartorial aspirations, and realised it would be too many unless he became his own boss. Cutting loose required a shrewd extrication strategy, which he worked on scrupulously.

If you have a bit of brain and lots of balls, you quickly see you can do it yourself. I learnt very fast the logistics and the steps to succeed in the business, and I took it very, very seriously. This was my passport to my freedom. Every time I was crossing borders transporting drugs I was thinking to myself, 'Why don't I just find someone to do what I'm doing and start my own enterprise?'

– Jorge

Jorge seized every opportunity to advance his career. First, he found horses for Marco for the payment of space in the bag for drugs he bought through Marco. Next, he started hiring horses to run for himself; Marco was cool with this as long as Jorge still bought the skunk from him, gave him space in the bag, and sold his drugs for him in Florianópolis. Marco had several horses doing this – it was easy, risk-free money and allowed him to keep his eye on their game.

Marco likes to be around the horses to control, to see where they're going, who they're talking to, trying to control everything.

– Jorge

Jorge wasn't planning to run again. He'd outgrown being a horse. Back in Amsterdam, he was now set to send his friend, Timi, when Marco got an unexpected bargain on eight kilos and swiped Timi – after all, he was still the boss. Jorge had to either bring in a new horse from Brazil or carry it himself. He decided to do one last run.

There were now three of them in the attic about to fly – Timi, Jorge and Bica, a journalism student from Porto Alegre, south of Florianópolis.

Bica was a natural horse, very pretty with an easy confidence. With a blond bob framing his chiselled face and a wide white smile, he could easily have landed a role in a toothpaste commercial, but airport catwalks were his thing. He strutted down them without fear. Andre had given Bica his first job after a fat sailing mate, Erik, had shown up at his house in Garopaba, offering up the good-looking guy – for a finder's fee, of course.

Bica was perfect; low-key, polite, and able to cruise through airports with the help of his good looks and fluent English. But Andre had soon lost his pretty new horse to the magnetic pull of Marco. As crazy as he was, he was fun and very funny. Andre shrugged it off – he'd still put stuff in his bag. But he watched in dismay as Bica became a cliché. He very quickly ditched his classic black Ray-Bans for $1000 24-carat gold-rimmed Oakleys, embodying his metamorphosis and his nickname – the Golden Horse.

Timi was a Joaquina surfer, slim but muscular and fit, with dark curly hair and a contagious laugh. He'd run once to Brazil with six kilos of grass and was ready for his second after spending a week of fun in Amsterdam. He would often get so stoned in the coffee shops that he'd hitch a ride on Marco's bike, teetering on the back and crying with laughter as the boss pedalled them back to the attic.

And then there was Jorge, who wasn't happy when he'd realised Timi was booked to fly several hours before him on exactly the same route. If Timi got caught, Jorge would be flying blindly into his red-hot slipstream. But tickets were booked, so he shrugged off his instincts.

The night before the runs, the horses and investors packed the skunk into paraglider sails. One group was in the attic, the other downstairs in the first-floor apartment that Andre, Dimitrius and Ryan, a good-looking curly dark haired guy from Rio, had recently rented to get some space away from Marco's raucous attic.

When we rented the first-floor apartment, that building became the biggest drugs link between Brazil, Netherlands and Indonesia.

– Andre

Early the next morning, Timi was first out of the gates. He was pumped and nervous as he took a tram then a train to Schiphol airport. He checked his backpack through to Brazil, then boarded and hit the skies. In Paris, he switched planes. Going via another European capital was a trick to reducing the risk, as Brazilian customs took far less interest in flights from cities like Paris, Rome or Frankfurt than those direct from the drug capital. On the plane, Timi sat down, happy to be on his way.

I did up my seatbelt and was thinking what movie will I watch, smiling and thinking, 'I'm going to have a very good Christmas.'

– Timi

But the doors didn't close. Two men entered the plane.

Timi started telling himself, 'These men aren't after me, my bags are checked through to São Paulo.' They started walking down the aisle. Timi stared blindly at the movie guide. 'Are you Mr Timi Silva?' one asked, stopping next to his seat. 'Yes, that's me,' he said, looking up. 'Please, come with us.' Timi unbuckled his belt, stood up, and walked down the aisle, telling himself, 'I'll be fine, they just want to talk to me at the front of the plane.'

He didn't feel the icy wind slapping his face as they escorted him out onto the stairs. He only saw the red and blue flashing lights of a Peugeot parked far below on the tarmac. With every step down towards his fate, reality hit him harder. The Peugeot's doors were wide open, waiting to envelop him.

'What are you bringing in your bag?' asked a cop, now flanking him in the back seat. 'Just clothes,' Timi muttered. 'Okay, well let's see.' Heavy silence fell until moments later, the car stopped and the agents led Timi into a terminal. Then he saw it. His heart skipped a beat. This was it, his nightmare. Sitting in the middle of a large table was his locked, bloated backpack.

'Open the bag,' the cop said, pointing to it.

I take off the padlock, there are dirty clothes on top; I put them in to confuse a sniffer dog. I take the clothes out and he tells me, 'Now open the flight equipment.' I open it out onto the big table. There's a seat . . . and there's the sail where the drugs are, and this agent comes directly to that part – sniffing, sniffing, sniffing like a dog. He knew I had something: drugs.

– Timi

Timi was sure the guy couldn't smell the skunk, as Marco had vacuum sealed it. He could maybe smell the anti-dog spray, a distinctive odour to repel dogs. As the agent took out a Swiss army knife Timi, in a last desperate move, slapped his hand down on the sail, objecting:

'No, no, no, you will ruin my sail. Are you crazy? Don't cut it!'
But he was sure I had something. He cut it and the weed bag too. It went poof.

– Timi

They snapped handcuffs on Timi, and started reading him his rights in French. 'I'm not understanding nothing but it was very sad that moment. I got desperate.' He collapsed to his knees, clasping his hands in prayer position, tears now pouring down his cheeks. 'Please, please, let me go home.' But the agent had undoubtedly seen it all before. 'You are arrested, you will stay here and you will meet a judge in a day or two.' He passed Timi a phone. 'You have one chance to call somebody.' Timi shook his hanging head. 'You must call to tell somebody you are arrested,' the agent urged.

I didn't have the courage to talk to my family or the guys who were with me in Amsterdam and will be waiting for me in Brazil. They will see I don't arrive, so they will conclude that I got a problem.

– Timi

So focused on his own bust, Timi wasn't thinking about Jorge coming through in a few hours' time. Right at that moment, Jorge was sitting in a coffee shop smoking a joint, unaware how scorching hot his flight path now was. He was departing at 8 pm.

I came back to the apartment to prepare myself for the journey, expecting it to be my last as a fucking horse. I arrive at Schiphol an hour and a half before my flight, checked in my giant parachute, walked outside the airport to smoke a big spliff and, completely stoned, walked back to board.

– Jorge

Heavy snowfall delayed take-off. An hour passed and Jorge started to feel anxious. He needed to make the connection in Paris to avoid rechecking his bags. Finally, the plane left and got to Charles de Gaulle 90 minutes late. He ran across to the Varig check-in desk. It was shut, flight gone. His drug-filled backpack was now in limbo. He raced back to the Air France desk, telling the woman there that he'd only missed his connection to São Paulo because her airline had been late. She coolly told him to take his bags, stay at an airport hotel and rebook his flight in the morning.

I knew I had to act and fast. I couldn't take all the risk of international check-in again, so I started to make a show, putting all the blame on Air France's delay. I order her to send my bags to Varig Airlines, cos it's a codeshare flight, and give me a hotel voucher. I refused to get my luggage, said they had caused me too much trouble. It was a great move.

– Jorge

At an airport hotel, he kicked off his new DKNY shiny silver shoes, lay back on the bed and phoned one of the richest girls in Brazil – they were having an affair in Florianópolis. This was the life Jorge desired. No nine-to-five ball and chain, not stuck with one woman but always able to indulge his insatiable libido.

In the morning, he returned to Charles de Gaulle, rebooked his flight and was soon in the air, relaxed, chatting with the flight attendant, who loved his silver shoes. 'She was saying wow, they're beautiful.' Twelve hours later, he performed his landing ritual – splashing water on his face in the bathroom, looking in the mirror and playing a short movie in his mind that would now be on loop until landing. He was the star, smiling, walking out of the airport, happy, rich and free – a Hollywood ending, every time.

It worked. He dropped the bag of skunk off for storage at his friend Lenzi's waterfront apartment, then phoned one of his partners, Rufino, to give him the good news, 'Goal!' Rufino reciprocated with bad news: 'Timi didn't show up.' Ice shot through Jorge's veins. He knew what this meant, and just how hot his trip had been – same route, same nationality and exactly the same bloated backpacks.

I didn't know how dangerous and hot that Paris catwalk really was. If I'd left that airport with my parachute I would have been arrested, but my instincts saved me.

– Jorge

Bica had flown another route and breezed home.

*

Help me, help me, help me.

The plea was scrawled across pages and pages of a letter from Timi to Salami, his close friend who was also an investor in the skunk he'd carried, and had been in the attic the morning he'd left. Prison life was tough and Timi needed cash. Salami showed the letter to Andre and Marco and they sent money.

Timi had plunged from living it up to down in the pits. 'I was in paradise one day; the next day I was in hell.' In a jail with some of Europe's most bloodthirsty criminals, working in the prison kitchen by day, watching his back – it was a far cry from the Christmas he'd imagined on the plane. One night after a shift, he jumped in the communal shower. Another Brazilian came in. 'Hey, did you see that? Did you see me punch the Muslim guy, the Arab?' He was laughing. 'Yeah,' Timi said, before shouting, 'Eh, eh, eh, look behind you, look behind you!'

> *I was in the shower watching the Muslim guy coming behind my friend; he has a big knife from the kitchen. I shout, and my friend turned and whoosh, he starts screaming. When he took his hand away, I saw his face is cut from mouth to ear, like two mouths.*
>
> *Another guy started screaming, 'No no no no no,' . . . and he ran to push the emergency button, and in one minute, 10 to 15 guards were there. They say, 'Hey, Brazilian, you go to infirmary, and you, Muslim, go to solitary.' They did many stitches in my friend's face and when I saw him after many weeks he had a very ugly scar; a mouth like the Joker.*
>
> – Timi

Timi's dark fate did not serve as a deterrent. It slowed no one down, nor gave them pause for reflection. The horses kept frenetically criss-crossing the skies with bags full of drugs. Within a couple of weeks, Jorge would be back in Amsterdam, but this time passing the baton of biggest risk and hiring a horse.

And Marco was about to give him the nudge he needed to commit the ultimate sin.

CHAPTER SIX

DARCY

It was an ambush. Jorge didn't stand a chance.

Marco was in Florianópolis to collect cash for his grass. Jorge owed him US $10,000 and didn't have it. He was on his way to meet Marco at a holiday villa by the lake, planning to tell him that he'd spent the cash but still had his skunk to sell. He didn't get the chance. Marco lunged at him with a knife, fury in his eyes. Jorge turned and ran. Marco chased him, catching him by his long ponytail, and slashing his arm. Jorge jumped in the car and sped off, bleeding. Not only had Marco just cut his arm; he'd cut the cord.

> *Before his attack I was feeling obligated to work for Marco. But after the attack I said, 'Fuck this guy, now I'm free to be who I'm supposed to be, a boss.' He just gave me the green light to be independent.*
>
> *– Jorge*

It was good timing. It was days after Jorge's last run and he was ready, seasoned, knew the ropes, and now felt no guilt. He felt free, even after learning that Marco's rage had been triggered by a jealous horse. Unhappy about Jorge's strong relationship with the boss, he'd stirred Marco up about Jorge splashing all his cash.

Jorge was already set with a new horse, who he'd had his eye on for a long time. Jorge and his friends Salami, Rufino and Zeta piled into a car and drove 30 minutes north to Jurerê Internacional, the Beverly Hills of Florianópolis, to talk to their new horse, Darcy. Jorge knew him from the Joaquina surf and from school, although Darcy was a few years older. He was ideal; an ex-surf judge, who counted professional surf stars Kelly Slater and Taylor Knox as friends. When they pulled up, Darcy was waiting for them on the footpath outside his parents' house. He jumped in the back seat, excited.

'We're ready to go, Darcy. We're each putting in a kilo. Are you still willing to go?' Jorge asked, as they drove off. 'Yes, yes. I need the money,' he replied. They cruised past the mansions in the ritziest part of the island. Darcy's only complaint about living here was the noise of helicopters constantly landing nearby to transport the wealthy elite in and out of their holiday castles.

After 20 minutes of going over the details, they arrived back at his parents' house. 'Darcy, you'll never get busted unless someone snitches on you,' Jorge said. This was meant as an upbeat parting pep talk, but those words would come back to haunt Darcy.

Three days later, Zeta drove back to Jurerê and gave Darcy a new wheelie sports bag, a ticket to Amsterdam via Paris, and US $2000 spending money. He was set to soar and felt completely confident.

Darcy spoke perfect English, having started lessons as a precocious kid wanting to read US *Surfer* magazine, which his grandfather bought for him. After high school, he did a surfing exchange to California, staying with Taylor Knox, then an ambitious young rising surfer, and in return Taylor came to Florianópolis and stayed with him. Later on, Darcy became a judge for the Association of Surfing Professionals (ASP), flying across the globe to assess the world's best surfers at the biggest events. It turned Darcy into a minor celebrity in Florianópolis, and he and his model girlfriend scored party invites for every night of the week. He started drinking and using blow heavily, and his star started fading fast.

Some nights, he got so lost in a haze of hookers, booze and blow that he didn't make it home. Soon he lost his girlfriend, and got sacked as a surf judge.

When I was judging, sometimes I would be all fucked up, get the results wrong because I was doing coke all night and my mind wasn't there.
– Darcy

He tried living in Auckland, New Zealand, for a couple of months to clean up his act, working as a barista. As soon as he came home, he fell back into his booze, blow and hooker habit.

He was splashing cash like water, so despite teaching English and living at his parents' ritzy house, he needed more. And he didn't have to look far for a way to get it.

Jorge would come to the beach with this long hair, these European clothes, silver shoes . . . I would look at him and say, 'Bloody fucking Hollywood, come on!' But he would laugh, 'Ah, Darcy, come on, it's el luxo,' that means luxury. 'See my DKNY leather boots, luxo, my watch.'

After a few runs he bought a four-wheel drive truck, Ford Ranger, full cabin, he would be driving that car . . . 'Oh there goes Jorge.' It was a big car, brand new.

Jorge would always tell me, 'Darcy, you're the perfect guy, man, you would go through borders so easily; you speak perfect English, you're a good-looking guy, polite – you're perfect.' So, one day I said, 'Yeah, okay, man, book me in.'

– Darcy

The timing was right for them both.

We went to Amsterdam with lots of energy and dreams.

– Jorge

*

It was a hot January day in Florianópolis when Darcy flew out to snowy Paris. He changed planes at Charles de Gaulle and sat at the KLM boarding gate, aware that only 15 days earlier Timi had lost his freedom here. His ghost didn't haunt Darcy, but he knew it put Brazilians on the radar and that his own tanned, sporty look made him conspicuous.

I was sitting in a terminal going to northern Europe, feeling like, 'Dude, I'm on another planet.' It was snowing outside, and all around me were just Nordic people; blond, blue eyes, all dressed in black suits and ties. I was a summer kid from Brazil, with dark skin, Nikes, Levis, looking like a surfer.

Then, I looked at the end of the terminal – here comes a guard with huge security walking around; they're looking for me. 'Excusez-moi' . . . he was speaking French, so I said, 'Excuse me, sir, this is an international airport, please speak English.' He says, 'Can I see your passport?' 'Yes, no problem.' I showed him. 'Is there something wrong with my passport?' 'No, no, it's okay.' So he hands it back and I went to Amsterdam. When I got there my bag had been fully searched but there

were just clothes in it. I knew it would happen . . . I looked different to the Europeans around me and 15 days earlier the Brazilian was busted.
— Darcy

Jorge and one of the partners, Rufino, met Darcy at Schiphol airport, and the three excitedly took the train and tram to the Quentin Hotel. For the next few days, they hung out together while organising to buy the skunk, the carbon paper and the dog spray. Jorge retraced the steps to places Marco had sent him. Darcy watched in amusement as the two bosses skulked around the streets wearing hoodies and sunglasses, nervously glancing over their shoulders. 'Why are you hiding?' he asked. 'I don't want Marco to see us,' Jorge replied.

After the attack I knew he could do something bad to me — especially in Holland — if he found out I was operating behind his back. And I knew that he liked shouting and screaming on the streets, so I was hiding, using alleys and small canals, wearing hoods and walking fast, looking over my shoulder all the time.

But I was working on his territory because I knew just the places he'd shown me — buying skunk in the same place, the plastic bags in the same market. I was afraid but I also liked this feeling of risk. I was even passing in front of his apartment to push my luck, sometimes. I felt uncomfortable, but I got pleasure from all this adrenalin. I always love the feeling of danger, to take risk, is like an orgasm and makes me feel alive.

— Jorge

After buying the skunk from Marco's coffee shop suppliers, he packed it exactly like his ex-boss, nestled womb-like in metres of sail fabric, and then gave it to Darcy.

The bag was so stuffed that I thought, 'Oh my god, I can't believe I'm doing this . . .' but I'm doing this. So I get all dressed up in the hotel, with my bag full of skunk, and go to Central Station to take the train to Schiphol airport.

– Darcy

Darcy flew out that night, excited to be making the fastest cash he'd ever made.

He arrived at São Paulo airport at 5 am rush hour, strategically timed to slip through customs in a riptide of travellers. He was tingling, alive, the adrenalin pumping hard. He collected his bag from the carousel. His eyes darted around looking for a wingman. He spotted a guy with a trolley loaded up with boxes of Sony electronics. He scooted in behind and tailed him, watching as the guy got stopped; the boxes were a sure target, and a perfect distraction. Then, it was his turn. Split seconds for fate, luck, chance to decide his future.

'Where are you coming from?' 'Germany.' 'You can go.' He breezed through, leaving customs officers busily searching boxes of electronics. They had no interest in the well-dressed guy with the nice leather jacket casually draped over a wheelie sports bag.

When I came out of the airport I shout to myself, 'Goal.'

– Darcy

It was easy. Too easy not to do again. Darcy loved it: the fast cash, the jet-setting to Europe, and an adrenalin shot as addictive as charging down a monster wave, the type he loved. Trafficking was the sport he was ready to play, fast and furiously.

'Ah, there's another trip? I'm the man, let me go,' he told Jorge.

When the guys called, 'Hey, would you like to go to Amsterdam?', I was frothing. 'Yessss, give me the ticket, give me the money and I'll go.' 'But you just got back?' 'Don't worry, I'm fine.'

I would go to Amsterdam, bring a heavy bag, that was my job – I loved doing that. I just liked the thrill of it, and the money, and travelling to Europe. It was such a trip just to go to Amsterdam, such a beautiful place, and I love going through the borders and talking to people.

When I landed in France, I'd say, 'Bonjour, comment ça va?' The first thing they do is smile, 'Oui, très bien', so it opens the door. After two minutes I'd say . . . 'Ah, do you speak English please, my French is only little.' Things would be so easy for me when I got to the check-in desk.

I was doing it twice a month, I did many trips, believe me, I did more trips than anyone here because I wasn't dealing, I was just carrying . . . I did the dirty job that nobody wanted to do, I was carrying the heavy bags. That's what I did.

There was a time I spent 24 hours in Europe and came back. I left Florianópolis on Tuesday night, I arrived in Amsterdam 2 o'clock Wednesday afternoon. Jorge said, 'Everything is ready, man,' and I was back in Florianópolis on Friday morning with four kilos.

– Darcy

As cash slipped through his fingers on clothes, watches, sunglasses, booze, blow and hookers, he was champing at the bit to go again. His relaxed confidence worked like a magic cloak of invisibility. When airport officers looked for traces of guilty fear on passengers, like a tiny drop of sweat or hint of angst, they found nothing on Darcy. Sometimes he became so blasé, especially after drinking on a flight, that he forgot he was even carrying drugs.

On one trip flying via Milan, he sat next to a hot girl who he guessed was straight off the Milanese catwalks. He started talking to her, using his flirty, cheeky charm, and she was soon giving him oral sex under the airline blanket.

We became friendly and we had sex on the plane; in the toilet, on the seat, we just hid under the blankets. She was a beautiful Brazilian girl, looked like a model.

When the plane landed she held my hand and said, 'Let's go.' We got outside and she said, 'Oh, here's my mum.' Then she took my card and left. As she walked off, I thought, 'Oh my god, how did that happen? Dude, I've made it, I'm through. Goal.' I was so impressed with what happened on the plane that I swear I forgot about what was inside my bag.

Did you see the girl again?

No, never.

– Darcy

Another time, Darcy blithely grabbed the wrong bag off the carousel at São Paulo airport. 'Ah that's my bag, that's my bag,' a guy called out, chasing Darcy. He looked down at the bag in his hands and just laughed.

My bag was full of shit and I took the wrong one . . . well, it looked similar.

– Darcy

Darcy was spiralling deeper into a lifestyle he loved with no plans to stop.

CHAPTER SEVEN
CHIEF FERNANDO CAIERON

Fernando Caieron arrived in Florianópolis as the new police chief of narcotics unaware of the rampant global trafficking emanating from the island. He had no clue that when he moved into a nice city pad, he was surrounded by the homes of many playboy traffickers.

Despite their flashiness, the playboys' game board was still invisible. Chief Caieron was focusing on the norm, like chasing the truckloads of grass roaring across the Paraguayan border and up through south Brazil.

After several months on the island, an agent came into his office proffering an ecstasy pill which he'd bought undercover at a club. No one had ever been busted with pills on the island. The new narcotics chief knew little about them, so googled and learnt they were Dutch imports. He wire-tapped the seller's phone and sent agents to his next drop. Angelo Pascoal Lorusso Neto was busted red-handed with 17 pills, and agents found a stash of 4000 more in a plastic whey protein bottle at his parents' house on the south of the island.

Caieron was excited. This wasn't just about busting Angelo, it was illuminating a new game and highlighting the potential financial bang of something so tiny. It was a catalyst to shift his focus in a new direction.

We were seizing trucks of marijuana and they were able to make the same amount of money with a very little bag.

— Chief Caieron

It was the start of the end for invisibility. Caieron got a glimpse of the playboy world, although he didn't yet have any notion of its scope. Angelo lawyered up and shut up, but Caieron's wire-tap on his phone had already yielded names of other small-time sellers, many who were now chirping on the phone about Angelo's bust.

The cops laughed at the codes they used, so transparent a kid could crack them. Clay Lopes Saraiva, a dealer now being tapped, got a call from a guy about the bust: 'Hey, did you hear Angelo was doing a manoeuvre with the car, and skidded on some oil and crashed.' 'Man, what a dumb arse,' Clay said, laughing hard.

It wasn't just the kiddie-code that Caieron and his agents found amusing, but the irony of Clay joking about Angelo's bad luck when the same fate was fast coming for him.

When Angelo gets arrested, Clay starts to laugh and laugh and laugh, making a lot of jokes about it. He was phoning people saying, 'What a dumb arse, he's fucked, he got into a car crash' with no suspicion he was on our radar – he was our next guy.

— Chief Caieron

Several weeks later, Caieron was set to bust Clay. From listening in to his calls, they knew he and his housemate, Martino, were picking up a buyer, Pedro, from Rio at Florianópolis airport. Caieron's agents went and waited. When the three guys got in a Ranger pick-up truck, the cops swooped. They found US $4400 on the Rio guy, no doubt cash for purchases, and at the house uncovered another US $4800, as well as 223 ecstasy tablets, 231 LSD units in red Tic Tac boxes, and ten grams of grass.

> *Everybody gets happy. 'Man, our first LSD seizure', 'Man, that's nice, good job'. We got satisfied.*
>
> – Chief Caieron

Three weeks later, Caieron was blindsided.

Two guys from Clay's home city Brasilia, Brazil's capital, two hours' flight north, showed up in Florianópolis, asking to talk to Caieron about the three busts. One was a civil cop, and Caieron didn't trust cops he didn't know, so he turned down a meeting. He passed on the message that he'd already given the file to the judge, 'so go talk to him'.

The next day, Caieron got bad news. The judge had released the trio, stating that Caieron had lodged his report to the court late. But he hadn't – by law he had 15 days, and he'd lodged it within 14 days. The judge cited an old, superseded law, allowing only ten days. Caieron was fuming.

> *It's ridiculous – the judge can't do this. So we called the press; I said to the reporters, 'Listen, you are always accusing us, "Oh, there's a lot of traffickers, where are the police?" Well, I'm going to show you we are doing our job, but it's quite difficult to do our job when the judges don't apply the law.' A reporter asked, 'Do you think the judge got some money?' I said, 'I don't know, but you can ask this question.'*

Then they did a story and the judge was moved to a different section. Just moved.

– Chief Caieron

Caieron later had his suspicions confirmed by an informant.

He told me those guys gave R $100k to the judge. And I believe it.

– Chief Caieron

Caieron knew that as much as he was fighting his targets, he was also up against a corrupt system, and people who were ostensibly on his side. Months of hard work, lost sleep and sacrificed personal life could all be obliterated in one dirty little deal. The system rewarded corrupt judges. If they were sacked for any offence, including after a conviction, judges in Brazil got full pay forever, essentially a paid holiday for life.

Caieron knew he couldn't stop the wheels of corruption spinning, but felt every win set a good example. This belief drove him, and he was fighting to get Clay, Martino and Pedro back behind bars. He soon got a warrant to rearrest Clay over the same drugs, but failed for the other two. It was better than nothing. 'We showed that it's outrageous, and it's not legal what the judge did.'

Clay went into hiding, but was still casually talking on his phone, unaware he'd been caught that way the first time. Caieron had kept his secret weapon out of his reports to keep the wiretaps viable. It worked. Clay gave himself away on the phone one afternoon, telling someone he was at his house collecting something. An agent called the landline, asking for Rodrigo. 'There's no Rodrigo here,' Clay replied. 'Oh sorry, man. Bye.' It confirmed his location. Agents who'd been on standby for days descended on the house, surrounding it and waiting for their boss to arrive. Caieron was at his office 45 minutes away. He jumped in a police car and tore down the highway.

The day was a scorcher, so one of the agents decided to try to expedite the bust. 'Clay, this is the federal police . . . We are surrounding your house. We know you're inside, so come out now,' he shouted. But nothing happened. He tried again. 'Hey, Clay, there's no chance of escape . . . Come out now, you're surrounded.' The other cops started laughing: this was definitely not smoking him out. Minutes passed. The sun was blistering, but they couldn't move from their posts. 'Hey, Clay, you mother-fucker . . . it's the police. Fuck you.' The cops laughed, but now just had to be patient. When Caieron arrived with several more agents, the teams split up, some surveilling outside, while the rest burst into the house and tore through the rooms.

There was no sign of Clay.

'Man, I can't believe this,' Caieron said, exasperated.

'No, no, he's here, Chief, he must be here,' one of the agents said assuredly. 'He couldn't have left.'

Another cop pointed up to a trapdoor in the ceiling. 'I'll take a look,' he said. He stuck his head up but came back down fast. 'No, nothing.'

'Man, did you lose the guy?' Caieron asked, frustrated.

'No, no . . . let me take a look,' another agent said. He asked the cops to shut the curtains to reduce the light contrast then put his head through the dark, narrow hole, and waited motionless for a couple of minutes for his eyes to adjust. He flashed a torch around and glimpsed something. A foot. 'Motherfucker,' he shouted. It was too narrow for him to climb up, so he just called out: 'Hey, motherfucker, I'm going to shoot your foot! Chief, he's here, can I shoot him?'

Caieron smirked, aware it was a bluff to spook Clay out. 'Give him three seconds, if he doesn't come out, shoot the bastard.'

It worked. 'No, no, easy, man, easy, I'm coming, I'm coming.' Clay climbed down, covered in dust.

'The only reason you're alive is because my chief didn't let me shoot you, motherfucker.'

'Easy, easy, easy,' Clay said, terrified.

Later that day, he was back behind bars, no longer laughing, and Caieron was happier – one out of three was better than nothing.

One of those other two, Martino, would soon become close friends with Jorge – working and partying together.

CHAPTER EIGHT

BLOW FOR BUCKS

In his InterContinental Hotel suite, Jorge grabbed a glass of freshly squeezed orange juice from the sumptuous breakfast spread, swung open the balcony doors and stood in his fluffy white bathrobe, gazing out across Amsterdam's Amstel River. It was a view of success.

Wow, man, fuck it, I am the king of the world. Now, I have a lot of money – what am I going to do on this beautiful day?

– Jorge

It was 2 pm. He'd woken half an hour earlier, hungry after an energetic night of sex in swimming pools at a high-end Dutch whorehouse. He couldn't wipe the smile from his face. There was €90,000 in his safe and electricity in his soul. A new business contact had opened the doors to Disneyland.

I was feeling like the happiest man in the world.

– Jorge

Unencumbered by Marco, he'd moved fast, twice sending a horse with three kilos of cocaine to Amsterdam. But his buyer could only pay in skunk and pills. 'It was a headache; I was not seeing money in Europe.' He got six kilos of skunk for one kilo of blow, so he'd been swamped with 18 kilos of grass each time, using three horses, including Darcy, to carry it back. It had set off a weed storm in Brazil.

> *I didn't know what to do, I had so much weed. I started selling it cheaper so I could get rid of it. And people got pissed with me. I understood that I was wrong, I was doing a low move to drop the price – but it was my business, I drop because I need to drop.*
>
> – Jorge

Marco, who was by now talking to him again, and Ryan had called him to a meeting in Rio, asking him to restore the price as it was too cheap. 'I came back to US $15 a gram.' Ryan also gave him a contact who'd pay bucks for blow, so it solved the problem. 'I'm like, wow, this is a totally different story.'

He'd done his first blow-for-bucks deal in the sophistication of Amsterdam's InterContinental Hotel with Ryan's buyer Rody, a large framed, fat, bald-headed Dutch man who wore expensive clothes, a Panerai watch and fancy designer spectacles. He turned up with a Gucci man bag full of cash and testing equipment. Jorge warmly invited him into his suite, then hung up the gold embossed *Do not disturb* sign on the door. Inside, he slung up the little security chain. The vibe was relaxed as they'd already met socially, and Rody had driven him here the day before after asking him to upgrade from a less secure four-star hotel, where *Do not disturb* signs were not as respected.

Jorge poured drinks into the crystal glasses he'd had sent up – a Perrier for Rody, who didn't drink, and scotch on the rocks for himself and Rufino, his partner in this deal.

Then Jorge went into the adjoining suite, where Rufino was staying, and got the plastic bag containing three kilos of blow. He gave it to Rody and sat back on the couch next to Rufino. Jorge wore his dark blue velvet Versace top, the one he'd coveted in Paris. With the elegant sound of ice chinking against crystal, the pair smoked cigarettes and watched the master work as precisely as a surgeon. 'Rody's very systematic, very calm. He does it step by step.'

The bald Dutchman took samples of blow from the bottom, middle and side of the bag to test the whole contents. 'He doesn't trust me 100 percent. It's our first business.' He did a couple of tests, using a lighter to cook it with ammonia on a teaspoon, and a simple water test – just dropping some powder into a glass of water. Pure blow dissolves, so if any reaches the bottom, no deal.

He got shocked because it was the best fucking blow he'd seen. It was so shiny that he was saying 'bling bling'. And it smelled like German ether, you know it's the top fucking blow you can buy because they wash it with special German ether. Was beautiful. He pays me cash right away – boom, boom, boom – one bunch after the other. €90,000.
– Jorge

Jorge sat like a king in the high-backed, black leather Victorian armchair, at a glass-topped wooden table covered in bunches of cash and a few lines of blow. Rufino stood beside him, ready to help. Jorge's chair faced the balcony window and tonight, the view was spectacularly lit up, the bridge and the city lights twinkling magically in the darkness. But Jorge barely noticed.

It was a pleasure to count the money – I was so into it that I don't even look around, I just concentrate on the money, feeling the notes to see if they're fake or not, and drinking whisky. These were brand new, good smelling notes, I count in thousands, 1,2,3,4,5,6,7,8,9,10 boom, 1,2,3,4,5,6,7,8,9,10 boom – 90 times. In Brazil I was dealing with a lot of money but was little by little; €10,000 here, €5000 there. This was the first time that someone opens the bag with €90,000 at once for me – puts it in my hands. The feeling was amazing, like, 'I am the king of Amsterdam.'

– Jorge

He counted it twice, as much to feel those tantalising euro notes as to double-check it.

Deal done, Rody left. He walked out through the palatial lobby, across a vast marble floor, under colossal chandeliers dangling from the soaring ceilings, past a pianist tinkling the ivories, with his black leather Gucci bag, now devoid of cash and full of blow. He didn't look out of place among the drifting guests, elegantly dressed for an evening in Amsterdam.

Upstairs, Jorge and Rufino were high and happy.

I was very excited, laughing, making jokes, feeling like a real gangster in this nice hotel . . . this guy was opening the door for me to become richer and richer, he was saying, 'Jorge, you can bring 10 kilos, 15 – as much as you bring, I'll buy everything.' So, I was feeling, 'Wow, now I'm really into the game.' Suddenly, I see myself as a boss.

– Jorge

Jorge put the €90,000, which he'd split with Rufino, in the safe. Then they went down to the hotel's riverfront restaurant to meet up with Rody, who came back after stashing the blow, for a night of fine dining, blow and hookers.

I went to drink wine and whisky and hang out. I ate very little because I was high already, and spent more time in the toilet sniffing than at the table.

– Jorge

The trio then moved on to the whorehouse where they had sex in the swimming pools, arriving back at the InterContinental just before sunrise. After counting the €90,000 one more time, Jorge hit his Egyptian cotton sheets.

Now, he was ready to do something with the glorious day. As he stood at the window with his glass of fresh orange juice, he knew exactly what.

First, he went downtown and bought a black leather Prada bag he'd spotted the day before. He returned to his hotel suite, grabbed €20,000 out of the safe, stuffed it into his new bag, and jumped in a cab to go downtown to P.C. Hooftstraat and indulge.

I went crazy. I went shopping like Pretty Woman; *I bought Gucci boots, a black leather Dolce & Gabbana jacket, Dior flip flops that cost nearly a grand, sunglasses, pants, t-shirts. I love to wear these long sleeve shirts, so I bought ten of them – Fendi, Dior, Versace, Jean-Paul Gaultier – €300 each. And then I went to Gassan and bought a Rolex, just a cheap one, €7000. It was my first Rolex.*

Rufino was also spending money like crazy but on different things – electronics. I have a bit of this woman's soul in a way – my friends don't like clothes like I do.

– Jorge

Jorge went back to the hotel, striding across the marble foyer laden with designer bags, met Rufino, then went shopping with him for skunk and ecstasy pills. His horse, Onion, so called because of his big head, was staying in a nearby three-star hotel and on standby to do a 'sweet return'. Onion had come with the blow and was leaving with pills, skunk and LSD. He got double his fee and the bosses got more cash – sweet for everyone. At the coffee shop, DeVito laughed at Jorge's sharp new look. 'He was making fun of me, saying, "Wow, how well dressed you are, my friend".'

Soon it was time to fly home. Jorge packed the skunk and 10,000 ecstasy pills into a bag and gave it to Onion, wishing him goodbye and good luck, then went with his partner, Rufino, to the Red Light District. It was becoming his practice to send horses off by having a 'bon voyage fuck' for luck. It'd worked so far, and was a convenient superstition.

Back at the hotel, Jorge packed, slipping the remaining €20,000 in his new Montblanc wallet and in the bottom of his Gucci boots. It wasn't much left of the €90,000, after splitting it with Rufino, shopping and buying drugs, but he wasn't fazed. He had bank accounts in Brazil, some with more than €100,000 in them, plus his investment in Onion's bag. And he was sure the cash was going to keep rolling in.

Money was coming so fast, and so easy, in a way. I have bank accounts, and I have so much money that I thought this will never end. I start staying in the most expensive hotel suites and showing off my money. I give huge tips to beautiful girls . . . I start to lose the value of the money. I stop looking at the price. I never before have money in my pockets and suddenly I have thousands and thousands of euros and I spend on clothes, watches, champagne, hotels, food. I start to lose my mind when I sell the blow for cash.

– Jorge

He was loaded up with gifts for Jéssica, so happy to see her after weeks away. All the sex with whores didn't reflect on his feelings for her: in his eyes, she was his true love. He adored her long dark hair, her beautiful face, brown eyes and tight arse. He knew the other guys lusted after her, but was unaware many thought he was a sucker for showering her with expensive gifts and cash. It circulated that he'd paid for breast implants, although he hadn't, but he did splash a lot of cash on her, including constantly paying off her debts at designer boutiques. Jéssica knew how Jorge got his money as he'd been honest with her from the start, aware that making excuses for all his trips would quickly turn tricky.

But he didn't tell her about his increasingly debauched sex life, and she kept her secrets too.

CHAPTER NINE

FLASHY IN FLORIANÓPOLIS

Jorge was headed to Joaquina beach in his shiny black truck with its silver trim, tearing around the island's roads, some cut like corkscrews into the steep hills. In the car park, he performed his morning ritual, ripping off his Gucci shirt, exposing his slender, muscular torso and, with music blaring from the cabin, kneeling down to wax one of his new China White surfboards, hand-shaped in Bali.

He ran to the water with his board tucked under his arm, Rolex glinting on his wrist, aware he was turning heads, and liking it. Surfing was no longer his only love, but it was his first. He was a natural on a board; he'd once dreamed of turning pro. He favoured surfing with his back to the wave, in surfer slang a powerful backside attack, twisting his body, turning the board sharply and breaking the lip of the wave – which inspired his first nickname, 'Break'.

He had a handful of nicknames, handy for confusing cops, like Cabelo and Cabeludo, Portuguese for hair and hairy, a nod to his long blond mane. Those who'd known him the longest still called him Break, although they disputed its origin. Timi was sure it came from Jorge's penchant for bad breakdancing during their school days. A couple of years younger than Jorge, Timi, Rufino and their class watched the seniors playing football, and when a fight broke out down one end, all eyes flew to the other, where Jorge spontaneously started dancing.

> *Everyone went crazy, laughing, when they see that figure break-dancing; very skinny, not a good dancer, just a clown, joking – he's completely funny. That was the first time I saw him dancing, and that's why we call him Break.*
>
> – Timi

Timi saw Jorge causing hilarity many times, like when the students left eggs in the sun for two weeks to use in the annual end-of-year egg war. It was raging when the cops showed up and Jorge hit one with a bad egg. They put him into the back seat of a police car but, quick as a flash, he slid across the seat, flew out the other side and sprinted off down the street, turning back to stick his finger up at the cops, to the howling laughter of watching students.

> *The crowd get crazy when they saw that. Break was a devil kid.*
>
> – Timi

Jorge's natural grace came out in the water, on a wave, where he had poise and rhythm. It wasn't lost on him that his signature move, twisting sharply, shredding the wave and spraying an arc of seawater as his long hair splayed out, created a bit of a show for anyone on the sand. He continued it out of the water, jumping up onto the back deck of his truck and, to the sounds of punk rock, stripped off his wetsuit and put on his designer clothes.

I stood on the truck like I was on a stage. People were looking at me dressing at the beach like a model; every day I was with different shirts, jackets or boots, in nothing like what the people were used to. I was all long hair, tattoo, piercings. I was very different, people thinking, 'Where is this guy coming from?'

– Jorge

He roared off, creating clouds of dust along the narrow road that snaked between Alps-like sand dunes, so steep and powdery that people sand-boarded down them, with stalls set up to hire out sandboards. Jorge drove fast and furiously, bypassing traffic jams by swinging the colossal wheels of his truck up onto the footpaths or, if he got stuck, aggressively revving the powerful engine, all with a joint dangling on his lips.

I was getting into that machine and going crazy, man. I was driving this kind of aggressive way, fast, surf music up loud, this rock'n'roll on my stereo – listening to Bad Religion, Green Day, Pennywise – punk rock. Always with air-con on, windows closed, smoking a spliff, feeling very powerful.

– Jorge

His overt displays even amazed Darcy.

He would pick me up in Jurerê in his big truck and we would go to the beach, putting punk rock music on and smoking a big spliff. I would just look at him, and think, 'Fuck, he's not scared.' He would go to the beach, go to clubs, to rich people's houses and light up a big fat joint of Dutch weed – smoking it everywhere.

When he arrives, people know who Jorge is, know he drives a big truck and 'Look at him! Wow, look at his clothes, look at his jewellery, look at his watch.' Everybody in town knew he was getting richer. Everybody knew what he was doing because he was showing off big time.

– Darcy

So far, Caieron and his agents were focused elsewhere and, despite being so visible, Jorge was still invisible to the federal police, although the boss of the civil cops was a surfer who regularly went to Bali, and was now aware of the playboys.

Jorge's flashy surf ritual was a marketing masterstroke, incidentally turning him into his own best advertisement. Wannabe horses were star-struck by his dazzle and his world travels, and more and more wanted to run.

I was not looking for horses, they were coming to me. I think my popularity was because people knew I was an ex-horse and thought if this long haired, tattooed, pierced, crazy fucker can succeed transporting drugs through borders, I can too. And when I'd decided to stop being a horse, I was already very popular in the scam scenario because I was a 'famous' surfer and I had a good, diplomatic character and also this shining aura – that is a gift that can't be explained. And news spread that it was safe to travel for me and the propaganda through mouth to mouth grows. So a lot of people began to look for me to find a job.

– Jorge

Jorge also widened the net by using Timi, who'd been released from the Paris jail after nine months. He got straight back into the game, working as a 'soldier' for Jorge and doing whatever he needed, including finding new horses. Jorge also encouraged customers across Brazil to offer up horses for a commission, having broadened his market now Florianópolis was so swamped with drugs.

While travelling around Brazil, selling my product, I made contacts everywhere – and in every city, I was explaining to my clients the way I operate, and if they find new horses, they would have a chance to use a little space in my bag to smuggle something for themselves as well.

– Jorge

With the bag of skunk and pills that Onion had just carried back, Jorge prepared for his usual delivery across the country. He unpacked and then repacked into pre-ordered amounts. He then jumped on and off flights, taking the drugs to clients in Rio, São Paulo, Salvador, Brasilia, Recife, Porto Alegre, Curitiba and Espírito Santo. Jorge always gave them time to do their own unpack, repack and pass onto small-time sellers who sold at clubs before returning a week or two later to collect his cash. He'd ditched global trafficking and was blasé about carrying domestically. But it was laborious, so he also hired Timi or Darcy to do these domestic deliveries by bus or plane.

Jorge's days at home between trips were hectic. He surfed, cheated with his mistress and hookers, visited his mum and ran his drugs business.

I was doing in one day what ordinary people do in one year. It was so intense, the travelling all the time, smuggling, packing our stuff – we got the horses, cross borders, we sell here, we sell there, we live this excitement.

– Jorge

Many of Jorge's friends were doing the same – creating little firms, hiring their own horses, often partnering up and offering space to other investors. But no one was working like Jorge. Break was travelling at breakneck speed, making south Brazil hot for all traffickers – and Andre, after years of working quietly, building up top restaurants to mask his drugs business, was worried about the noise emanating from the little island.

CHAPTER TEN

GAROPABA

Break was putting shit everywhere.

— Andre

Andre knew he was living in a house of cards that could be blown down by crosswinds from the zealous playboys of Florianópolis. Unlike Marco, who tried to control the uncontrollable, Andre saw the frenzy of activity as inevitable – you show a smart horse the ropes and you trigger a natural trajectory.

He'd always tried to keep a few degrees of separation from small-time sellers, like the Clays and Angelos, so that they knew nothing. But with horses being paid in drugs, they were selling indiscriminately. The secrecy and discretion were gone. And as the numbers of people exposed to the business exploded, so too could Andre's beautiful life.

He'd built up a nice little empire of boats, houses, cars and restaurants, creating the illusion of being a legit businessman to justify his wealth. From early on, he'd used a restaurant as a glossy front.

First, he opened a Thai place which won awards. Then, he moved to Garopaba, turning a small derelict flour factory into a showpiece restaurant. Perched on the tip of a tiny peninsula with sweeping ocean views and cosy candlelit ambiance, as heritage rules banned electricity, it fast became popular and was often used like a private dining room by billionaire steel magnate Jorge Gerdau Johannpeter. A lifelong surfer who was listed in the top 100 on Forbes Brazil's rich list, Jorge pretty much owned the beach next door.

Despite beaches being deemed public under Brazilian law, the only easy access to the stunning Vermelha beach was by a private road for residents of the few coastal mansions. Public access was on a long track across steep, rocky paddocks full of horned cattle, making the beach pretty much Jorge's. In summer, the billionaire brought an endless stream of rich and powerful people to drink Veuve and eat oysters at Andre's place.

> *Jorge doesn't know normal people . . . only the big ones — factory owners, airline owners, senators, the French ambassador.*
>
> — Andre

After a couple of seasons, Andre closed it down, tired of working around the heritage listing rules. He set up another restaurant on the beach in Garopaba after a friend and surf brand owner offered him a house. He called it Oriental Mormaii. Open just in the summer months, it had a large deck, stairs down to the sand, seating for 200 and a staff of 38, who were mostly naive players in Andre's masquerade.

One kid almost unmasked his boss after being sent to tidy up the pantry. A horse had dropped off a bag of 5000 ecstasy pills and Andre had put it in the pantry for a customer coming that night. He went home for a surf and shower, but received an urgent call to come back to the restaurant. The kid had found the stash and was going to call the cops. Andre tore back to his restaurant and took the bag, acting shocked, saying he'd give it to the off-duty police working security for him that night.

I got really worried. He was a new employee, and for that mistake, if he called the police, they will put me in jail. I felt fragile because one single mistake can make me lose all.

– Andre

Later that night, Andre did pass the bag on, but not to the cops. A regular buyer and his wife drove to Oriental Mormaii in two cars. After dinner, waiter Renato Pinheiro, also a horse, walked out to the deck with an armful of fresh beach towels, ostensibly to replenish the bathroom supply. He slipped one to the buyer with pills folded inside it. He and his wife then casually walked onto the sand and around to the road and left – in one car. The other car was Andre's payment. It was quick and slick.

There was naturally going to be slip-ups and problems which, in a normal business, might cause a bad day. In Andre's business they could cause a bad decade – behind bars. For Andre, it was the law of the jungle. Survival meant listening to his instincts and eliminating the problems fast, like the day he found a rat at home.

He was sitting at his desk, bagging 10,000 ecstasy pills – all top quality, denoted by the little M logo for Motorola stamped on them – when a friend called. He was coming for the weekend and needed to be picked up from the local bus stop. Andre raced out, leaving pills piled on the desk and the window ajar, reasoning he'd only be gone ten minutes, and his pool boy was just outside.

Two days later he got a call from a friend. 'Hey, brother, you need to take care.' 'Why?' 'Your pool boy was selling pills on Saturday night at Ferrugem beach.' 'What kind?' Andre asked, hoping he didn't say Motorola. 'Motorola.'

Andre was seething. It was the next beach, and if the pool boy got busted, it was a direct link to him. This was bad.

He set up a sting, just to make sure. He put a few hundred dollars in his wallet, reasoning if he stole pills, he'd take cash. 'Newson, I'm just going out to the beach,' he called out.

Andre checked his wallet on his return. 'Newson, come here,' he sang out from his office. 'What can I do for you, boss?' he asked, turning up at the door. Andre instantly shoved a pistol in his mouth. 'You fucking son of a bitch, you stole my money. Where is it?' Newson, shocked, eyes bulging in terror, fumbled desperately in his pocket and pulled out the two $100 notes.

'I should kill you, motherfucker. I know you stole my ecstasy too and sold it at Ferrugem beach on Saturday night.' Newson panicked. 'Please, Andre, please. I'm sorry. I have kids, please,' he garbled around the gun.

'You stole from me and now you're crying like a bitch. Get the fuck out of my house.' Andre ripped the gun out of Newson's mouth and stormed out his front door across to a motorbike. Newson followed him. 'First, I'm taking back the bike.' Andre pulled the keys out of the ignition. He'd bought it for Newson to use. 'Now, disappear. I never want to see you again. And if I do, I will shoot you.' The gun twitched in Andre's hand. He was furious – this fool had put everything on the line.

'No, please don't do this, Andre, please. I need the job.'

'Get lost, disappear. Fuck off.' Andre shooed him with a dismissive arm, turned away and walked towards the house.

Newson changed tack. 'Andre, I know a lot of things about you. Maybe I'll call the police.'

Andre turned back around, lifted the pistol, pointed it near Newson's head and fired.

'Ahhhh, man, you're fucking crazy! Crazy, you're fucking crazy,' Newson screeched, springing about like a mad cat.

Andre spoke calmly. 'No, man, I'm not yet crazy. I didn't hit you. But if you keep talking, I will show you crazy.'

'Okay, okay, but please don't tell my family why I got fired.'

'No, I won't. Just get lost and don't ever come back.' They both knew news of his thieving would bring shame on his whole family. This was Andre's insurance.

Andre never lost sight of the precipice he was living on. He knew that one misstep could send him tumbling into an abyss. That was why he always raised an incredulous eyebrow at the flippancy of most horses and the new generation of bosses like Jorge, who risked their lives for a nice watch, sunglasses and flashy designer clothes.

> *This is typical for the horses. This is famous: 90–95 percent of horses, when they get their first money, they buy something to show, 'Now I am someone, now I am good enough.' And this is really, really stupid. Because the guy puts his life at risk, to buy a $3000 watch.*
>
> – Andre

Andre saw one of his best horses become a cautionary tale. Bica, the pretty boy with the blond bob who looked like he should be in a toothpaste commercial, had fast morphed from polite and quiet into a playboy after moving to Marco's stable. He basked in the illusive power of being a drug trafficker, scoring VIP party invites in clubs across Europe, Bali and Brazil.

He looked like an American rapper, but blond, cap backwards, chains, rings, shirt open. His style changed totally, from a simple boy to a playboy. Even his posture changed from totally straight to swing, the way he talks too – 'Now I know the world' attitude.

I tell him ten times, 'Slow down, you're calling attention to yourself, take care.' 'No no.' And after that . . . I get a call, 'Oh, yesterday Bica was in this nightclub and gave ecstasy to me, my girlfriend' . . . 'Oh, no.' Why is the guy giving ecstasy inside the clubs? Bica is not the kind of guy who sells one by one, but he always keeps 20 in the pocket for a private party, you know, a club, put whisky bottle on the table, and give ecstasy to the girls, open your mouth, put it in.

This made noise for me, because Bica was my friend, he was always at parties in south Brazil, always coming to my restaurant and everybody knows he is the guy with the ecstasy, the guy with the skunk. They know about that – this is not good for me.

– Andre

Andre got another call, 'Your horse is selling skunk and candies in town. Is it your merchandise?' Bica was selling pills in his home town of Porto Alegre, renowned for its party scene. Andre had two guys selling there, but never a horse. It was way too dangerous.

We had created a monster. Not because of the market share – there was no difference for me – but because of the risk of having a young guy selling and carrying drugs, making parties where drugs fly free. Some shit will happen, I thought. I tell him, 'Be careful, man, you're carrying drugs, don't sell it. It's for your own safety. Don't give candies to every woman you see. Don't become famous.' But his answer was the same. 'Don't worry, I'm good. It's just some parties, nobody knows me.'

– Andre

Then one Saturday morning, Bica got ready to fly out of Porto Alegre to São Paulo. He pulled on a pair of boxer shorts, with a carefully stitched little pouch lined with carbon paper containing 500 ecstasy pills. At the airport, he walked to the check-in desk and gave the girl his ticket. She asked for his ID. This was odd – he'd never been asked for ID for a local flight. He felt uneasy, then he saw her give a hand signal. His instincts screamed, but it was too late; he was gone. Cops appeared, grabbed his arms, and snapped on cuffs. 'Come with us.' Bica saw a gun and their police ID. 'Why, what's happening, what's going on?' he wailed in cliché mock confusion. But the game was up. After more than 20 runs across the world carrying kilos of skunk, cocaine and ecstasy pills, he went down on a local flight with just 500 pills, with 493 more found at his house. Porto Alegre police had caught him talking on the phone with a guy they were wire-tapping.

Andre was in the car with his mum after picking her up at Florianópolis airport when he got a call. 'Bica's been arrested.' It was very bad news. 'Where is he?' Andre asked. 'Porto Alegre.' Andre didn't want to talk in front of his mum, so hung up. When he phoned back later, he offered to send a lawyer to help, and to see if Bica was talking. Bica sent a message back that he wanted no contact with dealers.

Bica didn't snitch on anyone and was sentenced to nine years' jail. Andre never saw him again.

Andre didn't know there was already a target on his own back. One of the top Florianópolis civil cops, the surfer who regularly went to Bali, had started a dossier on him. But international trafficking wasn't his jurisdiction so he passed it on to Chief Caieron.

The file was sitting at the bottom of a big pile.

For now the police chief was still blind to the matrix of playboys under his nose.

CHAPTER ELEVEN

MOTHERFUCKER

'The motherfucker federal police are listening. Fuck them,' a dealer spat down the phone as Chief Caieron listened in, sure the guy was posturing and didn't believe they really were.

Two weeks later, the dealer was sitting in Caieron's office. 'You have a right to make a phone call,' Caieron told him.

'I don't want to call anyone,' he hissed.

'Man, it's not a choice. You're obligated to make a phone call.'

'Okay, I'll call my wife.'

'Great, give me the number.' He did and Caieron dialled.

'Hello, it's Chief Fernando Caieron from Florianópolis federal police. We arrested your husband today for trafficking dope –' he paused for dramatic effect – 'with his girlfriend.'

Caieron got a bit of joy watching the dealer's face change from smug to panicked.

'Hang on, here he is.' Caieron passed the phone. As planned, the news of his bust was secondary.

'She's not my girlfriend,' the guy stammered.

Caieron swiped back the phone.

'Listen, he's lying. We've been investigating your husband for months, and he's fucking this girl. We can prove it. Here he is.' He passed the phone back.

The guy was busted and now, so was his marriage.

I was pissed because of what he called us. Oh, we're motherfuckers? Okay, man, I'll show you who's a motherfucker. And he was like a crying child.

– Caieron

The bust was insignificant until Caieron asked his standard question, 'What were you trafficking?' 'Skunk.' Caieron's eyes gave no hint of the thought flashing across his brain: 'What the fuck is skunk?'

Later, he googled and discovered it was marijuana up to five times the strength of the local stuff. A veteran agent told Caieron they'd probably unknowingly busted skunk before, unaware it was a potent strain from Europe, because they only tested marijuana for the presence of the active ingredient, THC, not the amount of THC.

It was another piece of the puzzle.

CHAPTER TWELVE

FAVELA GIRL

Jorge pulled his big black truck up at the bottom of Costeira favela and rolled down the window. 'What do you want?' shouted a skinny kid from a watch post. 'Tell Baby that Jorge is here.' Quick as a flash, the kid scurried off into the favela. Jorge lit a joint and sat at the wheel, watching and waiting. He wasn't scared, but felt adrenalin surging. Minutes later, an old man clutching an ancient fusil military rifle appeared, waving him into a garage. Jorge parked and followed him into the labyrinth of pathways.

It was steep and every so often Jorge couldn't resist turning to glimpse the vast bay sparkling across to the mainland. Costeira's erratic sprawl of crude shacks was a slum with a million-dollar view. Most favelas were built on the hills like this. The houses erected with no regard for regulations or the steep terrain, with many precipitously perched and vulnerable to landslides. Cables were chaotically slung up everywhere, siphoning off city electricity.

Jorge kept walking behind the old man and was starting to sweat. He'd chosen a low-key outfit, ditching his €1000 Dior sandals for a pair of Havaianas, white t-shirt and surf shorts. He didn't want the spotlight today, but got it anyway. Favela residents knew a stranger – heads turned to stare as he walked past. People here lived on alert, as violent wars between rival gangs, and gangsters and cops, were part of life. Police knew the favelas were rife with killings, drugs and dealers, but there was little they could do without a bloodbath, and even then, it solved nothing. Playboys like Darcy often popped up to buy party packs of blow from small-time dealers. Favelas were unsafe, but if you were just buying, you were usually okay. Jorge hoped so today. He wasn't coming to see some small-time dealer; he was here to see the king.

Soaked in sweat and puffing, he finally reached the top. The king of the Costeira favela, Sérgio de Souza, known as 'Baby of the Coast' – Neném da Costeira in Portuguese – was waiting at a small table outside a shack, drinking a beer and surrounded by four burly men with automatic rifles. He smiled at Jorge, saying, 'Sorry, man, it's just procedure,' as a guard started frisking Jorge. He quickly got the green light and Baby gestured to a chair and slid a beer across the table. Jorge hadn't expected this. It felt surreal as he sat drinking the beer, samba music playing in the background, listening to one of Brazil's most wanted fugitives chatting away about the Carnival party they'd met at five days earlier.

Baby's background was heavy. Born and bred in the Costeira favela, he'd risen to become one of south Brazil's biggest drug bosses, the island's godfather, after the slaying of a rival gang boss. He was accused of providing weapons to traffickers and ordering boys, known as his soldiers, to get into a bloody war across the island to wipe out a rival drug business, ending in the deaths of 50 young men.

Baby's devout followers often had 'N', for Neném, shaved into the backs of their heads, and tattoos of a baby in homage to their boss. He'd once been arrested with 16 kilos of blow, but was released thanks to an expensive lawyer. His hero status skyrocketed after a recent bust and escape. The story had spread fast; a fake pizza delivery guy showed up to the Florianópolis police cells with a raw chicken pizza – raw because the accomplice hadn't wanted to waste time while it cooked. The fake pizza boy pulled a gun from the box, went to the cells, took Baby out, locked a guard in, then fled with the king on the back of a motorbike. Days later, eleven people, including a cop, were arrested for helping him to pull off the brazen escape. Baby was out, free and on the run – after just five weeks in jail – and was now one of Brazil's most wanted fugitives.

Today, several months after that escape, Jorge was keen to move things along; drinking in the slums wasn't really his style, and just being here was heavy. 'So, what have you got to show me?' he asked Baby.

Baby stood up and led Jorge into the shack. Jorge couldn't believe his eyes. It was nothing like what he'd imagined. Inside was completely at odds with the clashing mess outside. It was high-end luxury – brand new furniture, a huge flat-screen TV – resembling a five-star hotel. But it all paled into nothingness when she appeared. 'This is my girlfriend, Maria,' Baby said. With her long blonde hair, mesmerising blue eyes and a hot body, very exposed in a micro mini, low-cut pink top and sky-high heels, she was one of the most beautiful girls Jorge had ever seen. He could barely tear his eyes away, but his desire to live was stronger than his lust – for now.

I was trying not to look at her because in the favela if you look in the wrong way at the boss's girlfriend, you are a dead man.

– Jorge

91

'Maria, get Jorge a cold beer,' Baby said, gesturing for Jorge to take a seat. Then he left to get a sample of blow. Jorge sat perched on the plush couch, waiting. Maria returned first. She came close to Jorge, leaving absolutely nothing to his imagination as she bent over right in front of him and placed a bottle of beer and three glasses on a side table. Jorge knew this beautiful girl was completely aware of the effect she was having on him.

Her arse almost touched my face. Then, she sat by my side, almost touching her legs to mine and I got hot and horny.

– Jorge

He barely heard her words as the beguiling 18-year-old favela queen started chatting about her desire to travel, and how Baby had told her that Jorge was living in Europe, that it was her big dream to see Paris one day. Right now, Jorge was having his own dream, and if he didn't stop, it would turn into a dark nightmare. But being forbidden fruit made her even hotter. She was brushing her bare leg against his leg. As she kept talking, Jorge struggled. She was too hot, too dangerous. He couldn't take it, he leapt up and flew to the other side of the room, quickly glancing up at the soldiers just outside the door to see if they were watching. They weren't. Baby returned with a brick of blow. It was a relief. In just minutes, business with the king had gone from feeling quite dangerous to comparatively safe.

Jorge looked at the one-kilo brick of cocaine. 'It was a beautiful brick, with a horse stamp on it.' 'Okay?' he asked, pointing to a knife. 'Okay,' Baby nodded. Jorge shaved some powder onto the shiny blade and sniffed. It tasted perfect.

Next he did a cooking test on a spoon. It was top quality. Baby confirmed it was 92 percent pure, the best available. They quickly agreed on the deal; US $5000 per brick, and Jorge would return in a few hours with US $25,000 cash for five bricks. They shook, both happy, with Baby offering to sell him an endless supply of bricks in the future. It was music to Jorge's ears. He had Rody wanting to buy as much as he could bring and now the king wanting to sell as much as possible. All it needed was the middle man to arrange its transfer from slum to glamour parties across the globe. The jump in status reflected a jump in price. The peasants who grew the coca leaves and turned them into bricks in the jungles of South America were barely able to survive on the price they got, in contrast to the extravagance it afforded those dealers transferring it to the high life.

As planned, Jorge and Rufino drove back to Costeira a few hours later, going through the same ritual: the skinny kid, the old man, the walk up, the pat-down, and the sexy siren driving him nuts.

She didn't stop staring at me, making me feel embarrassed, but I behaved straight. We counted the money, surrounded by heavy guns, and they put the bricks on the kitchen table.

– Jorge

Jorge and Rufino didn't get their hands on the blow until they met another skinny kid at the downtown petrol station. The drop was Baby's idea to ensure they weren't ambushed by any cops or robbers on their way out of the favela.

Jorge did a few more deals with Baby, always getting the kilo bricks, some of them wrapped in plastic stamped with a cartoon of a baby holding up two guns and sitting on a pile of money. Bricks were the preferred currency in Amsterdam, as international buyers could test one bit and were guaranteed consistent quality, whereas a bag of powder could be stacked with variable quality.

Jorge learnt more about Baby; how he was hiding here in the hills among his people, but suspicious, sure that danger and enemies lurked within. He was a moving target, never sleeping more than two consecutive nights in any shack, and always taking his armed soldiers with him. Shootings and murders were common; those skinny kids at the watch posts looked harmless enough, but could kill as quick as look at you. And Jorge heard stories of Baby's crimes, including the recent execution of a guy, shot in the back, for failing to pay a R $1000 cocaine debt. All of which made Jorge's move on Maria a few months later insane.

I was coming from the beach and Maria was sitting alone in this bus stop in Lagoa. It was almost dark, and I stopped my truck, open the window, say, 'Hi, do you remember me?' 'Yeah.' I say, 'Would you like a ride home?' She got in the truck and she sat with hot, beautiful legs by my side with a big smile. She looks happy to see me. Five hundred metres ahead, I stopped in the gas station to put gas in my truck, and she asked if I could get some beer, so I grab two Coronas – she drank hers really fast as I drove, and then asked me if I have some blow, she loves it, but Neném controls her too much and didn't allow her to use that. In my mind, I knew I was stepping on very dangerous territory and the consequences could be death, but the head of my dick was talking louder than my normal head, so I told her, 'I don't have any here, but I have some in my apartment – if you keep it a secret.'

– Jorge

Jorge drove towards an apartment in Canasvieiras beach on the north of the island that he'd started renting for stashing cash and drugs and having sex. He stopped a few hundred metres shy of it to conceal the exact address from Maria, just in case. 'Wait here,' he smiled, then raced off to the apartment, feeling more and more paranoid about this crazy move.

I started thinking, it could be a trap; she could be calling Neném now, and telling him some shit, and then I'd be in a big mess. But, my 'dick head' was still talking louder, so I got the blow and in five minutes I was back.

– Jorge

Her beautiful, beaming smile welcomed him, giving him the resolve to do this. He tore off to the perfect spot; a motel at Brava beach, where double-floored suites with jacuzzis, big round beds and room service were sold by the hour. Jorge slapped R $1000 onto the reception counter for two hours' rental and two bottles of champagne.

We got inside the room, and before the first line of blow, my hands were already under her mini skirt, and she loved it. I think she was in a trance, super relaxed, she gave herself to me. I was trying to relax, not to think about the risk I was taking.

We have sex for about an hour, having breaks to drink the champagne, and sniff lines. She was so horny that she seems like she had no sex for years. She was super relaxed, but I was not. After I came, I couldn't think about anything except Neném so I told her it was better we go. She agreed, saying that Neném was out of the city, but his soldiers would suspect if she didn't show up soon.

– Jorge

Jorge drove Maria to a downtown taxi rank, gave her cash for the cab fare and waved goodbye. As she vanished in his rear-view mirror, the haze of lust cleared and so did his mind. 'What the fuck have I just done?' In the morning, he shared the news of his romp with Rufino, who was known for being so paranoid he jumped at his own shadow. This news sent him into a wild panic.

He was putting his hands on his head, looking at me perplexed, in shock, telling me what consequences it could cause; 'Man, you're going to die, if he figures it out he's going to kill you and me.' Was true. It was very irresponsible. And, I was panicking too, because I was afraid she might talk and I would really be fucked.

– Jorge

For weeks afterwards, the Costeira favela cast a haunting shadow for Jorge. Driving past en route to the airport, he always thought about the sexy blonde siren, aware she now held his death warrant between her sweet lips. If she talked, he was dead. But several months later, Jorge got news that Baby had fled across the border to the criminal sanctuary of Paraguay, as Brazil was now too dangerously hot for him.

I was like – wow, thank God, because I was living with this ghost until then.

– Jorge

Jorge didn't miss Baby's blow bricks. He'd only done four deals with him anyway, never feeling very safe or enthusiastic to schlep into the slum, especially when he could sit comfortably in his city apartment and dial up blow as easily as dialling for a pizza.

His main supplier was Luiz Alberto Dias, a shifty-eyed dealer from the south of the island who carried guns as naturally as

Jorge carried man bags. Their introduction by a mutual friend, Lenzi, had been a boon for both. Jorge got blow on speed dial, and Luiz got a dialled-up lifestyle.

He grows a lot when he starts to work for us. He starts to live like us, to play like he got money. He bought a BMW, a boat – a big upgrade.
– Jorge

Before meeting Jorge, Luiz had sold to favelas, a long way from the global party circuit, where coca turned to nose candy and the price went boom.

Luiz worked with a Bolivian cartel contact nicknamed Alemão, who moved blow across the border by dropping kilos out of the sky from narco planes onto vast farms in Mato Grosso, a border state. Alemão also organised sending blow in trucks across Brazil on consignment to people like Luiz. Sometimes, Luiz drove hundreds of kilometres to a drop, hid kilos in his car boot and drove back to Florianópolis to sell to favela dealers – a lot of risk and work for little money.

He was dealing with heavy people, people if you don't pay they will kill you; the cartels from the west of Brazil, and selling drugs to favelas – very tough people. He got very different kind of business, and was always carrying a gun, always, everywhere he goes he's got a gun, two actually; a 38 Glock and a 32 revolver – was his habit because he needs to have guns. It's heavy going. And, he was quite a dangerous man actually.
– Jorge

Once Luiz hooked up with the playboys, everything had changed. His meagre profits turned mega when Jorge gave him a share in the Euro jackpot; not just selling at Brazil prices but the chance to invest in the space in the bag.

He was a very important piece in my business, so I wanted to make this guy happy. He was the one putting his face to go to the farms to wait for the planes dropping the cocaine; I never went with him to the fields, I never met the trucks – he was the one going there in the heat. I was not putting myself at risk. And, it's dangerous if people like Luiz see you making a lot of money, while they're just making a little bit. So, I came up with this proposition; 'Come with this good stuff, bring as much as I want, and you are going to have space in this bag and you can make some real money as well.' It was very easy – no stress, I don't need to go anywhere, negotiating direct with him, easy, very comfortable actually.

I started getting kilos for a lot of people – for Rufino, for Dimitrius, for Oscar, for all these guys sending blow to Europe. They come and pick it up in Florianópolis; it was easier than buying on the border, or a big metropolis. So, I was like central, if people want blow, they were coming to me, and everyone was coming to get that blow.

Did you take a big cut?

Yeah, of course, I'm not going to sell for free. On my friends and partners I was making like a thousand a kilo for myself.

– Jorge

Luiz and Jorge had a good working relationship. Jorge's big orders, of up to 25 kilos with cash upfront, meant Luiz could buy enough to warrant Alemão putting a narco plane in the sky or a truck on the road.

Jorge usually left the kilos at Luiz's old colonial house at Morro das Pedras beach in the south of the island, where he had a large backyard. Jorge guessed he buried it, but didn't ask. He didn't need to know. He had a blow bank and could make withdrawals any time he liked. He'd just ask Luiz, who acted like his personal blow banker, for a delivery to their mutual friend Lenzi's waterfront apartment.

Jorge sometimes drove 40 minutes south to Luiz's house to collect it, always giving him notice, and always at night, using the cover of darkness. They did business at a wooden table in the kitchen, always with a gun sitting on it and often with his girlfriend shouting abuse.

He was living with a simple blonde girl, and they were volatile with each other, always fighting and shouting abuse, 'you bitch', no class. Luiz was a tough guy, arrogant. He has one leg shorter than the other, so he walks like a freaky weirdo, big nose, black hair, and very big, dark eyes – shifty eyes, so I don't trust him 100 percent.

– Jorge

That was the paradox in this game. Survival was intrinsically tied to trust. They were forced to share life and death information and hold vast amounts of cash for each other, but there was often a pervading sense of distrust. Jorge held a latent suspicion of Luiz, which fast erupted on one deal when Luiz failed to deliver a pre-paid load for Jorge and Rufino, claiming, day after day, that the truck had broken down.

The days were passing, we had big arguments, shouting, saying that Luiz was robbing us. Then one day, I say, 'Yeah, so there's a truck broken down between Curitiba and Florianópolis?' 'Yeah.' 'And, they're waiting for that engine piece?' 'Yeah.' 'So let's go to see if this truck is really parked where you say.' So, I took him in my car, we went all the way to this place, three hours, and we saw the truck – it was there with the Mato Grosso plates, so I saw he was telling the truth.

– Jorge

Jorge's instincts were wrong that time, but he'd later discover that slyness he saw in Luiz's eyes wasn't imagined.

CHAPTER THIRTEEN

BIG EYES

Sharing almost 8000 kilometres of borders with the three cocaine-producing countries of Bolivia, Peru and Colombia, blow was ubiquitous in Brazil. Andre had many suppliers, ranging from drug lords to petty thieves. Their businesses were exclusively in South America, so they had to sell vast amounts to make a lot of cash, unless they could find global connections. They knew their cheap blow became a glamorous indulgence once it crossed the right borders, and its price skyrocketed in the same way a rough gem in a mine becomes a shiny diamond in Antwerp. But you needed the contacts.

Which was why Andre's suppliers often asked if they could invest with him and send their blow to cocaine's Antwerp – Amsterdam.

When South American drug lord Peacock started asking, Andre declined politely. 'Always I say, "Oh not now." He's number one, the big boss, he moves really big amounts in South America – so big risk. If he gets busted, big problems.'

Peacock was too dangerous but petty thief Parrot wasn't. When, out of the blue, he came knocking on Andre's Bali-inspired beach house door one day, Andre was more receptive.

He says, 'Andre, I know you don't like me.' I said, 'No, to be clear with you, I don't dislike you but I don't like people who steal in this area. My house was robbed twice.' He says, 'No, I don't steal here, I steal in Porto Alegre. I've come here because I have two kilos of cocaine.' I say, 'Yeah?' 'Yeah, and I don't want to sell here in Brazil, I want to send to Europe. Can you help me?' For his good luck, at this time I didn't have any cocaine.

So, I say, 'Okay, I have one guy who wanna run, maybe we can send this week.' And I call, 'Hey, bro, when can you travel?' 'I can travel today.' 'Okay great, just wait.' I click the phone and call the travel agent. 'Hi, one flight for me, São Paulo, Paris, Paris, Amsterdam, like usual.' 'For when?' 'This week?' After ten minutes the girl calls me back. 'Okay, Andre, I have for tomorrow, for Thursday and Friday.' 'Okay, Thursday. And book a flight for me for Friday, two seats,' because Parrot wanna travel too, he's never been to Amsterdam.

So, in ten minutes everything is all fixed. One day later the horse flies, two days later, he calls, 'Goal, I'm in Amsterdam.' 'Okay, tomorrow I'll be there.' The next day I take the flight, collect the cocaine, give it to my contact, take the money, pay Parrot, then, 'Okay, everybody, let's go eat some good steak.' It worked like tick, tick, tick, clockwork. Go Friday and back Sunday. Parrot has €35,000 in his pocket, he says, 'Oh thank you, Andre,' for him was a lot of money. I also have €35,000, but for me this is normal, day to day business. He never contacted me again after that.

– Andre

The travel agents also started asking for a piece of the action. Endlessly booking tickets, watching the playboys get richer, they knew what was going on, and wanted in. Jorge, Dimitrius and many others welcomed them, as it was quid pro quo. Olaf, a large, feminine-voiced partner in the travel firm Connexion in Florianópolis, turned himself into a VIP agent to the playboys and hit the jackpot. He won Brazil travel industry awards for selling the most tickets to Europe – while making vast amounts of cash from drugs trafficked on those flights. He accepted payment in blow in the bags. It didn't matter that he didn't speak English and had never been to Europe; his contacts were the playboys, who took his blow and sold it for him. He just had to put his hand out to collect the money after the run.

The playboys didn't stop to think that bringing Olaf and the other travel agents into the matrix was a dicey move, given the mass of potentially incriminating intel they kept, like dates of flight, names of horses, frequency of trips. A travel agent husband and wife team, Alex Conte and Fabrícia, were given the chance for even closer scrutiny of the game when they started, not just investing in bags, but carrying them. Their risk of busting was a lot higher than Olaf's, and they had plenty of sensitive information at their fingertips to cut a deal.

But Dimitrius wasn't thinking about that when he phoned blond-haired, blue-eyed Alex in Florianópolis and offered him his first run, carrying blow to Bali. Fabrícia was also soon taking blow in her leather boots to Amsterdam. Alex did a couple more runs and quickly got a reputation for being a pain in the arse.

This couple's got big eyes. Sell tickets, fuck that, sell drugs. But he's never travelled around the world. Sells tickets only, but then he goes to Bali and puts five kilos of cocaine inside. He came back, 'I am the man.' And after two times carrying, they think, 'Ah, we're very smart, we can do everything ourselves.' Second time he comes to Amsterdam, he already thinks he's the boss, knows everybody.

– Dimitrius

Alex turned up in Amsterdam with three kilos of blow, sent by Timi and Rufino, to sell through Dimitrius.

This guy Alex calls me. I say, 'I can sell for you for €24,000 today.' He says, 'No, no, I met a Portuguese guy, he's gonna buy it for €40,000 a kilo.' I say, 'I am working in Amsterdam for eight years, in and out, making contacts for eight years. You're here for eight days and you want to play boss? Okay, go ahead.

'But do you know what's going to happen if you break the law in another country and you don't have any contacts? You are going to be fucked. Be careful.'

– Dimitrius

Four days later, Alex was back. Standing outside Dimitrius' apartment window, he was a quivering wreck.

He shows up all fucked up, his friend all fucked up. The Portuguese guy gave them a drink, drugs them, beats them both in the hotel, took the drugs, don't give any money. Then he comes to my apartment to cry.

I look out the window on the street, and say, 'Don't come to my apartment. Never come to my apartment.' 'Ah, look at me, wah wah wah ... look at me, I was supposed to sell the drugs for €40,000 to the Portuguese guy. Now, I don't have the money', crying, 'Ah, the guys in Brazil want to kill me, help me.' I say, 'I warned you. Now, I don't help you. Get out.' 'Help me.' 'No, I told you be careful. €40,000 is too high. You have big eyes, not me.'

He got so pissed with me – but I'm not meant to help, I'm not the babysitter of drug dealers, I'm not his dad, I'm a businessman.

— Dimitrius

In Florianópolis, things unravelled fast. When Alex had called Timi and Rufino on safe arrival saying 'goal', it had been music to their ears. They'd quickly called the suppliers, three guys in São Paulo, with the good news.

We informed these guys, 'Okay, we got the goal, our horse is in Amsterdam. Next week we'll have the money.'

— Timi

This was new business. Rufino had found these São Paulo guys, who had pure quality blow and were keen to move it to Europe. Already they'd had one success and the future had looked white and bright until Alex got his big eyes.

Now the three São Paulo guys were furious. They'd smelled the euros, and now smelled a rat. Thinking they'd been taken for idiots, they wanted their money.

Alex caused a big shit. These guys didn't believe us.

— Timi

Rufino and Timi were the faces of the scam, and the São Paulo suppliers knew where they lived.

They hunted me on the island, caught me, kept me prisoner all day inside their car with a big knife on my neck. They almost kill me, almost cut my neck, the guys punched me. They catch Rufino, we go to his father's apartment, they punch us on the way up in the elevator.

This guy taking Rufino was a giant, Rufino don't fight, he's like a girl, you know. The guy goes to the door of Rufino's father's apartment, the doctor, Felipe. This giant is holding Rufino up in the air like a rabbit, by a big white gold chain Rufino wore around his neck. His father looks, 'Ah, what's happened?' 'This is your son? You want to see him alive? Well come on, Rufino, talk to your father, how much do we need?'

I'm standing in the elevator door with the knife on my throat. I didn't have a chain, so they just keep punching me, saying, 'Shut up, you don't talk nothing.' I can't do nothing. These guys, they kill. Rufino's father gave some money right away. I sold my car same day, Rufino sold his car, sold his watch.

Did they hurt you badly?

No, they knew that we could get a solution. But if not, for sure they would cut my neck. That's the rule when you work with that in Brazil. The guys had a mission; find a solution or eliminate us.

— Timi

Rufino and Timi wanted Alex to pay for what they'd lost by doing another three runs, but he refused.

Cos he's an asshole he says, 'No, no, I don't go, I don't go, I don't go,' and he put his nephew to run, to make what he should make. He's a shit man, trash. He told before he travelled, if he gets busted, he will talk about everyone, 'If I go to jail, everybody goes to jail.' And I discuss that with Break and Rufino — how can you send this asshole after he makes that comment? — but these guys don't care.

— Timi

Alex's story had an upside. It was like an advertising blitz for the bosses in Amsterdam who were now acting as agents in the surging 'ant business', where streams of young people were bringing smaller amounts of blow, often around a kilo, inside sleeping bags or just rolled in a pair of jeans and tossed in a suitcase. It scared them into dialling Dimi or one of the other bosses on arrival.

People in Florianópolis heard about it, so everybody starts to talk. Before they leave Brazil, people tell them, 'If you try to make more money alone, if you try to sell stuff in the street, and you don't have connections, maybe you're going to get hurt – it's not safe, you don't sell cocaine like you sell iPhones – don't get big eyes, cos the risk is too high. Call Dimi.'

So the ants say, 'I call Dimi because money comes to the hand for sure.' The ants know my phone number. 'Hello, where are you?' 'I am at the hotel.' 'Okay, don't talk on the phone.' I go to the hotel. Meet. Take a small sample, give to one of my agents. He shows to a buyer from outside Holland who come to buy – Italians, French, German. Does the test, 'Okay, I want.'

So, I did the middle thing. I make a lot of money because 500, 1000, 500, 1000, every day. These guys were coming every single day. Sometimes it's difficult because they bring stuff that's no good. So I have to look for people who like that. Sell to black people who do the crack thing. When it's very good quality it sells very fast, very fast – 24 hours.

I was doing this business like an oiled machine. Not big eyes. Big eyes don't go far. Everybody loves me because I don't have big eyes. I told everybody, like all the ants, 'You guys, you are just born, I've been here already for eight years. You think your contact will be better than mine!'

– Dimitrius

Travel agent Alex was in a new scam with the bent São Paulo cop and Andre. He again hired his nephew, Fernando Camargo Platt, to run. Andre would sell the blow for a commission as soon as Alex's nephew landed in Amsterdam, where the three men were waiting.

I know Alex from Florianópolis – just, but I don't like him the first time I saw him. When he arrives in Amsterdam, I feel the same instinct I feel about his wife. A bad feeling.

– Andre

Hours after he was due, the nephew was still a no show. 'Eh, this guy isn't coming, he's stolen all the stuff,' Andre said to Alex, before noticing he was acting suspiciously. Two days later, Andre saw Alex furtively looking over his shoulder as he sat down at a computer. Andre leapt up. 'What's this? What are you hiding from me, huh?' Andre saw in an email to his wife, they'd sent the guy via Portugal, not Paris as Alex had claimed – a suicide mission, in Andre's opinion.

It's the worst place for Brazilians, because all the mules who don't speak English go via Portugal or Spain. There are a lot of Brazilians in jail there. When I saw that, I knew what a motherfucker this guy was. I say, 'You sent your nephew with three kilos of cocaine inside a sleeping bag to Portugal? You just sent your nephew to jail.' And he starts to cry, 'Oh because I can't find the ticket via Paris, it's so expensive.' This is fucking bullshit. This Alex Conte is a total liar.

– Andre

Fernando Camargo Platt was busted in Portugal and sent to jail.

Arrested: Fernando Augusto Camargo Platt: 3.09 kg of cocaine concealed inside a sleeping bag. Seized also R $39.00, US $300

108

and €600. *According to Fernando: '. . . the trip, although organised by Claudio, had been prepared by his uncle Alex, Alex Sandro Conte.*
                                                    – Police report

But Alex was not finished. Soon, he would give the playboys a lot more to worry about.

CHAPTER FOURTEEN

BALI BLOW

*We are crazy. We smoke weed inside the bathroom of the airplane –
seven hours of flight, we couldn't wait. We make many bullshit and
nothing happens. Break was crazy. He got horses going, and he goes
with drugs too. Maniac. But the sensation, the feeling of the goal,
you know it's like making a score in a stadium full of people calling
your name.*

– Timi

Jorge was flying to Bali to meet with his horse, no longer
ignorant of the death penalty but practically flipping the bird
at it. He left his business-class seat to check out the dimmed
upper-deck, filled with people sleeping, except for one old man
smoking a clove cigarette. China Airlines was the last one to
permit smoking. With no sign of flight attendants, Jorge circled
back to his seat, sat down and lit up a joint. He took two deep
tokes, blowing smoke into a suction vent above, then passed it
to Rufino, who did the same.

Seconds after putting it out, a flight attendant appeared. Far from being subtle, Jorge waved her over and ordered two glasses of champagne.

It was an amazing feeling to be stoned, crossing the skies, drinking champagne, going to Bali.

– Jorge

Jorge was flying with half a kilo of skunk for personal use inside his own surfboard bag, so this act was more than dangerous, it was potentially suicidal. If the flight attendant alerted Indonesian authorities, he was gone.

I was a fucking crazy, insane maniac. I had no fear. We got fucking stoned, literally in the sky, with half a kilo of weed in the cargo compartment of the aircraft.

– Jorge

Transiting in Jakarta, Jorge stood at the baggage carousel, waiting for his surfboard bag. Watching the crowd fade as people grabbed their bags, he glanced at Rufino as the belt stopped. He prayed for it to jerk back into life and spit out one last bag.

I started to panic, but more about being without the weed in Indonesia, than being arrested. I couldn't picture myself surfing without smoking pot before and after sessions. The idea of being without weed in Bali or looking around the island to buy it, scared me. I was giving up hope when I saw a man coming with my bag and smiling at me. I grabbed it, gave him a tip, and passed through immigration.

– Jorge

Mission insanity wasn't complete, though. Jorge and Rufino slept overnight in an airport hotel and the next morning bought tickets to Bali. At the airport, Jorge blithely slipped off his Rolex and Prada belt and placed them on the X-ray conveyor next to his bag of weed now in his hand luggage. He'd decided to carry it on board to keep it close. He walked through the scanner, scrutinising the face of the customs officer monitoring the X-ray. He saw no change of expression and grabbed his bag, replaced his Rolex and belt and walked off to the boarding gate with a spring in his step.

I flew to Bali with half a kilo of weed above my head. On my arrival I passed the 'death penalty' sign and went through the gate without a problem. After carrying kilos, personal use quantities were a ride in the park for me.

– Jorge

As soon as he'd touched down in Bali, he was setting things up. He rented a luxury villa in upmarket Seminyak with Rufino and Dimitrius, his partners in the latest blow run. He booked two hotel rooms in different five-star hotels to stash the cash, and a third room in a three-star hotel for Timi to babysit the drugs, for the payment of a free surf trip. Then they went to collect the surfboard bag from the horse, Lucas, a handsome curly dark-haired guy from Florianópolis.

He was a good-looking man, popular with girls, like a Don Juan. He was tall, very strong, very defined, looks very healthy man and this worked in his favour. I think he never gets stopped in airports anywhere. He's got a beautiful presence actually, as a horse he was very good.

– Jorge

They would pay Lucas in a couple of days and also fly his ex-girlfriend out from Australia as a bonus. Back at their villa, they ripped open the lining of the bag, fast undoing Dimitrius' painstaking stitching, extracted the six kilos, sniffed a bit, then repacked it in plastic bags and hid it.

With the Bolivian blow rushing through his veins, Jorge sped off in his rented black Toyota Kijang van along the narrow, pot-holed roads, sipping a Bintang beer with Bad Religion blaring. Rafael's beachfront house was only fifteen minutes away. 'I was feeling powerful, untouchable, happy.' Jorge was keen to catch up with Rafael, his Swedish wife and their three cute kids.

> *We hang together around the swimming pool. The kids were eating a BBQ while adults were drinking and sniffing blow. I was feeling part of Rafael's beautiful family. Me and Rafael carry on until late, setting up the procedures for safe delivery of the blow to our contact, Chino, and calculating the payment figures. Rafael was like my older brother in Bali, he'd introduced me to the buyer and taught me how to 'walk' in such a dangerous place as Indonesia. In his presence I felt safe.*

– Jorge

The following day, Jorge and Rafael took the six kilos to Bali's M3 Car Wash Café in Sunset Road where the island's biggest drug boss, Chino, did business. Rafael sold most of his blow to Chino and they had a practised routine. Rafael got the first plastic bag of cash the next day at a petrol station in Seminyak, surrounded by tourists walking to villas and nearby spas. He took his cut then rode his motorbike to one of Jorge's five-star hotel rooms, where they sat together, counting US $250,000. Chino paid in instalments and would sell some of the blow before paying the full half-a-million dollars. Jorge stashed the cash in the safe. The ease of dealing in Bali truly made it paradise.

Now it was time to have some fun.

Jorge especially loved the parties at Ku De Ta, an upmarket beach club and restaurant where he hung out with drug dealers like Rafael, shared blow in the bathrooms and flirted with the hottest girls. He drew them to him with his sharp look and strategy of playing it super cool; watching other guys furiously flirt, while quietly sitting back, creating mystery, letting the most gorgeous girls come to him, the alluring, sexy, expensive-looking guy paying them no attention. It was a play that worked.

Perhaps because of the close bond with his mum, he understood women and had a natural affinity and empathy with them. He loved them, and they in return loved him, even when he'd prefer they didn't.

Barbara, the vulgar-tongued expat he'd met on his first run, was now a friend, but she didn't disguise her desire for more.

She was trying to hook up with me so bad, so bad. She was really trying to flirt with me but I never want to fuck her even when we were high on blow and you fuck just about whatever comes. No, not this woman, not going to happen — at all. So when she saw I was not going to play her game, she got more and more excited to hook up with me. Because in Bali, you can be pretty or not, there's always a lot of men who want to fuck you. Like, you can be ugly, but you always succeed in Bali, and I was always cutting her off, 'Come on, Barbara, leave me alone, leave me alone.'

And then one night I arrive at this party at Ku De Ta with a friend, and saw all these beautiful girls, and she was on the other side of the room, and when she saw me she starts running in my direction, and screaming and shouting, 'Cabelo, Cabelo, Cabelo, how nice you are here,' and jumps in my lap and I'm holding her so she doesn't drop on the floor. Then she starts to lick my ear in front of everyone. The girl was so embarrassing. And I say, 'Get off me, Barbara, please get out.' And, then I look around and everyone was watching this big scene and I think, fucking hell, she's already screwed up my party. No girls want to be with me after that.'

– Jorge

Many nights Jorge and Rafael went out to exclusive clubs and parties, places typically wall to wall with hot girls on holiday who loved bad boys with blow. They were a dynamic pair; Rafael, with his chiselled face and six-pack abs, and Jorge with his sexy smile and rock-star glamour. Both often left with the most gorgeous girls in the bar and no thought or sense of guilt for their girls at home.

When we go to parties, Jorge Break was always lucky with girls. He goes for the beautiful ones; he never takes ugly girls.

– Rafael

Jorge was planning to enjoy the surfing and partying in paradise for three months, organising another blow run and selling some of his own personal stash of skunk for the exorbitant prices on offer.

But things didn't quite go as planned.

CHAPTER FIFTEEN

ON THE RUN

Bali was electric. It was the high season, meaning a high rotation of gorgeous, wanton girls flying in for a week or two, keen to party. It was going off. There was great surf, great food, and Jorge had loads of Chino's cash to splash.

Then, one morning when he walked across to Bali Bakery for his usual breakfast, Jorge grabbed a copy of the *Jakarta Post* and glanced at the front page.

Within seconds he was running back to the villa, panicked. The moment he arrived, he could tell they knew. Dimitrius was with Rio playboy Ryan and they looked ghostly. They'd just had a call. The air was heavy, devoid of the usual happy ambiance. This was something they did not ever let themselves imagine. Living on the edge, yes; crashing over it? No, never. Especially not in Indonesia.

I was high on coca, panicked, I got my belongings from the villa and left to go to my hotel room.

– Jorge

Rafael had also heard the bad news. He was at home with kilos of blow from a new run with horse Psychopath and bent cop Claudio, who'd partnered up to bring it.

When we get the news, Psychopath and the police guy, they freak out, 'Ahhh, what we going to do, throw away the shit we have?' They walked back and forth like crazy, they nearly hit heads. I said, 'Calm down, we go slowly.' We have to be careful to sell it so we don't get bust, because was hot now. I wanna sell very smooth, not like quick boom, cos was too risky. Was so hot, Curumim was on TV everywhere.

– Rafael

ABOUT 40 HOURS EARLIER . . .

Marco flew into Jakarta airport with 13.7 kilos of blow in his hang-glider frame, high and agitated. Tonight, everything was being X-rayed. There was a bomb threat and his regular contact warned him anti-terrorism police were working the airport. When the glider went through the X-ray machine, dark shadows showed up. 'What's in here?' the officer asked, tapping the frame with a Swiss Army knife.

There's one officer, you know, a stupid guy, and he has this knife and he start to tap tap tap, tap tap tap, tap tap tap – the sound is different.

Where it's hollow?

Yeah. And I say, 'Man, I'm a professional. These are special tubes for aerobatics, for making a loop.' I show my book of photos.

– Marco

Marco was talking fast, good at it, using his book of more than 300 photos to show himself hang-gliding, surfing in Bali, driving his boat, proving he was a genuine sportsman bringing his equipment. He'd slipped through borders using this tactic hundreds of times, across the world. But not tonight. 'Wait here,' the officer said, walking off to get something to cut the tubes. Marco knew he was in deep trouble and now was his only chance. He had a choice: flee or bust with the biggest motherlode he'd ever carried. He watched the second customs officer, waiting . . . the split second he turned, Marco bolted, running like crazy through the airport despite his limp, and out the front door. He leapt onto the back of a taxi bike, rasping, 'Let's go.' 'Terminal One?' 'Yes, yes.' With the wind in his hair and blow in his veins, he felt alive and it struck him that this was just like a movie.

I'm David Copperfield, brother. I can disappear in one minute. I can fly with no wings.

– Marco

At the domestic terminal, he jumped off the back of the bike, tossed cash at the rider, and scrambled into the back of a taxi, gasping, 'Find me a cheap hotel.' As they took off, he looked maniacally out the back window for a tail.

The taxi soon pulled up at a hotel but cops were swarming. It had nothing to do with Marco, but they were not the kind of people he wanted to see. 'Oh my god, let's go. Take me to a shopping centre.'

Marco was soon inside a crowded mall. He bought a pink cap and sunglasses as makeshift cover then wandered aimlessly for a couple of hours. His panic was rising and he was unsure what to do. It reached 11 pm and the place was closing, shop lights being turned off and shutters pulled. It was no longer providing camouflage – quite the opposite.

He went up the escalator and grabbed a taxi, telling the driver to take him to a cheap hotel. At reception, he gave a fake name and avoided showing his passport, still in his pocket, by saying his girlfriend would bring it later. In the room, he grabbed a beer from the bar fridge and lit a joint he'd smuggled on the KLM flight from Amsterdam – an insane risk, especially given the kilos of blow in his luggage. He'd lost all of that now, nearly 14 kilos, after a marathon effort to get it here.

Weeks ago, he'd collected cash from investors and flown to Peru, buying the blow there and packing it into his glider frame. Then he floated on a tourist boat up the Amazon to north Brazil. He'd stopped to visit his grandma before flying out via Amsterdam to Jakarta. Now he was in this flea pit hotel with no blow, almost no money, on the run from the cops, and with a big problem with his investors. He took a final toke on the joint, then went downstairs to buy a phone card to call his main investor, Italian drug boss Carlino, who was waiting in Bali for his five-kilo slice of the load.

I call Carlino, 'Carlino, I have a problem.' Carlino says to me, 'Don't fuck with me, man. If you don't bring my glider now, I will kill you. Where is the fucking dope?' I said, 'Believe me, brother, I had a problem.' He says, 'You talk fucking bullshit. I'm going to kill you, motherfucker. You steal the cocaine.' 'No, believe me it's true, brother, the police caught the wing.'

– Marco

Back in his room, Marco lay on the bed. He was exhausted, but acute paranoia kept him staring at the ceiling until sunrise.

By 6 am, the Jakarta streets were already busy as he walked to a five-star hotel for breakfast – even in crisis, he had a taste for the best. Afterwards, he took a taxi to the Jakarta bus depot. As the only westerner, he still stood out, so quickly boarded a bus for the 25-hour trip to Bali.

A short distance from Denpasar bus terminal, Marco slipped the driver 100,000 rupiah to let him off, in case police were waiting at the final destination. The book of photos he'd left at the airport contained lots of shots of Bali, so he guessed police would tie him to the island. The bus slowed, doors opened, and Marco jumped out. It was a smart move; the police were at the terminal, handing out his profile photo.

On familiar ground, his insouciant confidence resurged. Hungry for calamari and beer, he took a taxi to his favourite beachfront restaurant in Seminyak, La Lucciola, patronised mostly by westerners. He called Rafael, an unwitting investor. He'd trusted bent cop Claudio to reinvest some credit, unaware he gave it to Marco, but Rafael planned to stay clear. Marco then called Dimitrius, asking him to come. Dimitrius was just leaving the villa when Jorge had come racing in from his aborted breakfast after seeing the front page of the *Jakarta Post*.

A Brazilian paraglider reportedly failed to smuggle in 13.7 kilos of cocaine through Soekarno-Hatta International Airport in Tangerang on Saturday afternoon, but did manage to escape arrest. His whereabouts is unknown, but customs and excise officers at the airport suspect that Marco Archer Moreira fled to Bali. It is the biggest smuggling attempt of cocaine in the country this year. If convicted, he could face the death penalty.

– Jakarta Post

Marco was sitting at a table at the front of La Lucciola, typically hyper, leaping up and down nonstop to look out over the bushes for his friends. Dimitrius, Sam, Marco's long-time dealer friend from São Paulo who'd been in Peru as back-up, and Andre came. Although Andre wasn't an investor, this debacle could impact him. As soon as Marco saw them, he dashed across the little footbridge to the car park.

He was happy like a kid. 'Hey, guys, I'm Mad Max, David Copper-field, nobody can take me, I'm the man.' Dimitrius the Greek, fuck he's angry. 'What the fuck, shut up. Are you crazy, man? You left the cocaine there. Sam tells me you sniff coke on the flight. What are you fucking doing with my money? You lose all the money for the operation, now the police are running behind you. You are fucking stupid.' He's really angry. And everybody is really angry, you know — me, Rafael, Greek, everybody, because it's not a happy situation, but Marco was happy . . . But he starts to be worried, when we go to the car and take the newspaper, 'Look, look, it's your face, it's fucking beautiful.'

— Andre

In Jakarta Post, *my name, my picture, everything; 'The Brazilian boy pilot, escape from airport, he left behind 13 kilos of cocaine, if he get arrest, will get 100 percent death sentence.' Whoa! I look at this newspaper, 'Oh my god.'*

— Marco

Marco saw one upside to the *Jakarta Post* headlines; at least now they'd have to believe his fantastic escape story.

When they see the newspaper I tell them, 'You see now, now you have to help me.'

— Marco

Despite being angry, they had to help. Not only was he a friend, but this could be mortally dangerous for them all.

'Marco, you have to run away, man. Let's go, let's go, let's go,' Dimitrius said, wanting to get him out of public view fast. They jumped in the car and Dimitrius drove to Carlino's house.

I say to Marco, 'You cannot stay with me, because the police are running after you. I want to help you. I give you clothes and I can hide your passport.'

— Dimitrius

We gave him money, weed and moral support. He was laughing, laughing, actually saying he was 007, joking about his James Bond escape, asking if we liked it — completely ignoring the danger he was in. He was out of his mind, he had no consciousness of what was going on around him.

— Jorge

The air was charged with fear and anger. Not only had they lost a US $40,000 investment, but the expected US $1.5 million profit. They were furious when Sam told them Marco had been high since Peru, using the glider blow. He'd dug into the tubes with a knife to extract it as he'd travelled. They were all sure it wasn't a terrorism alert that brought him down, but little holes in the compressed blow showing up on the X-ray, as well as Marco acting hyper and high at customs. Sam had flown into Jakarta just behind Marco and straight on to Bali after hearing from their airport contact what had gone down.

Sam told me that when they were in Peru packing the blow inside this hotel room, Curumim told him, 'Don't interrupt, leave me alone.' He wants to do himself. So Sam left and after two days he starts to get very worried about Marco, so he knocks on the door, and Marco opens in a state of complete craziness. All his nose is white, his eyes wild, saying, 'Let me finish my job, don't fucking piss me off.' Marco from the beginning was very high, since he left Peru. So imagine the state he was in in Jakarta.

– Jorge

He told me, 'I did a lot, man.' He sniffed cocaine in Peru, he sniffed cocaine in the flight. The hang-glider was full and he's going there with a knife to dig and pick up cocaine to sniff. He's so crazy because he bought 14 kilos; by the time he got caught it was 13 kilos and 700. Three hundred grams he sniffed and gave away.

– Dimitrius

Everyone knows Marco was using drugs while bringing it. Fucking stupid. Every time, sniffing, sniffing inside the aeroplane, not normal. Call attention. Marco was really, really high on cocaine when he fell. Stupid. Totally. Because you are playing with money, millions of dollars, and you are using. It doesn't make any sense.

– Andre

They had to figure out what to do. First, Dimitrius hid the passport. 'I dig a hole, put his passport and tickets, seal the hole, but the maid saw everything.' He wanted Carlino to send Marco off to safety in his luxury catamaran.

'Put Marco in your boat and go out of Indonesia,' he said to

Carlino. 'Fuck, man, if I give away the boat, what am I going to do? I have no money?'

Carlino was the big, big, big boss in Italy. He says, 'I used to ride a Ferrari, now I'm in Bali broke cos Interpol is chasing me, I sold everything, no riding a Ferrari, I ride my scooter. My boat is in the ocean so they don't see it. The boat is the last thing I have.'

– Dimitrius

Instead of sending Marco cruising off into the sunset on the catamaran, Carlino drove him to a cheap, nondescript hotel in Sanur, visiting twice a day with news plus little stashes of blow and grass to keep him happy.

Carlino come and go, come and go, he helps me.

– Marco

As days passed, the island was only getting hotter. Police were following the photo trail, searching Marco's hotel, the Bali Village, his rooms, his friends, chasing down every tiny clue, determined to catch the Brazilian fugitive. He'd embarrassed the Indonesian authorities, slipping by customs, airport police and anti-terrorist police on a day of heightened security and creating international news. Authorities were going to hunt him down, no matter what it took.

The Customs and Excise office have closed down access to all airports and seaports in the country in an effort to find Moreira, who is still at large.

– Jakarta Post

Marco was getting bored and agitated in the hotel. He regularly went downstairs to the lobby to watch TV, bizarrely covering his face in coloured zinc cream.

Sometimes I come down in the lobby, I watch the television. I already dyed my hair red, and I have make-up on – not make-up – you know, Australian people use for sun protection, have white colour, red colour, green colour. I put cream all over my face, try to hide my face, because they had many pictures in my professional book.

– Marco

When he saw himself up on the TV screen, he knew it was time to leave Bali. He pushed Carlino for the boat.

I say, 'Brother, now give me your boat. I can go to Brazil – me and Sam.' But Carlino, motherfucker, is jealous of that boat, so he makes many stories; where is the boat, where is the boat, where is the boat? He didn't want to give the boat, he wants it in Bali, for the girls. The boat is like – killer boat, like a catamaran boat, 47 foot, you know. Big one. Fantastic boat. Oh you don't believe it . . . US $250,000. But he won't give me the boat.

– Marco

Andre suggested he flee shrouded like a Muslim woman.

I tell him, wear a burka and go to Thailand. Go to Sumatra by bus, take the ferry at night-time, go to Malaysia or Thailand, go to Brazilian embassy, tell them 'I was with a prostitute, she robbed all my documents.' That's it – finish. They will send you to Brazil. But Marco, 'Ah no, I go to Lombok.'

– Andre

Marco was set to go island hopping with loyal back-up man Sam. He had a vague plan to go to Timor and then Australia, but no real strategy. He started an erratic hopscotch of islands with his bag of essentials: cash, blow, grass, surfboard as cover, and a healthy dose of arrogance.

I escape by motorbike, car, motorbike, car, and Sam come together with me.

– Marco

They had daily beach BBQs, surfed, used hookers and took them back to their rooms, where they smoked grass and sniffed blow. Far from staying invisible, Marco attracted attention, wearing a sombrero and telling locals he was American tourist John Miller, a name inspired by Miller's Beer. He made an attempt to fracture his trail by jumping islands, using a boy to take them across on his boat.

The police were in his slipstream, catching up fast, forcing locals to talk. Marco knew things were getting hotter, so sent Sam back to Bali to collect more cash and his passport. He had to leave Indonesia. But by then his passport was ash. Dimitrius, afraid of being caught with it as police raids intensified and aware his Balinese maid had seen him burying it, had dug it up and burnt it.

Marco was now on the move. He found a toothless old man to take him across to Moyo Island, a short boat ride away, he was told. Two hours later, as the sun was setting, they were still chugging along. The old man was lost and circling. They could run out of fuel soon. Marco was anxious, then they saw lights.

On arrival at Moyo Island, a small gathering of people helped pull in the boat. An Australian man introduced himself as the manager of a six-star Aman resort, the only hotel on this nature-reserve island. Marco knew the Aman resorts, he'd stayed at one in Bali. Tonight, he couldn't afford it, but the manager offered him a bed in the staff quarters. Marco accepted, kicking himself for using the name John Miller – it created a trail right to him. He organised a fishing boat to pick him up at sunrise. He didn't sleep. He was starting to panic.

As darkness lifted, Marco stood on the sand, waiting, squinting into the distance. He started waving furiously as a boat approached. When he realised his mistake, it was too late. It wasn't the fishing boat. It was an ambush. 'Get down, get down on the ground now.' Cops were leaping out of the boat, pointing guns, screaming. They finally had their airport Houdini, 15 days after his vanishing act.

On the boat trip back, Marco saw the familiar faces of those who'd helped him. The cops had snared them along the way, and anyone who didn't want to talk was beaten into submission. Marco was taken to a hotel and questioned. He told his cliché story: his boss, American John Miller, had made him carry the cocaine, but he had no idea where he was now. Marco would stick to this. Those close to him knew the truth. Marco was John Miller; he was Mad Max, David Copperfield, 007, king of Lemon Juice, Marco Archer Cardoso Moreira. He was a man of many names; a fun, crazy guy who was now facing the death penalty.

Jorge heard the news of the bust as he was getting ready to go for a surf.

I was preparing my equipment to go to Uluwatu when Dimi came in the villa with the Jakarta Post *in his hand. On the cover was a picture of Marco. I was devastated, I got confused. I couldn't go surfing – we sat in the living room, astonished, looking at each other without saying a single word. The silence was so deep, so intense. I made a big line, grabbed a beer and got high for two days.*

I drove to Rafael's house searching for advice: 'Should I leave the island? Would there be an investigation?' Rafael told me to calm down, and get out of our group for a bit. So me and Rufino went to Lombok to surf Desert Point for ten days. After I returned I stayed in Bali until September, pretending nothing had happened, avoiding Marco's name and any relation with him. The whole island was talking about the Brazilian busted in Jakarta with 13 kilos of blow, and the local people were coming to me, knowing I knew Marco, to ask me questions. I was denying I knew him and I felt shame denying our friendship, but it was necessary for my own protection.

– Jorge

Bali blow boss Rafael froze his business temporarily, waiting for things to settle down.

Everybody was freaking out. Everybody was scared he will give us up too, I was very scared because if he wanna fuck me, we had many deals together.

– Rafael

CHAPTER SIXTEEN

OPERATION PLAYBOY KICKS OFF

Chief Caieron was sitting in the recording room in Florianópolis, listening to the incessant chatter on the wire-taps.

'Man, have you heard what happened with Curumim?' 'Yes, oh bad luck. He's fucked.' 'Shit, poor Curumim, he's a good guy.' 'Curumim's not in a good way.' 'Man, it's going to be tough for Curumim.' 'No, Curumim's going to make it.' . . . Curumim, Curumim, Curumim . . .

Caieron turned to his agents and asked, 'Who the fuck is Curumim?'

We don't have a fucking clue who Curumim is, or where he is, or what he did – never heard of Curumim. One guy googled and could find nothing. But we are very suspicious it was related to drugs because of the guys we were listening to. But it was another name coming from space and landing on our table. We know that sooner or later, someone will say something to us, and we'll find out who he is.

– Chief Caieron

He couldn't have known it would be quite so fast.

'Hey, chief, Tadashi wants to talk to you,' one of his agents said later that day.

'Me, why? What's he want?'

Tadashi, a surfer who regularly visited Bali, was sitting in the federal police cells after being rearrested by Caieron's agents. He'd just lost his appeal against an old trafficking conviction for 20 kilos of marijuana seized in the ceiling of his house.

I didn't give a fuck about Tadashi. It wasn't my investigation. It was two to three years old, but my guys said he wants to talk to me. 'Okay, bring him to my office.'

– Chief Caieron

'Man, this must be a mistake, you can't arrest me, I was free. Why are you arresting me? This is bullshit,' Tadashi argued.

'Man, you are being arrested because there is an order from a judge.'

'Come on, man, let me go free. I know many things. I can help you.'

'You are under arrest and going to jail. Nothing you can say can change this,' Caieron said, set to dismiss him.

'I know a lot of names. I can give you a lot of people. I know everyone. Let me help you.'

'Okay, what do you know?' Caieron asked, expecting nothing.

'Do you know Curumim?'

Caieron flinched, a bolt of electricity lit up his veins. He was wired, on high alert, but he kept a straight face. He gave Tadashi a blasé look and shrugged.

'Yeah, so what about him?'

'You know he was arrested in Indonesia with cocaine and he's going to be sentenced to death?'

132

'Yes, I know. Tell me something I don't know,' Caieron said, showing no hint of the acute excitement inside him.

He starts to sing like a bird telling me all the Curumim story. Everything he said, I said, 'Yes, I know, tell me something I don't, tell me more.'

He told me how they operate, how they first started to bring skunk, then after a little while those guys with skunk and pills in Amsterdam say if you bring me some coke, I can pay you in this. So, those guys realised they could take coke, and bring pills. So the firms boom. It was like a Wall Street boom.

I start to see the system, that every horse one day, sooner or later, is going to start his own business, travel for himself and after a while hire someone else, and then that someone will do the same. I saw it's like a cancer. I thought, we have to combat this, we have to fight this.

Tadashi said the guys are sending it to Indonesia, to Europe. I said, 'Man, this is huge.'

– Chief Caieron

Tadashi's story also helped Caieron put in context a snippet he'd read in a local gossip column – 'another young guy from Florianópolis arrested in Europe for cocaine'. The global picture crystallised before Caieron's eyes. He'd known Amsterdam was in the frame, but not Bali. He'd known he was missing something and now, thanks to the synergy of Marco's bust in Indonesia and this guy in Brazil trying to save his own arse, the matrix was exposed.

Was this how Operation Playboy was born?

Yes, yes, yes, after this. Because Tadashi told me everything – all the big picture. Every guy we arrest before gave me a small detail, a small part – we have Angelo, we have Clay, we have another guy here, another guy there and some guys being arrested abroad, we are collecting pieces ... but suddenly, Tadashi gave me that click. Suddenly put these pieces together for me – opened up a big window.

The moment he said to me how the organisations are working – how much money they are doing with a single kilo of cocaine – I said, well, welcome to the future. I realised, man, this is huge, we need to start a new thing, a fresh new thing ... I said this is going to be our priority. I guess if I have to establish how Playboy Operation starts inside me – I can say it was when I talked to Tadashi.

– Chief Caieron

At federal police headquarters, Caieron and his agents typically tossed around names for their newest operation, and in that moment someone sang out 'Operation Playboy', it was quite possible the playboys felt a collective cold shiver.

One of Caieron's older agents was bemused that they were going to hand over cases involving hundreds of kilos of marijuana to the civil police in order to chase little pills.

He said, 'Hey, boss, now you're going to give these small pills priority?' I said, 'Man, you're not following. You know how much money they get with those fucking pills?' 'No.' 'Man, from this one kilo of cocaine, the guy will bring like 25,000 ecstasy pills and he's going to make more than a truck of marijuana. And, the guy can't believe it. This was the beginning of our deep dive into that world.

– Chief Caieron

Although Operation Playboy was now launched, it was kept secret so as not to give the playboys any warning.

'Smile!' Jorge poses in front of pot café The Bulldog on his first day in Amsterdam for his inaugural drug run. Big House snapped this photo then took Jorge to the attic apartment to meet Marco and the other bosses.

Kathryn Bonella

Marco's Amsterdam attic apartment with its big round window from which he would shout, 'Drugs, drugs, I love Amsterdam, free drugs'.

When we [also] rented the first-floor apartment that building became the biggest drugs link between Brazil, the Netherlands and Indonesia.
– Andre

Florianópolis is the classic Brazilian mix of wealth and poverty. The favela slums crawl up the hills behind expensive waterfront apartments and office buildings. The federal police headquarters, where Chief Fernando Caieron played his mind games with the playboys, stands on the shoreline in the centre of the photo (also pictured below).

Downtown Florianópolis: Chief Caieron and many of the playboys lived just streets apart, close to the waterfront, in this upmarket area of town.

Kathryn Borella

A slum with million-dollar views. This is the outlook that Jorge glimpsed each time he went up the steep paths of Costeira favela to talk to fugitive and island drug boss, Baby.

Koldewey A. C. / Agencia RBS

Sérgio de Souza, aka 'Baby' – Neném in Portuguese – was one of South Brazil's biggest drug bosses and the godfather of Florianópolis.

A baby sitting on a pile of cash, holding two guns and wearing a pendant with 'NC' (Neném da Costeira), was often stuck to the wrapping of Baby's drugs.

Jorge surfing at his beloved Joaquina beach.

Surfing was a bridge to get into this drug trafficking story . . . because surfing gave me the desire to go around the world, and smuggling was the bridge to get there.

– Jorge

This photo of Jorge was confiscated by Chief Caieron's team in the raid on Big House's home.

. . . that picture got famous because it's the first picture of Break [Jorge] in the news.

– Chief Caieron

Joaquina beach was the surfing playground of the playboys. They made no secret of their drug running at Joaquina, wearing The Bulldog t-shirts, flaunting their cash and smoking skunk.

Glossy magazines describe Florianópolis as a cross between St Tropez and Ibiza. In summer the island's population can double, with the rich flocking there for its famous nightlife and stunning beaches.

Andre's career started the night he discovered hundreds of cans washing up on a beach. They were full of top quality marijuana. Here, some of the cans retrieved by police are put on display for the media.

Kathryn Bonella

The 'pockets' in the paraglider sail were put to use as perfect receptacles for packages of marijuana.

Kathryn Bonella

Paraglider pilots fold up a sail after soaring through the skies over Florianópolis. The playboys used the large swathe of fabric as the perfect cover for smuggling. [Note: the people in this photo are in no way implicated in drug trafficking.]

Andre opened an exclusive restaurant in an old flour factory, seen here in the background, to mask his drug business.

Andre's restaurant sat between two beaches. One beach (top left) was effectively private because a billionaire, one of Andre's regular diners, owned the only access road. The other beach (bottom) was open to the masses. These two shots were taken on the same day.

Jorge (left), Timi (right) and a friend check out the waves of Uluwatu, Bali, from its famous clifftops.

Jorge and Rafael's favourite bar, Ku De Ta, located on the beachfront in trendy Seminyak, hosted some of Bali's best parties. It was usually wall-to-wall with hot babes on holiday who loved a bad boy with blow in his pocket.

CHAPTER SEVENTEEN

GHOSTLY SURFER

Weeks after Marco's bust, Timi flew home from Bali with US $70,000 of Jorge's cash strapped to his legs, and was soon plotting with Zeta, Rufino and Dimitrius to send a horse back to Bali.

'No thank you, dude. I'm not going to Bali,' Darcy replied when Rufino pitched the job to him.

'But man, it's so much money,' Rufino enthused.

'There is no amount of money you can pay me to go to Indo with a bag. I'll keep going to Amsterdam. I'm fine with that, thank you,' Darcy said, resolute.

Despite putting his freedom on the line with every run, playing Russian roulette with a firing squad gave Darcy a bad feeling. 'It's like surfing big waves. There's no time for hesitation, either you do it or don't paddle out. On a trip like that, if you're scared, if you have a bad feeling, don't go. That's the feeling I had about Bali.'

They found another guy, Luis Alberto Cafiero, a DJ, with a

pregnant girlfriend who needed fast cash. He'd carried weed in a backpack to Amsterdam for Jorge three times.

Rufino and Timi took him on a morale-boosting car ride around the lake area and up to Joaquina beach, stopping for coffee, giving tips and assuaging doubts, all despite the fact that there was no way in hell they'd be paddling out in Marco's wake.

We have a very long talk with him in the car, explaining all. I used myself as an example to the guys all the time. 'Look, I got busted in France, and they sent me money. Now, I'm here, I am alive.' The horses look at me like 'Oh, this guy went to jail but he's okay.'

– Timi

Despite motivating him, Timi was having doubts not just about this run, but about the whole game. He loved the endless free surf trips, the nail-biting excitement and fun, but this life was losing its gloss.

Seeing his mentor Marco bust, watching other people fall and the bosses washing their hands of them despite promises, gave him a new sense of disquiet. It was starting to play on his conscience, and now he was uneasy about sending Cafiero to Bali with surfboards because he looked nothing like a surfer.

He was a DJ, small, feeble, short, very skinny, very white, no sun, just the moon – not a surfer, not athletic – a big risk for that operation. We all talked about his profile and knew it was not appropriate, but they don't care. At that moment, they are sending two other horses, so if they get two out of three, that's okay. I told them, but they say, 'Hey, you don't like him to be a horse, you have another one today?' 'No.' 'Okay, we use him.'

– Timi

In one word I will describe this – greed. The shit's here, let's do it fast. And, they get the first one who is available.

– Darcy

Dimitrius was now a partner in the new Bali run, despite having just lived Marco's bust up close and personal. He was in Florianópolis packing the surfboard bag, and asked everyone to clear out of the apartment to avoid a previous problem.

One day when I opened up five kilos all the guys look at it, and start farting. I say, 'Oh my god. No, no, no, get out.'

Why were they farting?

Addicted, excited and they start to fart. It's normal for addicts. I start laughing. I say, 'Go to the kitchen.' But they come back wanting to sniff and I say, 'Man, you have to get out because you're making me stressed.' When I'm with drugs, I'm not relaxed. I'm okay but if I hear a noise, a bang, I get scared. So most of the time I tell people, 'Get out, I'll do the work and call you guys when I finish.'

– Dimitrius

Dimitrius knew Cafiero's life was in his hands and he was patient, scrupulous and organised – the perfect demeanour for a blow packer. First, he crushed up seven one-kilo bricks into powder, necessary for this method of trafficking, flattened it all into iPad-sized plastic bags and vacuum sealed them. Then he took a smoke break to let his mind and fingers relax. Before restarting, he washed his hands to remove any blow as even a faint trace on the bag cover could alert sniffer dogs. He lay the plastic bags side by side and bound them together with cling wrap, then slid the whole thing into the lining of the bag's divider cushion.

Lastly, he stitched it up, using exactly the same holes he'd unpicked to avoid incriminating double holes. Once it was all perfectly done, he called Timi and flew to São Paulo, exhausted.

The next day, Timi delivered the bag to Cafiero, who wished his pregnant girlfriend farewell then flew out from Florianópolis to São Paulo's domestic airport, Congonhas. Dimitrius was waiting for him. Together, they rode the bus between airports so Dimitrius could give him his ticket – South African Airways via Johannesburg to Bali. He instructed Cafiero to email him on arrival so Zeta could fly out to Bali to pick up the bag and pay him US $7000. It was easy. Now he just had to ride the wave.

When the bus pulled up at Guarulhos airport, Dimitrius wished him good luck. Then Cafiero was on his own, lugging the board bag into the airport terminal.

Federal police were watching the kaleidoscope of international passengers moving through the vast terminal, alert for anything suspicious. About five hours earlier, they'd busted a Thai woman trying to board a Swiss Air flight to Bangkok with 5.1 kilos of blow in the false bottom of her backpack. Police said she'd fit the 'mule profile' – a young woman, alone, carrying a backpack. They were trained to see tiny clues. When the pale, skinny DJ covered in piercings carried the huge surfboard bag across to the check-in desk, it was a wipeout.

> *The pale complexion of a man who tried to check two surfboards on an international flight aroused the suspicion of Brazilian airport security officials, who said they found nearly 7 kilos of cocaine hidden in a package between the boards. Luis Alberto Faria Cafiero, 27, was arrested boarding a flight to Johannesburg, South Africa, with a connection to Bali, Indonesia. 'He did not look like a person who's always on the beach,' said Federal police officer Isaias Santos Vilela.*
> *– AP Worldstream*

Dimitrius was sure the bust had nothing to do with his meticulous packing.

> *I did a very good job. They first catch him because he doesn't have the surfing guy look. The problem is not my packing.*
>
> – Dimitrius

São Paulo airport police caught their third trafficker for the day two hours after Cafiero's bust, a Dutch guy going home with 9.2 kilos of blow in plastic bags tossed in his suitcase among underpants, towels and packets of coffee, which were supposed to deceive sniffer dogs.

Jorge was still surfing in Bali. He didn't hear of Cafiero's bust until he flew home a couple of weeks later.

'Are you fucking stupid?' Jorge yelled at Zeta. 'You think Cafiero looks like a fucking surfer – white, pale, skinny? What the fuck were you thinking?' Zeta stood mute on the doorstep of his parents' house as Jorge shouted furiously. Jorge's three-month surf trip to Bali had been very profitable. He'd just carried home US $200,000, plus he had the $70,000 Timi brought back. One of his horses had also arrived with a big bag of pills and skunk, but now any feelings of satisfaction were obliterated. If Cafiero talked, he could expose them all.

'You'd better tell Dimitrius to hire a lawyer to help this guy and to see if he's gonna talk. I'm not taking any responsibility. I'm disappointed in you, Zeta. Big mistake. They will link us with Marco's arrest. You're a dickhead. You and Dimitrius brought heat to our business. Do something and do it now.'

Jorge spun on his heel and left, not interested in hearing anything from Zeta.

Zeta and Dimi planned this behind my back and made a huge mistake. I was in shock, not because they decided to make another operation without my knowledge. I was surfing the best waves on the planet, had made a small fortune – they were free to do as many scams as they like. Same for Cafiero, he could run for anyone he wants. But to send Cafiero as a surfer, loaded with seven kilos of blow, to Bali was irresponsible and stupid.

Even I would stop him in the airport – what the fuck, where are you going? – he was a horrible looking person, pale and ugly, with all these piercings, in the eyebrow, in his nose, in both ears he put these tubes that makes your ears giant like the native people. He was full of tattoos and skinny. They sent him with this surfboard bag probably twice his weight. He probably could not even carry that. Was a big mistake.

– Jorge

The timing made it a possible cataclysmic mistake. Another Brazilian flying out to Bali with cocaine in sports equipment, just weeks after Marco's bust. Jorge could see it was going to crank up the heat, put them under a blowtorch of scrutiny and possibly expose them like never before. Someone would start connecting the dots. He didn't know that Caieron already had, although Tadashi hadn't given their names.

No one sent a lawyer to see if Cafiero was talking. The days passed and nothing happened. They all assumed he'd kept his mouth shut.

They were wrong.

Straight after his bust, Cafiero spilled names, email addresses and many phone numbers, comprehensively stripping the playboys of invisibility. Caieron was sent a copy of the statement and saw some names he'd never heard: Rufino, Zeta and Dimitrius.

Cafiero had told the cops anything they wanted to know, revealing Dimitrius had hired him for this run to Bali, that he was nicknamed 'the Greek' and used two passports, sold Balinese furniture in Brazil, was 1.7 metres tall, between 30 to 35 years old, had short black hair, a strong Rio accent, and that he'd told him he'd trafficked drugs more than 30 times through São Paulo airport. In a move that would turn out to be the most damaging, he also gave the cops Dimitrius' email address, the one he was instructed to send a 'Goal, I'm here' email to but never got the chance.

Cafiero also described Zeta to the cops. He was the link between himself and Dimitrius, 25 to 30 years old, with black curly hair, dark skin and green eyes. For some reason, he didn't betray Timi, but the police got his number from Cafiero's phone anyway.

Even with this detailed statement, Caieron needed more proof to guarantee bringing them down in the Brazilian courts. He would have to assign a team to target them, and right now, his agents were all busy with other cases. It would have to wait. Caieron was relaxed. He knew that sooner or later, more intel would land on his desk and was sure these traffickers wouldn't be stopping anytime soon.

His lack of fast action was inadvertently a smart play. It gave the playboys confidence that Cafiero had shut up and kept their invisibility intact.

But their names were now in the Operation Playboy file.

CHAPTER EIGHTEEN

JÉSSICA

Jorge was standing in the bathroom of Jéssica's apartment, about to jump into the shower, when the intercom buzzed. He grabbed it. 'Jorge, the cops are down here with me.' It was the concierge. Jorge tensed. This was bad news. The concierge then gave him some good news – he was refusing to let them up without a warrant. 'Okay, thanks. Bye.' Jorge flew across the room, stark naked, spying out a window. He saw two unmarked police cars and several plain-clothes cops standing below.

His heart was pounding. He had to get out. He threw on some clothes then, agile as a cat, sprang down the back stairs to the car park. Checking the coast was clear, he made a run for it, sprinting through a side gate. It was a slapstick scene for anyone watching, the lithe, long-legged, skinny guy hurtling down the street like a maniac, frantically swivelling his head to see if he was being chased. Two hundred metres later, Jorge jumped in a cab, gasping to the driver, 'Brava beach please.'

Jorge felt sure it was an extortion exercise. He now knew the cops were aware of him. He knew some surfed at Joaquina, and also in Bali where one of the top civil cops often holidayed. He was conscious of how overtly flamboyant he was, and right now that seemed like a big mistake.

In the weeks since Cafiero's bust, he'd got busier and flashier. He had the ability to push personal tragedies, like the possible execution of his friend and incarceration of his horses, to the back of his mind, eclipsing the dark side of trafficking with the bright sun of Bali and bling of Europe. He suppressed his fear and angst but couldn't eradicate them.

From his secret apartment on the north shore, he was figuring out his next moves, both with the cops and Jéssica. After coming back from Bali a few weeks earlier with all that cash, he'd splurged on her, bringing back expensive gifts including a Cartier watch, buying her a new car, paying her bills and for big improvements on her apartment. He loved spending his cash on Jéssica, and she loved it too.

I treated her like a queen. I was happy, she was happy — or that's what I thought.

— Jorge

But others knew he was in for heartbreak. Some, like Tizzy, a lawyer working at the Tribunal de Justice, were intimately aware of what she got up to while Jorge was away:

Did you know Jéssica?

Yeah, I know her. Everybody knows her — she's very fast.

She had lots of boyfriends while Jorge was away?

Yeah.

You?

Yeah, sometimes me too. Everybody.

For a while now, Jorge's close friends had been telling him she was unfaithful and making a fool of him, urging him to dump her.

Break was an idiot with the girls. He makes much money and gives to the bitches.

— Tizzy

Everyone was criticising me, saying, 'Why are you giving her a car, man?' I heard rumours about Jéssica, people came to tell me she was cheating. Lenzi was saying for a long time, 'Jorge, you have to break up with her, she's a slut.' But I think I was in love and trying to fool myself, trying to believe that these people were lying. And I was confronting her and she swears, 'No, I'm not, it's lies.' We broke up twice, but I regret and return, believing her because I was blind and very attached.

But I was starting to get very anxious and paranoid that she was cheating on me, I wanted to believe she wasn't but I had all this in my mind and it was haunting me, I couldn't even fuck her.

— Jorge

The rumours didn't abate and he was becoming more upset, while justifying the hypocrisy in his reaction, given his own wild sex life, as the Latin way. It wasn't a reflection of a bad relationship or his fading love; he was just satisfying his Latin lust. Of course, this in no way gave Jéssica permission to do the same.

I was in love with her, but at the same time I was fucking around at parties everywhere I went. It was my instinct. I can't really be with just one girl, I like this diversity – and I always need sex.

– Jorge

Jorge also now had the cops onto him, direct heat that he couldn't just deflect or suppress. It was changing his game, in Florianópolis anyway.

Before I was thinking it was Disneyland, I was untouchable. But after this, everything got really hot for me on that small island. Everything changed after the raid at Jéssica's apartment – my mentality changed. I started to be very afraid, looking over my shoulder. I stayed more away from the weed, I tried not to touch it too much – just for my own use, giving jobs to other people, to hold the weed, separate, deliver, collect money. I was more distant from it because police were on my neck, they knew my activities and they wanted me bad.

– Jorge

It wasn't slowing him down, though. He had blow and was set to make another quick trip to Amsterdam via Paris, with a new horse simultaneously flying on a different plane. Timi was on that flight too, acting as 'horse watcher'. If Jorge had a new horse he didn't fully trust, or thought they might get confused or lost, he would move Timi into play. In Florianópolis, he'd be taken to surreptitiously see the horse's face on a beach so he knew who to follow.

I'm a very good physiognomist, I'm like an FBI agent, never forget a face.

– Timi

In Amsterdam, Timi stalked the new horse along the long airport corridors, through customs and out. Then he swooped, taking the bag of drugs and quietly telling the horse, 'Come with me.' Timi loved this job – no risk, and a trip to Europe. They went to check into one of Jorge's favourite hotels, the Krasnapolsky.

Break brings me there. He wants to stay in this hotel, the Krasnapolsky, in front of the Queen's palace, very near the Red Light District. Big hotel, very traditional for celebrities, very nice service, and the girl says, 'We just have one room at the top, the expensive one.' Break says, 'Come on, let's go, that's what I want.' I say, 'Break, you're crazy to pay all that.' 'Ah, just let's enjoy, you can stay with me, okay.' He is a crazy guy, a very funny guy. His passion is spending money . . . he spends all his money on hotels and expensive clothes. He didn't think of tomorrow.

– Timi

A few days later, they flew home. Jorge went via São Paulo where he met the horse and dropped off the skunk, then on to Florianópolis. When he switched on his phone, he saw a message from a loyal school friend, Marcio, saying, 'We need to talk.' Jorge stayed the night at Jéssica's and went to meet Marcio in the morning. It was bad news. All his niggling doubts exploded into reality.

Marcio gave Jorge painful details. At 3 am the previous morning, he'd driven past Jéssica's new car and noticed she was inside kissing a guy. Marcio didn't recognise him, but drove past twice to make sure. The news ripped off Jorge's delusional blinkers. He knew Marcio had no reason to lie.

I just gave her a brand new, beautiful fucking car and went to Amsterdam to do my job, and she's with some guy in that car. The fucking whore. I had no option, I couldn't stay with her any more. I went to the flat when she was at work, picked up all my belongings and went to my mum's apartment. I could go back to the Brava beach flat, but I wanted to be in the city centre cos being alone wasn't a good idea, I was devastated, I was sad, and feeling stupid. Being with my mum was the best option.

When Jéssica figured it out, she came to my mum's place, making a scene, acting, crying, saying, 'It's all lies,' she still loves me, people are just jealous of us and blah blah blah. I didn't buy it. I'd made up my mind there was no way back. So, she started to play the victim. She said if I really want to leave her, I should sell the car or pass it into my own name. I told her, 'You know what, you can stick this fucking car up your ass, I can buy a car like this every day of the week. I don't care about the money, get out of my place.' I felt devastated, I was broken hearted.

But I soon realised for the first time since I started making money I was free and single. I could go anywhere in the world without giving an explanation to anyone, I had power, prestige and cash. I started to party hard, and I was hanging with a group of young, rich, beautiful Florianópolis society girls.

I soon began to date Julia Sirowski, the richest girl in my state, daughter of the owner of Globo TV. Before, she was dating someone, and I was dating someone, we were just cheating and hiding – meeting, fucking and that's it. But I could start to be more open about us, go to her house, be with her circle of friends. Her house was a mansion in Lagoa da Conceição and it was always crowded with girls, in the swimming pools, one indoor, one outdoor with a sauna, jacuzzi, big boat in front of the lagoon that we used for wakeboarding. It was parties all day and night long. So I realised, after a short time, I'd made the right decision. And, I turned the page.

– Jorge

CHAPTER NINETEEN

DARCY DOES BLOW

Around 2 am, Jorge left his mum's apartment and drove across to the lake area for an intense night of making magic in a surfboard factory. As he walked through the metal gate, the place was still and quiet, the secretaries and shapers and lingering surfer clients long gone home. Only Jorge's good friend, the boss, Igor, was here, waiting for him. Tonight, they were going turn blow invisible.

Jorge loved this place. Shiny, colourful boards lined the walls and equipment like saws, sanders, scissors and foam blanks was scattered everywhere. The distinct, intense aroma of fibreglass and resin hung in the still air. It was a surfer's heaven.

Jorge saw the newly shaped bare foam board on the table. This would shroud his blow. He was switching to using boards since Cafiero's bust a few weeks ago had ruined surfboard bags. For a while at least, the linings of the bags would be given extra scrutiny at São Paulo airport.

Using surfboards was an old way of smuggling blow that

came in and out of vogue, depending on busts. Jorge was here to help with the meticulous job. He knew blow and Igor knew boards. He was a top shaper with a busy client list, including some of Brazil's top pro surfers, even one on the World Tour. Tonight was just for a bit of extra cash. Surfboard shapers were the poor cousins of the surfing world, making little money.

They quickly set to work on the first board. Jorge sliced a kilo brick in two, then they figured out where to insert each half. For balance, the blow needed to sit either side of the stringer, a thin strip of wood that ran down the centre of the foam. These boards would never hit the water but had to look and feel genuine – a lopsided board could send a horse down as fast as a customs officer picked it up. Horses' lives were in Igor's hands, and he knew it.

He had to custom-cut the cavities in the foam for a perfect fit for each brick. Another crucial step was laying carbon fibre across the entire deck of the board for camouflage during X-rays.

It was slow work, but the hours flew. The sun was rising and soon Igor's staff would arrive. They finished off by spray painting the clear board with crazy bright colours, then called it a night. They'd come back that night to fibreglass and sand it, and start all over again on the next board.

I spent about five hours on each surfboard from cutting the blow, to measuring, finding the right position in the foam, cutting the hole, putting in the blow and putting a little layer of foam on the top. After that you put carbon fibre on the top and then this glass-like resin, and wait for it to dry, then put resin again, it's a process that takes hours.

– Jorge

When the three boards were done, Jorge gave them to Darcy, who was set to do his first blow run to Europe.

I finally thought why not? It was the beginning of the end.

— Darcy

Unlike Cafiero, Darcy would look a natural carrying surfboards. The only thing working against him was the destination. Taking boards to Bali was normal, a surf trip to Amsterdam was not, but if anyone could talk their way through, it was Darcy.

He woke up at his parents' Jurerê Internacional home and gazed out of his upstairs bedroom window at the familiar view; his mother's beautiful garden and beyond through some trees, a glimpse of the ocean.

Every time I went, I opened the balcony door and thought, 'Oh my god, dude, look where you live, you are nuts because if something goes wrong, boom, there's going to be iron bars. I always thought about that, but then, 'Ah, who cares, let's go to the Netherlands.'

— Darcy

He went downstairs, told his parents he was going on a surf trip up the coast for a few days, then left with the board bag. He drove north to Navegantes airport preferring, like most of the playboys now, to avoid Florianópolis' small airport. He flew to São Paulo's Guarulhos, unfazed by Cafiero's recent bust there, and then to Paris.

'*Bonjour, comment ça va?*' he said at customs, using his scant French to help charm his way through Charles de Gaulle.

'*Très bien, et vous?*' 'Good, and you?' the officer said perfunctorily.

'Ah, *très bien*. Do you speak English please?' Darcy asked.

'Yes,' he said, looking at the huge surfboard bag. 'Where are you going?'

'I'm going surfing in Hossegor. My friends are there.'

Darcy was ready to put on a show, pull out his Rip Curl wetsuit and his favourite board, which he'd packed on top of the others in the board bag just in case he needed to prove he was a genuine surfer. He could talk about that board with unfeigned passion.

> *It was high performance, with six deep channels, super light, an amazing board made for me with my name engraved on it, worth US $600. My favourite board, I loved it.*
>
> – Darcy

But the officer waved him through without any more questions. Undoubtedly the Hossegor cover story was bolstered by the fact the surf resort, seven hours' drive from Charles de Gaulle airport, had just hosted the World Tour's Quiksilver Pro tournament and a lot of surfers had been coming through.

> *They didn't check anything. I got a taxi to a train station in the centre of Paris, Gare du Nord, and walked in with that bag like a coffin, with four surfboards inside, and took a fast train from Paris to Amsterdam.*
>
> – Darcy

As the train flew along at 300 kilometres per hour, Darcy sat quietly sipping beer, seemingly a relaxed tourist enjoying a trip. It belied what was going on underneath; he was ecstatic, buzzing. He wanted to scream, to celebrate, but he knew cops watched these European trains. One of Andre's horses had recently been busted getting on a train in Madrid with a bag of blow.

So Darcy gazed serenely out the window, watching France, Belgium and the Netherlands flash by in three and a half hours. Then he was there, in Amsterdam. He'd done it. He grabbed the board bag, went straight to the hotel and called Jorge. 'Goal,' he sang out. The little word was music to Jorge's ears. 'Okay, man, great job. We'll see you tomorrow.'

Jorge was buzzing. Goals never lost their thrill, no matter how many he made. He phoned Oscar, one of the partners who had a kilo share. 'Goal.' Oscar called the third investor, Tizzy, with the good news. Later that day, the three of them met in KLM's business lounge at Guarulhos airport, Tizzy wisely never mentioning his fling with Jéssica.

Darcy was already celebrating; he was in a laneway in the Red Light District doing a deal to buy some blow. 'I bought €100 worth of cocaine and had more than US $150,000 worth in my room, can you believe it?' He jumped in a black Mercedes taxi to head back to the hotel, but couldn't wait. 'Excuse me, man,' he said to the driver, then sniffed. The driver was blasé – he'd seen it all before. Cabbies in Amsterdam often found dope in the back-seat pockets, left by tourists en route to the airport who suddenly remembered their coffee shop dope was still in their pocket or handbag.

The next day, the three guys met Darcy at the Quentin Hotel. Tizzy and Darcy were mates from school days and surfing at Joaquina. Darcy and Oscar were meeting for the first time, with a fateful handshake.

Later that day, a Dutch contact of Oscar's turned up to collect the boards. Tizzy and Oscar lugged down the bag, minus Darcy's board, and tried to fit it into the back of a little red Fiesta, kicking and shoving it hard. 'Ah, gently, gently, be careful with my car.' 'Ah, fuck your car,' they laughed.

The buyer eventually drove off with the surfboard bag across the seats, and soon came back to pick up the guys. Despite protests from Jorge, Oscar refused to let him come. This was his contact and he would not risk Jorge poaching him.

When Tizzy and Oscar returned to the Quentin a couple of hours later, they were fuming.

'What the fuck, man, what did you do with the drugs? Three hundred grams are missing,' Oscar shouted at Jorge. They'd cracked open the three boards at the buyer's apartment, extracted the blow, tested it, weighed it, and discovered the deficit. Jorge was as shocked as them, and it made no sense for him to have swiped a bit in Brazil. Jorge thought it was perhaps Lenzi, an addict, who'd helped with the last board.

> *Lenzi was Break's right arm and he has too many addictions; burning money with drugs, women and casinos. But I put my money in Break's hand, he needs to be responsible for the money, for the drugs, for every-thing . . . he makes the operation.*
>
> *– Tizzy*

After a heated argument, they agreed to split the loss between all of them, including Darcy.

> *I was pissed because I delivered the coke to them in a hotel in the centre of Amsterdam. I did my job perfectly, 100 percent, and the agreement was not honoured.*
>
> *– Darcy*

Darcy grudgingly took a pay cut, sensing what many in the game believed – blow blew bad karma.

I believe coke is what brought all the greed, and the bad karma. When I came with weed, I felt that it would make people happy. But when I was taking coke, I thought, 'Dude, this shit is bad.' Rivalries started, it brought up a bad vibe among us. We weren't laughing as hard.

– Darcy

The four guys stayed together to shop for skunk and pills for Darcy's return run. Despite tensions, they all shared the same religion – hedonism – so enjoyed their time in the city, using hookers, smoking grass in coffee shops, shopping and clubbing.

One night, Oscar and Tizzy went to a party hosted by a friend of Oscar's buyer, in a tall house on a canal. Tizzy couldn't talk to anyone as his English was sketchy and he didn't speak Dutch. He sat down to roll a joint at a table opposite a black American guy who was covered in gold chains and nubile girls. The American was talking a lot, but Tizzy couldn't understand a word, so smoked his joint and left for the hotel. He found out much later, while watching a music video, that the black guy at the party was superstar rapper, and ex drug-dealer, 50 Cent.

A week passed as they struggled to find kilos of skunk, and Darcy realised his parents would be worrying. He borrowed Oscar's phone; 'Hey, Dad, I'm driving my friend up the coast, we're still here in São Paulo.' His dad bought the story, he hoped. Darcy's family was far from naive about his lifestyle. One of his sisters had once staged an intervention, telling him, 'I know what you're doing Darcy. I know you're travelling, I know you're dealing, and I want to take you to a rehab clinic. If you don't want to come, then get your bags and get out of Mum and Dad's house, right now.'

Darcy had marched upstairs, packed a bag and left. His

soft-hearted dad asked him to stay. 'Don't worry, kid, you can stay here.' 'No, Dad, I'm moving, I don't want to hear all that shit.'

Darcy had no plans to stop trafficking, but soon moved home again. 'If you're addicted to that shit, you're in a dark hole but it seems like a party.'

After ten days in Amsterdam, the guys were finally ready for Darcy to carry the bag of pills and skunk. Darcy left the hotel, entrusting his favourite surfboard and Rip Curl wetsuit to Jorge.

> *I wasn't bringing a board case from Amsterdam when I had weed on my back. So I say, 'Break, you take it back.' He says, 'Yes, don't worry. Just leave everything here, I'll take care of the board case, I'll bring it back.'*
>
> – Darcy

As always, Darcy breezed back to Brazil and took a taxi to Onion's apartment, where the drugs were stored. Onion and Lenzi, who'd come up from his own apartment a few floors below, were waiting and Darcy nonchalantly tossed the bag at their feet.

> *I always deliver like, 'Ah, here it is, dude.' Boom. Throw it on the floor like it's just a wet towel. 'Here's your shit, bye, guys, see you tomorrow,' leaving them with big smiles on their faces.*
>
> – Darcy

The three investors were also ready to fly home when Tizzy's dodgy track record with Dutch justice caught up with him. As Oscar and Jorge cruised through immigration, Tizzy was taken into custody.

For a smart lawyer, Tizzy made some dumb moves. His shady Dutch story had started a year earlier when he flew to

Amsterdam for a cash run, hired by his friend, Big House, to carry €80,000 back to Brazil. Big House had bought him a return ticket from São Paulo to Amsterdam, but told him to use only the first leg then toss it. He bought him a second return ticket from Amsterdam to São Paulo, just in case the original was compromised. With €80,000 at stake, the cost of two return tickets was cheap insurance, and pretty standard procedure. It worked. Tizzy made a home run with the €80,000.

Things started to go awry when Tizzy tried using the two unused legs for another trip a few weeks later. For Tizzy, this was just a fun trip, although he took $9000 for Onion to buy him two kilos of skunk and carry it back for a fee of 200 grams of skunk.

Tizzy was stopped by immigration on arrival in Amsterdam. There was no crime yet, but he was escorted to an office and told to strip naked.

He then sat on a little chair as airport officials came in, one after the other in quick succession, prodding his stomach and asking questions. 'Why are there so many stamps in your passport?' 'Why do you come to Amsterdam so often?' 'Do you have a job in Brazil?' 'I'm a surfer.' 'I'm always travelling.' 'Yes, I have a job. I'm a lawyer.' He was polite and cooperative, but they weren't satisfied. They kept asking and prodding. Tizzy felt sure it was the odd ticketing that had red-flagged him; why was a Brazilian finishing his return trip in Amsterdam? They were suspicious, sensing something was off. After almost three hours, they told him to get dressed and let him go.

For his return to Brazil a week later, he'd tossed up whether to buy a new ticket or risk using the old return leg. He chose to save cash and risk it. As soon as the KLM check-in guy scanned his ticket, Tizzy knew it had been a false economy.

The guy broke with the routine, picking up the phone. He said something in Dutch, hung up and then gave Tizzy his boarding pass and a fake smile. Tizzy knew something was very wrong. Two burly men were striding his way as he walked across to immigration. By the time he gave his passport to the officer, they were there. One stood, surly faced, arms crossed, right beside him; the other was looming airside. As a black belt in Jiu-Jitsu, Tizzy could wipe the floor with both of them, but knew that wouldn't be a smart move right now.

Tizzy accepted his passport back and walked towards the lurking agent. He told Tizzy to stop and took his hand luggage. Tizzy watched as, one by one, his daughter's chocolate bars were pulverised in the agent's big hands. 'This is a lot of chocolate,' the guy stated. 'Yeah, my daughter loves it. Is it a crime to carry chocolate now?' Tizzy was trying to seem cool, but he wasn't. Through an office window straight ahead, he saw the other man searching his checked-in bag.

'Okay, you can go to your gate,' the chocolate pulveriser said.

Tizzy couldn't believe it. He grabbed his bag and walked off, thinking, 'Is this a trick? Why have they let me go? How did they miss the grass?' He kept walking. He was in a surreal bubble. Nothing felt real.

It wasn't.

'Excuse me, Brazilian, you have a problem. Please come with us.' The men were right behind him.

He retraced his footsteps back to their office, where the bag of skunk was now on full display on a table. 'Where are you hiding the pills?' one of the guys asked. 'I don't have pills.' 'Who's your supplier?' Tizzy quickly made up a story. 'A Brazilian guy, a total stranger, came up to me in Leidseplein and asked me to carry two kilos of grass. He was going to contact me when

I arrived in Brazil.' Tizzy knew it was lame, but like most busted traffickers, he was sticking to it.

They handcuffed him and took him back down the airport corridor, past his boarding gate and downstairs to a waiting police car. On the ten-minute drive to the cells, the cops lit up a joint and smoked it. Tizzy was shattered.

> *It's a strange feeling of peaceful when it all cools down, but it's a fake peaceful, there's no way out. I wanted to be dead.*
>
> – Tizzy

They locked Tizzy up alone in a cell where he spent a dark night of deep regret. He thought nonstop about his pregnant wife, his beautiful little girl and his proud father who, like Jorge's, was a top prosecutor in Brazil.

But this was Amsterdam, Europe's drug gateway. The rest of Europe often cursed Holland's soft attitude to drugs. Tizzy was about to bless it.

'You're free to go.' They were words Tizzy wasn't expecting. A cop explained that he was charged, but could go home to Brazil and hire a Dutch lawyer to represent him in court. If convicted, he'd be fined €6000. Tizzy couldn't believe it. He went straight to the KLM desk and rebooked his flight.

The first was at 11 pm, so he grabbed a taxi to the Rokerij Coffee shop, where he spent the whole day, too scared to call anyone or go anywhere in case he was being watched. That night he flew home with his freedom and reputation intact. 'Fine. Happy ending. My family don't know – nobody knows.' But he failed to hire a lawyer to represent him.

Many months later, on this latest trip with Jorge and Oscar, they'd flown via Madrid, clearing immigration in Spain. On their departure, Jorge warned Tizzy not to go through Dutch immigration, but via another European city. He ignored the advice and tried his luck.

'You have a problem,' the immigration officer said after checking his passport. It was the same counter, then the same office as he was escorted to last time, but this time with a sickening new sense of déjà vu. 'I'm so fucking stupid,' he thought. They explained that he'd been sentenced to 60 days' prison for the two previous kilos of skunk because he hadn't hired a lawyer. They searched him and found his cash from Darcy's run, advising him they'd give it back if a lawyer proved it was clean.

They failed to find 50 grams of skunk in his socks, despite six body searches between the airport and the cells. They made him strip naked, but let him keep his socks on when he complained it was too cold to take them off. As soon as he got to his cell, he flushed the skunk but quickly regretted it. He wasn't searched again, and could have done with a skunk haze to soften his harsh new reality.

It was hell. Fluorescent lights shone around the clock, and prisoners only got two 30-minute spells outside each day. Releasing him into this prison yard was like putting a seal pup in a shark tank, or so it seemed. Tizzy was the only white guy, and a smallish build, in a yard of huge, angry Africans. They immediately started pushing him around. His look masked his power. He was dangerous. His black belt in Jiu-Jitsu gave him techniques to maim or kill in a flash. He badly hurt two big black guys in self-defence, but it made Tizzy a high-risk inmate. He was moved to a maximum-security isolation cell. Before any outing, he had to stand with his back to the door and put his hands out a flap to be handcuffed.

Days passed. He wasn't given fresh clothes or the chance to see a lawyer. After the daily 6 am showers, he was given paper towels to dry himself. If he thought the magic wand of soft Dutch justice was going to sprinkle fairy dust again – he was right.

On day ten, a guard opened the door, and told him, 'You're free to go.'

Tizzy couldn't believe his good luck – again.

CHAPTER TWENTY

HANGING WITH KELLY

Darcy tore down the highway, surfboards rattling on the roof of the hire car. Abruptly, he swerved to the edge of the road, stopped, jumped out, and yanked the ropes tighter around them.

These boards were valuable, even more so than those he'd just carried to Amsterdam. Arguably, these were priceless, magic boards, hand-picked by Kelly Slater to ride his way back to world number one. Darcy jumped back into the car and sped off.

In the back seat, taking a white-knuckle ride through south Brazil, was Kelly Slater himself.

Riding shotgun was his good friend, American pro surfer Taylor Knox. Darcy was euphoric. Cashed-up after his first blow run, plenty of party drugs in his pocket, and now escorting Kelly and Taylor.

The World Tour's itinerary was serving Darcy well, reinforcing his cover story in Paris and now bringing the A-list to his home turf after the contest was moved south from Rio.

Darcy's chaperoning gig came at the request of Taylor, who was putting him up with all the surfers at the Praia Mole Hotel. Across the road was one of the likely contest spots, Mole beach. Organisers would announce each morning the beach with the best conditions, triggering the fanfare of surfers, judges, media and thousands of fans to head there for the day's contest.

Andre's front yard beach, Silveira, was chosen on day one. As Darcy raced the 90 kilometres to Garopaba, Andre was already on the beach in front of his house helping to set up a VIP area for Mormaii, his friend's surf company.

Darcy pulled up, let the guys out and parked the car. He was looking forward to hanging out with the elite pro surfers for the next ten days. He already knew many of them, and some of them knew him and his grassy pockets. 'Hey, Darcy, what have you got for me today?' one of the surfers had asked him back at the hotel. Darcy didn't ever sell but generously gave the guy a gram or two of White Widow.

Darcy had stayed close to Taylor since their exchange days. Surfing had first aligned their paths, but their stars went on very different trajectories. Taylor's shot to world number four, and Darcy's shot to champion horse. Their shared passion for surfing was also fading, as Darcy rarely hit the water anymore.

Kelly accepted Darcy as an integral part of their close crew in Florianópolis. Darcy escorted them around the island, translating, making introductions, even taking them to his parents' house for dinner. They were relaxed together, Kelly sometimes pulling out his ukulele and singing.

The closeness gave Darcy a glimpse into the fanatical Brazilian worship of Kelly Slater. He was in the eye of the fan storm.

I saw things when he was around me that I have never seen before. It was amazing, amazing.

– Darcy

Famous people, like a sexy MTV host and the state governor, were keen to meet Kelly. Darcy's phone rang nonstop. Crowds of people gaped and took photos wherever they went. Darcy got the chance to put his lead foot to good use, tearing off to escape school kids chasing them, or fans leaping out at red lights, taking photos.

On the final day of the contest, Kelly and Taylor were in the quarter-finals. Darcy was driving them 100 kilometres south to Imbituba in a bigger, more powerful van, with the boards now lying across the folded seats. Darcy was going faster and faster.

There were six trucks in front of me, so I got behind, in third gear and 120, fourth gear, 170, fifth gear and I overtook six trucks, and Taylor goes, 'Look, look, Kelly, we're going 190,' and Kelly says, 'Oh shit,' and was holding on. I was almost at 200, and he says, 'Come on, Darcy, slow down.' And I say, 'Sorry about that, I just got excited.' I love to drive fast.

But with precious cargo like those guys in the car?

I was out of my mind. It was part of my excitement, I was a very excited man. Speed thrilled me. Surfing, driving or flying with huge bags under my belt, it was exhilarating for me. I was totally irresponsible. I was living my life and enjoying every minute. But he asked me to slow down, and I did straight away.

– Darcy

When they pulled up, Kelly and Taylor started waxing their boards. It was a pivotal day for Kelly in his fight to regain the world title. Six times he'd won it, five in a row just before he'd taken a three-year hiatus. No one had possessed the talent and drive to beat him, until now. Hawaiian Andy Irons was young, clinching the crown with his raw, explosive talent while Kelly was away, and had no plans to let him snatch it back. Their rivalry was deep and fierce.

There was a time when I really would go to sleep at night thinking of ways to punch him in the face.
— Andy Irons on Kelly Slater

I remember I was in France one time. I remember, I was, like, hitting this bag, I just was training one day and I was hitting it and I was just like imagining it was Andy.
— Kelly Slater (*A Fly in the Champagne*)

It was now a two-horse race for the world title. Out of the year's nine completed tournaments around the world, Kelly and Andy had won seven between them. With only two left after Brazil, a win today was critical.

It was thrilling to watch. Taylor was first up against world champ Andy. If Taylor could knock him out, the contest would be wide open for Kelly to win. Darcy smiled as he heard Kelly offering Taylor a bit of extra incentive.

Kelly says, 'Taylor, if you beat Andy, I'll pay you a business-class flight home.' Taylor goes, 'Darcy, did you hear that?' I said, 'Yes I did.' Taylor says, 'See, Kelly, Darcy heard it, Kelly.' Kelly goes, 'I'm serious, man.'
— Darcy

Whether the thought of a business-class seat helped him or not, Taylor won.

Kelly was stoked, and so was Taylor.

– Darcy

Andy was out. Taylor was knocked out in the next round and Kelly was up against a Brazilian in his semi-final. He gave Darcy a high-five and Darcy wished him luck, then watched the super-hero, flanked by security, run to the water. Darcy walked behind them through the rowdy crowd, carrying Kelly's back-up board. 'Ah, you fucking asshole, why are you helping the American?' someone shouted. Others were ogling the board and yelling, 'Can we take a photo of the board?'

Kelly won the heat, then the final against Aussie Mick Fanning, to the roar of Brazilian fans.

'This is the craziest crowd I've ever seen in my life,' began Slater, over the deafening sound of thousands surrounding him. 'I thought it was mad when I first started, but this is heavy . . . I couldn't hear the scores . . . it's a pretty awesome feeling to come off the beach to applause like that . . . This sea of people is incredible though. You come to Brazil and feel like a rock star.'

– Kelly Slater, *Surfing Magazine*

While Kelly was speaking, Darcy was busily putting the boards in the van, and helping to set up an escape route. He drove the van to a spot on a Port Authority property next to a fence, which they'd gained permission to cut. Kelly's security team ushered him through the crowd, through the fence, and into the van. Then, Darcy hit it.

I drove pretty quick on the way back. Not 200 but pretty quick.

– Darcy

Kelly and Taylor flew out of Florianópolis and left Darcy with unforgettable memories.

He kept a keen eye on the last two contests in Hawaii. It was a nail-biting finish, coming down to 30 minutes and their best two waves. Kelly lost to Andy and was shattered, seen just afterwards sobbing in an outdoor shower.

Darcy understood that passion and love for surfing, and his time with the World Tour guys inspired him to get back on his board. But he was soon crying too – he tore a knee ligament while surfing and was out of action. On crutches and after a costly operation, he desperately needed to do a run as soon as he could walk unaided again.

CHAPTER TWENTY-ONE
PLAYBOY COVER GIRL

Bernardo, a Joaquina surfer, was sitting on a Varig plane on the tarmac at Charles de Gaulle in Paris with blow strapped to his legs. He came with extra baggage – famous connections. If he got busted, it could unleash a blowtorch of scrutiny, possibly leading to his bosses. They knew this, and had argued over sending him.

While Bernardo, a shy, skinny guy, stayed low-key, his sister, Maryeva, was high profile. Across Brazil, men were in love with her. She'd shot to fame in a beer commercial that became a sensation. It used an extreme close-up shot tracing a drop of sweat rolling down her body as she stands on a hot beach in a tiny red bikini. After she takes a sip of Brahma beer, the drop – still in extreme close-up – reverses up her cooler, smoking hot body – giving every viewer an intimate ride. Overnight, Maryeva became the 'droplet girl' and every man's fantasy.

But her love life fast eclipsed that when she started dating Brazilian tennis superstar, Gustavo Kuerten, aka Guga. The

Florianópolis boy had already won the world number-one spot, three French Open titles, and the hearts of Brazilians.

Maryeva was snapped meeting him at airports and parties, and was suddenly on the cover of gossip magazines. No longer the droplet girl, she was Guga's girl. While he competed across the world, Maryeva was stripping off for magazine covers, and her brother was secretly running as a horse.

Sometimes Bernardo would arrive and Guga and Maryeva would pick him up from the airport.

– Darcy

Maryeva and Guga didn't last, but she stayed high profile. She'd been the July cover girl for Brazil's *Playboy* magazine and in an interview about the shoot for *Veja* magazine, showed just how close she was to Bernardo.

My brother is very jealous. But I sat him down on the sofa, with my mother, and showed them all of the photos. Both of them approved of the work.

– *Veja* magazine

It was five months later that two investors, Big House and São Paulo cop Claudio, argued about sending Bernardo. His sister was hot, and could bring reflective heat if Bernardo got busted. But they'd buckled to bucks, rationalising he was a good horse, and ready to go. They'd booked him on a Varig flight to Amsterdam, one Jorge favoured – departing São Paulo with a brief transit stop in Paris. It was fast, almost direct, with no change of planes or need to get off, and on a new Boeing 777 jet. Given Jorge had a Varig Diamond member's card, this flight was perfect for him, but for a horse it was very dangerous. The last leg was invariably almost empty, increasing a trafficker's visibility and vulnerability.

Bernardo was a sitting duck when French immigration officers entered the cabin to do their routine passport check. For them, it only took a tiny clue, a glint of fear. Clearly they saw something in Bernardo. He was taken off the plane and searched. It was just days before Christmas and it wasn't going to be a happy one.

Word spread fast in Florianópolis that Bernardo had gone down. Tizzy, who was only recently back from his own European troubles, bumped into Bernardo's girlfriend on the beach the day Bernardo had left. 'Bernardo went to Europe today,' she'd told him. Tizzy knew what that meant. The next day, he saw her again.

She tells me, 'Bernardo hasn't called me, I think he has a problem.' I thought, 'Oh yeah, big problem!' France has very hard police, they hate Brazilians . . . hate, hate.

– Tizzy

When Darcy got the news, he shrugged it off. When you walk a tightrope, you don't look down at anyone else's fall.

My twin brother was in town from California and told me, 'Dude, Bernardo got caught.' I say, 'What?' 'Yeah, Bernardo is in prison in France.' I say, 'Wow.' He looked at me, 'Dude, you fucking stop doing this shit.' It's funny as hell – he loved getting a few joints for free, and 'Dude, stop doing this'. But I didn't think about stopping. I wanted to do the parties here, wanted to carry on that life – and I needed money.

– Darcy

Darcy was still managing to hobble up into the favelas to buy little party packs of blow, but he wasn't ready for a run. Limping through airports with a bandaged knee and a bag of surfboards would make him stick out as badly as Cafiero.

The two bosses, Big House and the cop, were keeping a low profile, glad Bernardo's bust hadn't exploded in the media but still fearing it might, aware things were volatile. Maryeva was as protective of Bernardo as he was of her, and was on the warpath.

She was, 'Ah, who did that with my brother, I want to know. I'm going to give them to the cops.' She starts asking around, 'Who's involved?' She was trying to find out and the boys were very scared.

– Rafael

Just five months after Maryeva's July *Playboy* cover, her brother was also a 'playboy' pin-up – on Fernando Caieron's wall; December was Bernardo's month. Caieron had heard about the bust, not through Maryeva's campaign of wrath, but via the usual international police channels. Adding Bernardo to his expanding playboy wall gave Caieron another piece of the puzzle. But, so far, neither Caieron nor Maryeva knew who'd sent him, although the cover girl was fast to point her finger at Jorge, who'd introduced Bernardo to the bent cop, but had no part in his last run.

Bernardo's arrest brought me lots of headache with Maryeva, she was making a lot of problems. She starts to blame me for his arrest, she says I sent him . . . blah blah blah. She accuses me one night in a nightclub and I say, 'Listen, Maryeva, I didn't send your brother. I know who did but I'm not going to tell you. When Bernardo gets out of jail, you're going to talk to him and you're going to see that I have nothing to do with this trip.'

– Jorge

Despite the island getting hotter, Jorge wasn't slowing down. He was now busy organising ten blow boards, five for Darcy to carry when he could walk properly, and five for his recent Bali runner, Lucas. Jorge was using a different shaper after Igor quit, deciding the extra bucks weren't worth jeopardising his legit surfboard business. The new guy worked out of his backyard and wasn't as good as Igor, nor was Jorge supervising like the first couple of times.

After spending Christmas with his mum in Florianópolis, Jorge flew to Amsterdam, using the same Varig flight via Paris that doomed Bernardo. He decided to have a bit of fun, on Bernardo's account. He sat back in his business-class seat, and waited for the agents to do their routine checks. 'May I have your passport please?' one came up and asked. 'No,' Jorge affably replied, watching confusion flash across the agent's face. 'What did you say?' he asked. 'I said no. I'm on Brazilian territory, going to Holland, and I have no reason to show anything to the French authorities,' he said, smiling politely.

I wanted to play with them, tease them. The agent's face went red, a river of fury running in his eyes. He looked to his partner with a confused expression, then looked at me again, then after a deep breath, repeated the same question: 'May I have your passport please?'

— Jorge

Jorge pulled his passport out of a pocket and passed it to him. He'd had his bit of amusement, and had no wish for this to escalate into being escorted off the plane. They'd find nothing, but he could do without the inconvenience.

CHAPTER TWENTY-TWO

BLONDIE

The inconvenience came when Jorge got back to Florianópolis.

Home was getting hotter for Jorge, not just from Maryeva mouthing off, but a growing intrigue about his endless cash, and the busts of horses like Cafiero.

Florianópolis was too small for me. Too small. My flash cars, designer clothes, spending my whole time surfing and partying, spending crazy amounts of money. I was creating lots of attention.

– Jorge

Jorge was still keen to spend summer on the island. He'd just arrived from his trip to Amsterdam, dropped the skunk in São Paulo, flown to Navegantes, and driven 100 kilometres south in his shiny black truck to his mum's basement car park. Exhausted and sick with the flu, he went upstairs, stripped naked, and passed out on his bed.

When the doorbell rang at 6 am, he had to get up; his mum was away. He pulled on some underpants, still half asleep, then shuffled bleary eyed to the door. 'Who is it?' he sang out, wary. It was the concierge, so he relaxed, remembering he'd parked a car in when he'd arrived. He swung open the door to his worst nightmare.

A scrum of cops burst in, pushing him backwards into the wall, gripping his arms, yanking him through the small apartment to his bedroom. They pushed him to sit down on the bed. One cop, clearly in charge, sat next to him and flashed a search warrant. Jorge glanced down at it, suspecting it was fake. He knew these guys were the civil cops, the ones who'd tried to get into Jéssica's flat, but failed because they didn't have a search warrant.

'Where are the drugs, Blondie? Where's the money?' The guy's fingers wrapped tightly around his arm.

'You're wasting your time. I have nothing here,' Jorge said. It was partly true – he was careful never to bring drugs to his mum's place, but a bunch of cash was hanging in her closet. He'd stashed it into the pocket of one of her many blazers last night.

The cop's fingers were needling his arm. 'Blondie, we know everything about you. People have snitched, your friends snitched.' Jorge recognised one of the cops as the son of a famous old local cop. He started telling Jorge how he envied him, seeing him around town with sexy girls and fast cars. Jorge stayed calm, wondering if they thought this would actually work. It wasn't an episode of *CSI*, where they lay a few baited words and the perp gushes his entire guilty story. Jorge simply shrugged, saying his dad was a rich prosecutor and, 'Yeah, girls like me because I'm a good surfer.'

Moments later, they tried a new tack, ripping through drawers and closets, hurling his expensive clothes into a jumbled pile on the floor. They tore his bedroom apart, then went to the lounge room, flipped the couch, pulled pictures down, and emptied out cabinets onto the floor. Jorge felt upset for his mum; her usual pretty, pristine apartment was a catastrophic mess.

The cops went from room to room with Jorge trailing them in his Armani undies. They moved into the hot zone: his mum's closet. Jorge watched them pulling out clothes on hangers, trying to stay calm when one cop picked up the loaded blazer. Jorge didn't look directly, but in his peripheral vision, he saw the guy's hand lingering near the pocket. He waited, held his breath. Then the cop just tossed it onto the heap on the bed, no inkling his fingertips had come within millimetres of €30,000. Jorge's emotional rollercoaster was all internal. His face gave no clue of his panic and then relief. But he knew this wasn't over.

They were growing more pissed off and frustrated; obviously they'd been sure of finding something.

I could see in their eyes, they had adrenalin rushing through the veins.
– Jorge

Jorge felt the boss's clammy fingers clutching at his bare arm again, dragging him back into his bedroom. The guy went straight to the wardrobe, already searched, but this time he reached inside and, hey presto, pulled out a small plastic bag of weed. The cop turned and smirked at Jorge. 'Okay, cuff him,' he said to one of his juniors.

It wasn't mine. I knew it, they knew it.
– Jorge

Jorge showed no emotion as they pulled his hands behind his back and snapped on cuffs. Then the boss told the other three to leave the room to give them a moment alone. He sat down on the bed next to Jorge, who by any body language playbook was at a deep disadvantage – naked, except for his undies, and hands cuffed behind his back. The cop looked him in the eye, put his hand on Jorge's bare leg and broke into a sadistic grin.

Jorge looked straight back at him. 'We both know that's not my grass,' he scoffed.

'Well, how can you prove that, Blondie? It's your word against four police,' he smirked, 'but you're not under arrest yet. I know exactly who you are and what you do – a playboy like you has a good life, travelling around the world, good cars, clothes, beautiful women. Your friends tell us you've just arrived from Amsterdam with five kilos of grass.' Jorge showed no hint of a reaction, but wondered who'd been talking. He'd left all the skunk with Hugo in São Paulo.

'Where is it, Jorge? Where's the five kilos?'

'You're wrong. I don't have anything.'

'Well, Blondie, tell me about your friends, Rufino, Onion, Zeta?'

'I have nothing to say to you. You're wrong about all of this, and making a big mistake.'

'Jorge, do you want us to take you out of the building now, in handcuffs, when all your mum's neighbours are leaving for work? You will get three years in jail for that bag of grass or . . .' He paused. Jorge was waiting for it. '. . . we can negotiate.' Jorge stared blankly at him. 'Come on, Blondie, I get paid a miserable salary. If you want, I can do your security. I can safely transport your drugs, I can collect money from people who owe you, I can work for you. You need it.'

Jorge shook his head. 'I don't know what you're talking about.'

'Blondie, I have two kids and a wife to pay for,' he pushed.

Jorge realised he had no way out. He wasn't guilty of this five grams, but the cop was right – who'd believe him?

'Okay, how much?' he asked.

'Twenty grand. US.'

'Are you crazy? I don't have that much.'

'Okay, fifteen.'

I start to think really fast about all the consequences. If I give him money now, he will always be knocking on my door, and I don't deal with cops. But I had to get rid of these rats from my flat.

– Jorge

'Okay, ten grand,' Jorge said.

'Okay, but give it to me now.'

'I don't have it here. You've searched, you know I have no money here. I need time to make some calls to friends to lend me the money.'

The cop grinned. 'Blondie, Blondie, Blondie. Don't you try to fool me because I'll find you in hell if I have to. I'll give you until 5 pm today to meet me in the Angeloni supermarket in Beira Mar Avenue, okay?'

'Okay, I'll be there.'

'Don't fuck with me, Blondie,' he warned again.

'Man, I swear to you I'll be there at 5 pm with the money.'

Before walking out to the others, the cop told Jorge to go along with him when he told them the deal was $8000, so he could pocket the extra $2000. Jorge nodded, unsurprised. Before leaving the apartment, the cop called his office, reporting they'd found nothing. Jorge suspected he was talking to dead air and this whole thing was an off-the-books treasure hunt, just as their attempted raid on Jéssica's flat had been.

After two hours of torment they finally left, stepping over the scattered heaps of his mum's precious possessions. The cop called out from the lift, 'Don't you fuck with me, Blondie, or remember, I'll find you in hell, and I will kill you.'

'I'll be there,' Jorge promised as the lift door shut.

He had no intention of ever seeing him again.

In the same afternoon when I was supposed to show up in the Angeloni supermarket, I drove my truck to a lawyer friend of mine, a surfer and my client, and asked him to hide my truck at his house. He drove me to my apartment in front of Brava beach, in a nice condominium with swimming pool, tennis courts, gardens, where rich people spend the summers, to hide until things cool down.

– Jorge

Jorge imagined the cop standing at the front of the supermarket, rubbing his clammy hands together in glee, hungry for his blackmail money, then checking his watch and waiting, growing angrier by the minute until he was incandescent, with no choice but to accept he'd been outplayed by a playboy. Jorge knew he'd created a mortal enemy, put a target on his own back and made Florianópolis a red-hot danger zone, but it was his only choice. If he'd buckled and slipped cash to him today, he was sure he'd be rat-trapped; tomorrow and tomorrow after that, they'd hit him up again.

He was also angry and upset about the mess they'd made of his mum's apartment. Fortunately, she was in Portugal, visiting Jorge's sister, so he had time to get it cleaned up. He rang his mum's maid and warned her not to be scared when she next walked into the apartment.

Was just like a hurricane. Everything was on the floor – a mess. Usually, we see this in the movies but this is what they really do.

– Angela, maid

For now, hiding out in a luxury beach condo was Jorge's best bet. He had a view of the waves and could surf early each morning, then hang out playing tennis, swimming and getting fit. It was large, three bedrooms, with a stunning view. It was hardly the hell the cop threatened to find him in – it was heaven. But Jorge's flamboyant lifestyle on the island was finished and eventually even this flash condo would become a cage. Right now, though, he didn't want to run. He had ten boards waiting to fly, and Rafael was arriving soon from Bali.

Rafael was one of the rare people Jorge agreed to see at the condo. They'd become close friends. Onion brought him from his hotel downtown and, on the balcony while smoking a joint, Jorge filled him in on the raid.

Fuck, Break's the best. The way he talks, he's a clever guy, funny guy. Nice guy to hang with.

– Rafael

They both knew their islands were getting hotter: Bali after Marco's bust – causing Rafael to now keep a constant eye on his rear-view mirror – and Florianópolis after Cafiero, and now Bernardo.

Rafael knew about Bernardo and his famous sister, Maryeva. He was staying in the Florianópolis Novotel downtown with Bernardo's boss, the bent cop, who was Rafael's partner on this deal, and their regular horse, Psychopath. In the lobby, they'd spotted Maryeva. She knew none of them, so it was more just a panic reaction when they all scurried behind a column then stood watching her famous arse.

We see her in the hotel lobby – through the glass, we see her pass, going to the elevator; they say, 'Look, look, the girl.' I say, 'Wow.' I look a lot, she was so beautiful, so hot, she's the Playboy *cover girl. Fuck, she was very hot. People sometimes come with the magazine,* Playboy; *naked – wow, she was perfect. They show me – 'Look, the sister of Bernardo.'*

But she was looking for the people who put her brother in the situation – for the cop, so we were hiding so she doesn't see us. We know she don't know us but imagine if she suspects, she calls the police and says go to the apartment, they're going to fuck us, you know.

For me it was no problem, she doesn't have any clue who I am . . . she doesn't know the other guys either, but they were shitting their pants, scared, like, 'Fuck, she's here, the girl's here, she's looking for us.' Was just a coincidence, but too close, they didn't want to give a chance to make a problem, they were worried she'd get suspicion, so we moved hotels.

– Rafael

Rafael and the cop were in town to buy some blow from Jorge, who was planning to on-sell from Luiz Dias, but as he needed to stay invisible now, he put another deal on the ocean-view table. He'd sell Rafael four blow boards for the same price as unpacked bags of powder – Jorge would take the hit on shaper costs. Rafael negotiated. He had upfront cash for three kilos, but could he take one more kilo on credit? Yes, if he took a fifth for Jorge and sold it for him in Bali. Sharing a joint, they shook on the deal. Onion and Rafael went off to get the five boards while Jorge went down for another dip in the condo pool.

At the apartment downtown, Onion gave the boards to Rafael. 'Let me see,' he said, grabbing one and holding it up to the light.

I say, 'Fuck, you guys are crazy. I'm not going to send this shit. This shit isn't going to work; they're going to catch. I don't even want to send this to Rio.' But they say, 'No it's okay, we've been doing it like this like crazy. It works.' I was like, 'Shit we're going to get busted.' Was too easy to find, you don't even need to put in the X-ray. Just take the board, put it in the light, the boards have one brick in each, black carbon paper to avoid the X-ray but this makes more evidence, you see black squares in the middle of the board, should put all the way across. And, they're too heavy, man. Bad job, I was not trusting these boards.

– Rafael

Even if they were perfect, Rafael wasn't a fan of sending blow boards to Bali. The method had been exposed way back in the early 90s, when Brazilian surfer Frank de Castro Diaz got busted at Bali airport. He'd made the mistake of carrying a saw to cut the boards open, which caught the eye of customs officials. Rafael still sometimes received blow boards, but these ones in Onion's apartment were death boards. 'Was so bad, shit was so easy to find.' But he came up with a plan.

I think, 'Okay, let's go . . . the domestic flight is easy, and we can change the packing in Rio.' So I bring to Rio, and we break the boards – just put on an angle [against a wall] *and pow with feet. I help take out the shit, and pack in the surfboard case.*

– Rafael

The five kilos of blow arrived safely in the lining of a surfboard bag, and Jorge would soon fly to Bali to collect his share of cash and stay there surfing for a few weeks.

For now, he was still sitting on the remaining five blow boards, which he'd promised to Darcy. But not yet; it was too hot to move them. Darcy was ringing Jorge incessantly, desperate for the promised run. He was flat broke and needed cash to buy party packs of blow.

I was calling him and calling him, and he wouldn't take my call, but I needed him to answer me because I needed money. And he still owed me about US $1500 – not much but when I was short of money, I would call people who owed me but he didn't answer.

– Darcy

Out of the blue, Darcy got a call from Tizzy asking if he wanted to do a run for Oscar, the investor he'd met in Amsterdam three months earlier. Darcy didn't hesitate. 'Yes, I'll go. I need the cash.'

Within an hour of accepting Oscar's run, Darcy got a call from Jorge, asking him to come to the apartment. Jorge had been hearing from Onion that Darcy was desperate to talk. Darcy knew the building as his sister owned one of the penthouses. He went, they talked, but somehow, wires got crossed. Darcy left feeling he'd made it clear he was running for Oscar. He needed cash and Jorge wasn't ready to send him. Jorge was sure he'd made it perfectly clear that he needed to lay low for a couple more weeks, and that Darcy had agreed to wait to run then.

The next day, Darcy was set to run. Oscar drove to Jurerê with three hastily made boards, parked outside Darcy's girlfriend's flat, and phoned him. Darcy limped downstairs to meet him at the car.

So Oscar arrived. I spoke to him, he said there was another guy who went two days ago, and he was already there, everything had worked.

He gave me the board bag, and I dragged that thing to the apartment. Any bag with three boards is heavy. I opened up the zipper of the board case, and I saw the boards, the rails and the work, and it wasn't very well done, but I'd already committed to the job.

— Darcy

CHAPTER TWENTY-THREE

CLOWN SHOW

So I took this big bag and I went. They issued the ticket to Lisbon, Portugal . . .

– Darcy

As Darcy limped through São Paulo airport, it felt good to be flying again. Cafiero, Marco, Bernardo; none of them gave him pause to look down from the high-wire he danced on so elegantly. He had no doubts today he was going to pirouette through airport checkpoints with his smile and slick repartee.

But at the federal police headquarters in Florianópolis, Darcy's name was suddenly flashing on the radar. One of Caieron's agents had just taken a call, an anonymous tip. 'Chief, a guy named Darcy Santos is flying to Europe with cocaine today.' 'Darcy' rang a bell for Caieron: he'd heard it in wire-taps. 'Call Florianópolis airport,' he said. Soon the agent came back reporting there was no sign of Darcy at Florianópolis airport. 'Okay, call São Paulo airport.'

Darcy was checking in at São Paulo, refusing to give space to negative thoughts: the rough boards, the fact his ticket was via Portugal, or the perennial hiccup when carrying blow boards to Amsterdam – its lack of waves. He breezed through, walked to the gate, showed his boarding pass and was ushered onto the plane. With his slight limp, he went down the aisle to his seat and collapsed into it, glad to be resting his sore knee.

On the ground, Caieron's agent was alerting São Paulo airport police.

As they started searching for Darcy's name in passenger manifests, he was buckling up, ready and waiting for the tilt upwards.

The plane undocked from the jet bridge, rolled back and swung around. Within minutes, it was hurtling along the runway, lifting off into the big blue. Darcy felt happy and relaxed. He watched out the window as puffs of white clouds started obscuring the sprawling metropolis, soon making it vanish completely. Darcy lay his head back against the seat, enjoying a glass of wine and ready to sleep, unaware how close he'd come to running out of luck.

Can you imagine how crazy the airport is in São Paulo? A few police to do a million things.

– Chief Caieron

Ten hours later, Darcy was wide awake as the plane landed in Lisbon. He was ready for his usual routine; walking across to immigration with his contagious smile. But when he handed over his passport something was up – he didn't get the usual return smile.

The lady says, 'Oh, can you wait just one minute,' and she left. All the other lines kept moving, but I was stuck there. It was really weird. I knew something was wrong. Then, five minutes later she comes back with my passport. 'Okay, that's fine.' She stamps my passport, and I felt 'that was weird' but since she let me in, 'everything is fine', and I went upstairs to get my flight to Amsterdam.

I was hungry, so I had a slice of pizza and a beer in a café, bought a big Toblerone and went to my gate. I saw 'Amsterdam' and stopped at the gate, and was relaxed, sitting, eating a slice of chocolate and reading a magazine . . . and then two guys came, one said, 'Mr Darcy Santos?' 'Yes.' 'Can I see your passport?' 'Yes.' So, he looked at it.

'Okay, can you stand up?' As soon as I stand up, two guys put my hands behind my back and handcuff me. I go, 'Fuck, oh my god.' They start walking me out, and one guy says, 'You know what this is all about, don't you?' 'No, I don't.' He says, 'It's all about your little surfboards.'

– Darcy

Darcy's heart was racing. His life, his future, his family flashed through his mind. He didn't notice if people were watching. He didn't care; he was consumed by his predicament and in a whirlwind of confusion, a rushing in his head, a sense of vertigo, spinning off balance on the high-wire – for the first time, he was forced to look down. They frogmarched him, two cops, two officials, through Lisbon airport. 'Oh, I was feeling bad. I had my hands in handcuffs, and wow – I felt like shit.' He was barely conscious of the steps or his sore knee as they led him downstairs to an official area.

Inside the room, Darcy glimpsed a row of plastic seats stuck to the wall like a bus stop, one occupied by a black guy. Then his eyes flew to his surfboard bag on the floor. It struck him that it was still padlocked shut, so how did they know? Why was it even here when it was checked through to Amsterdam? He shut down these thoughts. There was no time for analysis now.

They sat him down, but didn't go straight to his bags. They started focusing on the other guy, trying to interrogate him, a Nigerian who'd been busted on the same flight with half a kilo of blow in his suitcase. He didn't speak Portuguese, they didn't speak English. Darcy offered to translate. As an English teacher it was his instinct to help, but it might also win him some points. It did. 'Take his handcuffs off,' the boss ordered. Darcy began translating, his own bag sitting two metres away like a ticking time bomb. It was at least 90 minutes before two more cops arrived.

Darcy watched as they started twisting and banging one of the surfboards with no hope of breaking it despite the board's natural fragility. It was like a clown show. Under other circumstances, Darcy might have laughed at their slapstick performance, but right now he was just hoping, 'Maybe I'll get free if they can't open it.'

But they weren't giving up, and finally got a prop for their unintentional theatrics: a sledgehammer.

They started boom, boom, just strong hits with the hammer, ruining the board, but still not breaking it. It was surreal. Then they figured it out — one held the nose of the board up to his stomach, and the other boom, boom, boom. After three, four, five hits, they finally broke it and then the fibreglass was sticking out of the foam and they almost got hurt, and whoa! A bunch of powder comes on the ground.

– Darcy

Darcy felt as inversely miserable as they looked happy. One cop dipped his finger into the blow, licked it, then grinned at Darcy:

'Wow, your shit is good, isn't it?' Darcy shrugged, not wishing to inflame things by being rude, but thought, 'Well, dude, I'm hardly going to bring bad shit all the way to Europe, am I?'

He saw again the reality that he'd dismissed in Jurerê, that the boards were badly made – unsanded and rough, an obvious red flag to anyone with the vaguest clue about boards. But this Laurel and Hardy duo clearly knew something long before they'd opened the bag.

Employing their newfound skill, the pair quickly broke the other two boards. They carefully extracted the blow bricks from the foam and swept powder spillage up off the floor, picking out the bits of dirt and fibreglass with their fingers. Then they put the lot into two plastic supermarket bags, and weighed it in at 3.49 kilos. Darcy watched from his wall seat, feeling as shattered as his boards.

> *I felt like shit. I felt depressed, I felt angry, I felt bad, I felt stupid, but there was nothing I could do. There was no way out.*
>
> – Darcy

After almost five hours the cops packed up, leaving the broken boards and bag on the floor. They took the bags of blow, Darcy's suitcase – which they hadn't bothered unlocking – and the Nigerian's blow and bag, out to the boot of a waiting Ford Focus. Another cop snapped handcuffs back on Darcy and escorted him and the Nigerian out and into the back seat, then drove off towards the city.

> *In the car, I felt desperate, but I couldn't scream. I couldn't cry, nothing – nothing I could do would help. So I just thought, 'Keep your mouth shut and take it like a man, because that's what you are.*

You knew what you were doing. Now it's survival mode. Change the
button, it's now survival.'

– Darcy

They pulled into the Judicial Police station and, as Darcy walked
in a surreal daze along the passageway with the Nigerian, he felt
the glare of eyes.

Everyone knew what was happening . . . 'There's the surfboard man.'
They took me into one office and the black into another office. I could
hear them screaming at him. A guy started speaking to me, 'Ah, don't
worry, no handcuffs for you,' and 'Ah, this is good shit you have here.'
And, 'What's your address? Your job? Name of your mother, father? Do
you have brothers and sisters?' Then he gets his gun, 9 mm, puts it on
top of the table . . . and says, 'Wait a minute, I'm going to the toilet,'
and leaves. I knew what was going on, they were testing me to see if I
was stupid enough to try something. And, I thought, 'Yeah, what can
I do with a gun? Where am I going to go?'

Maybe they wanted to beat me up, because if I had a gun, they
could do whatever to me, and say I was going to shoot them. After five
minutes he walks back in and sits down. I just look at him, like go
ahead, ask more questions, what do you want to know? They thought
that they were dealing with a little Brazilian kid who didn't know
shit. Portuguese people, they have no idea.

– Darcy

Around two hours later, they gave Darcy food, which he
hungrily ate as he'd had nothing since the pizza and Toblerone
at the airport that morning – a parallel universe now. Then
they told him to grab a few things from his suitcase and put
them into a plastic bag. 'I took underwear, a couple of trousers,

a jacket, three or four shirts, my toothbrush, toothpaste, my Havaianas, my Birkenstocks – German leather sandals because they're comfy at night and you can wear with socks. I had good clothes.' They were remnants of his cushy life and all he had of home. He clutched the bag as they escorted him down the corridors. He was scared, fragile and raw. The soundtrack to his new reality blasted through his soul.

Jesus, that noise I will never forget. There was this big, huge green gate – it went booooom, like iron noise, clack . . . booooom, and this echo sounds. When I heard that, I thought, I'm here, I have been arrested, my life is over. I'm going down, I'm dead, it's all over. I felt angry, I felt bad, I felt sad – all those things at the same time. I thought how stupid and cocky I was, I thought, 'See, you asshole, you fucking prick, there you are, this is where you are ending up, fucking prison. Here you are, welcome to hell.' I was angry with myself.

They put me in a cell with 12 other people. And there was a bunch of Africans in there looking at me . . . looking at my clothes, my shoes, and they were like, 'Are you Brazilian?' 'Yes.' I start telling my story, 'Oh man, I just got busted with my surfboards.' 'What did you have in your boards?' 'Oh, I had three and a half kilos of cocaine.' 'What!' Everyone started coming down, out of the bunks, 'Fuck', 'Fuck', 'What happened, how, how come?' The Angolans were excited. 'What, three and a half kilos?' 'Oh my god, what's your phone number?' 'Can I have your contact?' It was funny as hell. I tried to entertain myself, but at the time, I was worried about my family.

– Darcy

With all the beds taken, the guards brought in a mattress and a thin blanket that left Darcy shivering. 'I was so tired but I had a bad night of sleep.' When he opened his eyes, he wasn't shaking off the vestiges of a bad dream. He was lying on a mattress in a freezing cold cell crammed with Africans. It was all too real as he was taken out to face a judge that morning to give a statement. Typical of busted traffickers, he had a story ready to pull from up his sleeve. But unusually, he was taking the blame.

I put up all this fake story that I met a guy in Mole beach, his name is Pineapple. I invented him and made up a lot of shit. I said, 'Yeah, it's mine, I did it myself, I bought cocaine from this guy Pineapple, I built those boards myself, I have the contacts in the Netherlands.' I was lying. I fucked myself, I ruined my life myself, I chose that direction, and I'm not a snitch.

When I got back from the judge, I thought my life is ruined, and I have to call my family now. So in the afternoon, I went downstairs and I called Brazil. Mum answered the phone and I said, 'I want to speak to my dad.' That was devastating. It's total loss of everything. It is a bad feeling. I felt really bad for my family and really bad for me. It was the start of a lot of pain in my heart.

– Darcy

The following day he was suddenly a jailhouse celebrity, being looked at and questioned in the communal area dubbed 'the patio' – a large concrete slab, open to the skies, with goalposts at each end. Inmates were asking, 'Are you the guy?' 'Did you have the boards?' 'Ah, how do you know?' Darcy asked, baffled. 'We saw you on TV last night, the 8 pm news.' 'Oh dude, I'm famous,' he joked.

The inmates were a distraction, but at night he was alone with his devastation after being moved to a single cell. In those interminably long, dark and lonely hours, he thought of nothing but this hell and his reckless arrogance in blowing off warnings from friends, from his brother, his sister – people who dearly loved him. It had been a mistake. Now it was all too late – his life was finished. Dark thoughts thrashed nonstop around in his mind, tormenting him.

Jesus, you have no idea. I had everything and I lost everything. Two months before, Kelly Slater and Taylor Knox were having dinner with me in Jurerê. All of a sudden, I am in jail with Africans who didn't shower, couldn't write, and I had to fight just to make sure someone didn't kill me.

– Darcy

As the winter sun set, he stood at the barred window, looking across the patio at seagulls flying around 'shitting on the concrete', and remembered that he'd somehow always known this was where he'd end up. All those times he'd stood on his bedroom balcony, gazing at his mum's beautiful garden and the glimpse of azure ocean, he'd wondered when he'd be looking through bars. But he'd always just shut down his thoughts and go. Now, invading his reminiscences of the world outside, was the bang, bang, bang of the cell doors being systematically slammed shut for the night.

I felt really sad at night when I was by myself, thinking about everyone back home and I was in this tiny little room with those bars and I would look . . . and say, 'Remember, remember your window – you knew, you knew – you knew it – and here you are.' My life had fallen apart. My mum was pissed, my brothers and sisters were so pissed. I was feeling so alone – I didn't have anything because my money had finished. I was 10,000 kilometres from home, I was lost and locked and a few tears rolled out.

– Darcy

Compounding his torment was gnawing doubt about how the hell they'd found the drugs. It didn't add up. The bag was checked right through to Amsterdam – why was it even pulled off the connecting flight? How was it still locked, still intact, if they'd X-rayed the boards? How did they know about the blow? He filled the long, empty hours with mental acrobatics. Maybe it was bad luck, a random pick, and they X-rayed the huge bag. But no matter how much he circled, he always ended back at the same place: did Jorge snitch on him? And those words Jorge had uttered as assurance before his first run: 'You will never get busted, unless someone snitches on you.' Had these words become contaminated with a dark twisted irony? Was it fury he'd glimpsed in Jorge's eyes when he'd said goodbye at the Brava beach condo? Maybe he'd been so angry that Darcy wasn't waiting to run for him that he snitched. Or maybe it was just bad luck. His mind went round and round and round.

Until one night, it stopped. He got his answer while watching the news in his cell. He saw a story about Lisbon airport's X-ray machine for oversized luggage being out of order for the past nine months. Suddenly, he knew there had to have been a snitch. And he was sure it was Jorge.

It hadn't been bad luck or bad boards incongruously going to Amsterdam. Darcy was right, there had been a snitch who'd savagely clipped his wings. São Paulo airport police passed Caieron's intel from the anonymous caller, a woman, to Lisbon airport police. All Darcy's mental anguish was justified.

But there was little he could do. Right now, he was fighting for survival, waiting to be moved to a jail, constantly hearing, 'Pray, just pray that you don't get sent to Caxias.' A rich Dutch guy – busted with 40,000 ecstasy pills, who Darcy had become friends with – was moved first. 'We had the same shoes, same kind of clothes, he spoke English – we became friends.' Darcy heard in patio gossip the next day that immediately after entering Caxias, he'd been brutally bashed and robbed, found bleeding, in just his underpants. 'The guards, they put you in there, they close the gate and there are 15, 20 Africans, they want whatever you have, and they will take it. They took him inside a cell and they ripped him off, they took his bag, they took everything.' Darcy prayed he wouldn't be next.

In Florianópolis, his devastated father was doing all he could to help his boy. He collected character references from a congressman, a doctor Darcy had taught English, the Federal University, and the Association of Surfing Professionals, to send to the judge. Darcy didn't know what was going on until he was called to a meeting one morning, and introduced to a lawyer. She gave him cigarettes and €50, and explained that his brother in California had hired her and she'd try to get him freed, but warned the chances were slim.

Straight after she left, Darcy phoned his brother, and learnt that he and their father had agreed to hire her for €10,000 to get him four to five years in jail.

'What? Forget about it. You're not going to spend €10,000. I don't know what's going to happen, but please, I don't want any lawyers.' Darcy didn't want his family to pay for his mistakes. But giving the lawyer the flick wasn't so easy. She clung to the lucrative job with some leverage – Darcy's dad had sent an expensive box to her, full of chocolates, granola, contact lenses, socks, shirts, jackets and euros, and now she refused to give it to Darcy.

That's the Portuguese people. She ended up charging my brother €1000 just to send the box. He could afford it but I told them, 'Listen, please, this is my thing. I'm going to use a state lawyer.' But Dad sent another one who was going to cost €3000 and I said, 'Dad, forget about it. I don't want a lawyer – this is my fault, I'm here because I did this, thank you but don't spend money on this please.'

– Darcy

As the days passed, Darcy started thinking that maybe things wouldn't be so bad. He'd grown up witnessing the justice system in Brazil, perfectly pliable for rich people with power and influence. Paying lawyers who would then pay judges for exoneration or a soft sentence was the norm. Darcy began hoping his family's influence could work its magic all the way across the Atlantic.

I started thinking about it, and feeling, well, the judge will look at me and he will say, 'No, he's a teacher, he's a good guy,' I'll be free, I'll be free, I'll be free. Some guy said, 'Dude, you are in for four, five years.' And I was like, 'No way, no no, my dad is going to do something.' I had no idea, no idea of what was going to happen in court.

– Darcy

CHAPTER TWENTY-FOUR
SURFBOARDS IN THE SKY

Jorge heard about Darcy's bust while still hiding in his Brava beach condo. He was shocked, but even more so by what Darcy was accusing him of doing.

> *Yeah, it pisses me off. I'm fuming — I'm not a grass. For me, it's a war, I hate police, I never deal with police, it doesn't make any sense me calling them — 'Hey, there's a guy running' — and jeopardise my whole business. And, I was running from police.*
>
> *I've known Darcy since childhood and he was a guy I admired — but Darcy was a fucking horse. I have another fucking 100 horses to run for me. In life, no one is irreplaceable, everyone can be replaced.*
>
> – Jorge

Jorge guessed it had been Darcy's limp, looking suspicious with a bag of surfboards, that had brought him crashing down. But Jorge didn't have time to worry about Darcy's problems, he had his own war going on and not just with the cops. He couldn't get hold of Onion or supplier Luiz Dias. He'd been ringing both relentlessly, with no luck, and the last five blow boards were in Onion's flat. His frustration overtook his fear of the civil police and he left his foxhole to go downtown for the first time in 20 days. It was time – the world of blow didn't stop blowing for him.

He jumped out of the cab at Onion's apartment and rang the bell. No answer. He rang again. Nothing. Confused and irritated, he skulked off down the street towards Toca da Garoupa, his favourite fish restaurant, for lunch. 'Jorge, Jorge.' Jorge turned, on high alert, and saw a welcome face. Rufino was pulling up in his car. 'Get in,' he said. Timi was in the passenger seat, so Jorge jumped in the back. What they told him next sent him into a frenzy. 'Get me a ticket. Get me a ticket on that plane.'

Twelve hours later, he was sitting in a Lufthansa first-class seat jetting from São Paulo to Frankfurt with a sly smirk on his face.

In the car, Rufino had broken bad news; Onion and Luiz were sending the five boards to Amsterdam tonight with one of Jorge's horses, Lucas – ripping Jorge off while he was off the grid and vulnerable. Jorge didn't take it well. This wasn't just war, it was personal. He'd given both those ingrates their start in the international game, and now they were screwing him.

I thought they were loyal to me, would wait for me.

– Jorge

Rufino had got the tip-off from a travel agent, a guy who they regularly used and who invested in Jorge and Rufino's runs. He'd revealed Lucas' flight details and now Jorge sat many seats ahead of him – or so he hoped. With the last minute scramble to get to the airport, Jorge had arrived at the gate after everybody else had boarded, so he still wasn't absolutely sure if Lucas was here.

When the cabin lights dimmed after the meal service, Jorge made his move, walking from the pointy end down to the back – unfamiliar turf these days. He was looking at faces, his heart thumping. He didn't see him. He got to the end of the plane, and circled back up the other aisle, scanning the faces, worried now the horse wasn't here. Then he saw him. Jorge felt a burst of elation. There was Lucas' handsome face, eyes closed, sleeping. Jorge wanted to punch the air, but suppressed the urge and glided quietly past with a faint smile on his lips.

Back in his first-class seat, he called the flight attendant and ordered a glass of champagne to celebrate. As he sipped, the thrill disappeared with the bubbles. 'What the fuck am I going to do now?' He hadn't thought this through – just acted on impulse. He guessed Lucas was unaware of the double-cross but that he'd fight to finish the job for which he'd been hired. Lucas wasn't exactly a soft target – he was a black belt in Jiu-Jitsu – so Jorge knew he had to play smart. With fury in his veins and the element of surprise up his sleeve, he started coming up with a circus show to beat those conniving clowns, Onion and Luiz.

By the time he disembarked at Frankfurt airport, he was ready. 'Hey, Lucas,' he said to the horse, after surveilling him for a few minutes in the immigration queue.

'Hey, Jorge, what are you doing here?' Lucas said, surprised and happy to see him.

Jorge didn't return the smile. 'Hey, bro, listen. I know what you're doing and I need to talk to you. There's very serious shit going on.'

'What? What's going on?' It wasn't something a guy with five kilos of blow in his bag, and standing at an airport border check, wanted to hear. But that was Jorge's plan; freak him out a little and tip him off balance.

'For your own security and mine, it's best we don't talk here. I'll tell you everything in Amsterdam.'

'No, no, bro, we can talk now.'

'Bro, just carry on in the line. I'll talk to you in Amsterdam,' Jorge said, then briskly walked to the back of the queue.

Lucas stayed in line and cruised through immigration. Jorge was watching him, impressed by the horse's cool-as-a-cucumber confidence, even after Jorge had rattled him, and with Darcy's bust so recent. Now he was through into the EU, with just the domestic leg to go. Jorge went through too and sat a few seats away from Lucas at the boarding gate to Amsterdam. Lucas was keen to know what the hell was going on, looking at Jorge, mouthing, 'What? What?' Jorge mouthed back, 'Wait, just wait.'

On the next leg, Lucas sat a few seats in front of Jorge and intermittently craned his neck, catching Jorge's eye, mouthing, 'What? What, Jorge?' Jorge just put his hand up, mouthing, 'Wait, wait.'

Lucas got off first at Schiphol airport and waited on the air bridge for Jorge. 'What's up, man? What's going on?' he asked as soon as Jorge reached him.

'Listen, bro,' Jorge said, as Lucas instantly fell into step beside him. 'I know you have nothing to do with this, but you are carrying my blow.'

Lucas was blindsided. 'What?'

'Listen, don't ask me questions now, but those surfboards are mine. Onion and Luiz robbed me, and I know you're just doing your job, I respect that, I'll pay you, but I'm taking the bag.'

Lucas shot back, 'No, you're not. This is my job, Jorge.'

They strode side by side down the airport corridors to the luggage hall, palpable tension between them now – two alpha males set to defend their blow and egos. They appeared an uneven match, Jorge positively waif-like next to the pit bull horse with big stocky shoulders, a solid neck and cauliflower ears – a status symbol among Jiu-Jitsu fighters. But appearances could be deceptive; Jorge's frame was lithe but supercharged with fury at Lucas' refusal to give up the bag. Right now, he was a match for any heavyweight.

I'm not a guy who plays tough. I play with the mind, but that day I was out of my mind. I was putting my ass on the heat because I was so furious and so focused on getting my boards that I didn't care about anything else. I was like twice my actual size. I was big.

– Jorge

Jorge strode back and forth to the oversize luggage flat belt, where the boards would come out. Lucas didn't seem to realise this, staying with the main baggage carousel. Jorge came back and stood beside him, pushing. 'Bro, you are going to give me those boards.'

'Sorry, Jorge, I'm not. I told you, this is my job.'

Lucas' obstinacy was infuriating Jorge – they were his boards, not Lucas'. Jorge raised his voice. 'Bro, this is my stuff and you're going to give me the fucking bag. You're right in the middle of a fucking big problem.'

'No, Jorge, no.'

'Bro, just let me take the boards.'

'No.'

Jorge tore back and forth between the carousel and the belt like a maniac, shouting in Portuguese at Lucas each time

he got back. 'Man, it's going to be better if you give it to me.'
'No, Jorge, I'm not going to give them to you.' Other passengers
were starting to stare. Jorge ignored them. He knew if Lucas got
outside with the boards, he'd lose his blow.

'Listen, man, you might be the black belt in Brazil, but in
Amsterdam I'm the black belt. I have people waiting outside, so
just shut up, and let me take the boards.'

'No. Don't put me in this problem, Jorge.'

'Man, you have no problems yet, but you're gonna have one
big fucking problem if you don't give me the boards, cos we are
both going to be arrested. And I don't give a fuck.'

*I was so out of my mind that I thought it's better to be arrested than let
this guy go with the boards. In that moment, I didn't care. But I was so
over the top that I think the cops thought this was a normal argument
because usually if you have drugs in your bag, you try to be low profile,
not shouting and walking around like a crazy fucking nutter.*

– Jorge

He stormed back over to the flat belt and this time the bag
rolled out. Juiced with rage, Jorge scooped it up as if the five
boards weighed nothing, slung it over his shoulder and walked
across to Lucas, glimpsing a sudden droop in defeat.

*When he looks at me I saw, boom, he gives up, kind of puts his head
down, like 'Fuck, I can't do anything.' He looked a bit upset.*

– Jorge

Jorge nodded towards his wheelie bag on the ground next to
Lucas. 'Bring that and follow me.' He strode to the airport doors,
pumped and smiling, singing out, 'Good morning,' to the two

cops at the exit, then walked to the cab rank and lit a cigarette, proving again that confidence was key to successful trafficking.

Lucas came out pulling Jorge's wheelie bag, looking deflated. In the taxi, the air was tense. 'Jorge, where are you going?' 'Listen, man, I'm not talking in the taxi.' Given the scene he'd just made, he had no intention of creating a trail to his hotel. He stopped the taxi at Leidseplein, paid the driver, and strode off.

'Where are you going, Jorge?' Lucas called, traipsing behind with the wheelie bag and his own sports bag.

'Bro, just follow me and don't worry. You're going to get your money.'

Jorge walked across a canal bridge and 200 metres on to the Marriott Hotel, just near the three-star hotel he'd first stayed in as a horse. The Marriott was now one of his top picks, partly because of its strawberry waffles. The staff didn't bat an eyelid when they turned up with the big bag of surfboards. They just smiled and took his cash for the room – and a huge deposit in lieu of a credit card, which Jorge never used. He went up to the room with Lucas shadowing him. They'd stay together until Jorge sold the blow. He was acutely aware that once his adrenalised superpowers wore off, Lucas could turn on him at any moment, although right now he was humiliated and abjectly submissive.

In the hotel, I was talking about his money all the time because he could just knock me out and grab the surfboards and go. But he got no balls. And I was so out of me, I was like evil – I was doing everything I need to rescue the blow. I didn't really think about risks. But he was quiet, he wants to receive his money. I was in ecstasy; I was so happy. I got my blow, and instead of having €60,000, I had €150,000 all to myself.

– Jorge

Jorge couldn't help smirking, thinking about his feat, outfoxing Luiz and Onion. He decided to amplify the moment. He took the phone and called Brazil. 'Luizinho,' he laughed. 'Eh, Jorge, how're you doing?' Luiz was amicable, unaware of the reversal of fortunes, but not for long. 'How am I doing? I'm in Amsterdam and I'm with Lucas, you piece of shit.' Jorge paused, letting Luiz absorb this. There was silence. It was a blow, a blindside – just as Jorge got the day before. Jorge was basking in it. 'Luiz, you think you're smart, but I'm smarter. You tried to rob me, but now I'm taking your blow, I'm taking Onion's blow and fucking you both.' A sudden blitz of expletives turned the line blue. Jorge laughed uproariously. All the stress and jangling nerves of the past 24 hours evaporated as he listened to Luiz's screaming abuse and impotent threats. 'I know people, dangerous cartel people, who will kill you. I'm going to kill you, you don't know who I am and who I am involved with. I'm going to kill you, man.' Tears were welling in Jorge's eyes as he laughed, a little crazed, but relishing this moment. He knew Luiz had never been to Amsterdam and had no contacts or power here. Nor did Lucas, who was sitting on the couch, emasculated. 'Motherfucker, talk to your horse,' Jorge laughed, still almost crying as he held out the phone. Lucas shook his head.

Later on that night, Jorge started work, cracking open the boards and extracting the blow. It was a noisy job, but he felt protected by the *Do not disturb* sign. It wouldn't take a genius to guess something fishy was going on. A sharply dressed, long-haired dude with a perpetual glint in his eye walks into a hotel in the heart of Amsterdam carrying surfboards, paying cash, and now loud banging was emanating from his room. That was the beauty of a five-star hotel and its *Do not disturb* signs. They worked. They were worth their weight in gold for a trafficker.

Jorge put all the broken bits of board back into the bag, and went downstairs with Lucas. With the now-sagging bag hanging over his shoulder, Jorge strutted across the foyer, past smiling staff wishing them a good evening and out into the dead of night. Where did the staff think they were going with a surfboard bag at night in the middle of Amsterdam? It wasn't their job to ask.

The pair, now colluding out of necessity, walked down a laneway and deep into the sprawling Vondelpark, to an area safely devoid of security cameras. Jorge had used this spot before. They hurled the incriminating bag into a huge rubbish bin then quickly walked off, taking a circuitous route back to the hotel in case of a tail. The staff wished each of them a polite 'Good evening, sir' as they walked back across the foyer, minus the bag, 15 minutes after leaving with it. Again, no one gave any hint of suspicion. Jorge just gave a nod as he marched straight past.

My attitude in hotels was always authoritarian and a bit arrogant because I was all the time in expensive suites and paying cash. I thought I could do anything, I was moving through hotels, airports and restaurants like a rock star – a drug star. I was behaving like one. But I was taking lots of risks.

– Jorge

Jorge soon learnt more about the depth of Onion and Luiz's betrayal. They'd not just stolen his blow, but lined up his own guy to buy it. Leo, a Brazilian married to a Dutch woman, was Jorge's trusted middle man. He'd introduced Onion to him when Onion was a horse, never suspecting this dirty double-cross. Leo had apparently known nothing of the duplicity and would now simply pay Jorge. But, clearly under pressure from

Onion, Leo urged Jorge to at least pay Onion his share of the investment. Leo wasn't keen to burn any contacts, especially as Onion was bringing business too.

Leo and Jorge exchanged cash and blow at the Marriott, then Jorge paid Lucas and bid him goodbye. But with €150,000 cash, he didn't like them knowing his hotel, so switched to the L'Europe, another favourite, this one because of its gooseneck feather pillows and Egyptian cotton sheets. He hid the cash in the safe, then went to the Red Light District to celebrate, taking brutal amounts of MDMA, blow and grass, partying nonstop for days, aware he couldn't go back to Florianópolis now that both the cops and Luiz were after him. Jorge had no intention of paying Luiz for his share of the blow, since he felt sure the rip-off was his idea, but came around to agreeing with Leo to pay Onion. But only if he came to Amsterdam and faced Jorge.

He did.

Onion was soon sitting next to Leo on Jorge's couch in his plush hotel suite. Jorge had woken late in the afternoon, showered and dressed sharply, and was now high – and ready to give it to Onion. With a glass of scotch in one hand, and a cigarette in the other, he paced back and forth in front of the couch, and started his show.

'You are a greedy bastard, Onion. Very disloyal.' Onion was looking at the floor, muttering an apology.

'How can you expect me to forgive you, Onion, after everything I did for you? In any other organisation, they'd invite you here to Amsterdam and kill you but this is your lucky day.'

I was in a bad mood and started to humiliate Onion as much as I could. He was avoiding looking me in the eye, apologising with shame on his face, trying to explain himself, saying that I was out of reach, that he wasn't going to rob me because Luiz promised him he'd replace the blow they were taking from me. Bullshit. I was enjoying that moment, but I didn't want that rat in my room any longer, so I opened the safe, took out an envelope with his share that I had counted and separated the night before, and threw it at him. He thanks me, and I told them, 'I have to go.'

Onion was as guilty as Luiz but you know he came to Amsterdam, asked for forgiveness, all this shit. Luiz didn't act smart. He made an uproar, he kicked up a fuss, and he lost. Onion used the diplomatic way and it worked.

– Jorge

After they'd left, Jorge did some more lines and his paranoia about the €100,000 in the safe deepened with Onion knowing his hotel. There was almost zero chance that Onion would come back and rob him, but Jorge packed up and switched to another five-star hotel. Just in case.

CHAPTER TWENTY-FIVE

SOCAS DA SILVA

Jorge's hostile horseplay didn't slow Onion down. He was working with Luiz and on a roll. Even as he'd obsequiously sat apologising on Jorge's plush couch, their new horse was already in Amsterdam with blow boards for Leo.

The horse, Eduardo Socas da Silva, jetted back from Amsterdam to Brazil with €50,000 for Onion, but his feet barely hit the ground before they spun him around to run again. 'I had a lot of doubts, even though Onion told me it was safe.' Onion assuaged Socas' doubts over coffee in a Florianópolis bakery, dangling the lure of more fast cash; 'Three blow boards at €2000 each, so €6000 fast, easy, safe – let's go.' 'Okay.'

A couple of nights later, Socas was packed ready to fly. He rendezvoused with Onion and Luiz in Florianópolis to start the journey and met their second horse, Achylles Nucci Avila. Socas' three blow boards were in a VW Golf, with Onion's cousin Golden at the wheel. Socas climbed in next to Golden while Nucci got into Luiz's VW Santana, which had his four blow boards in the back. The two horses were flying together – two Brazilians on a surf trip to Amsterdam, one of whom had flown in a couple of weeks earlier – definite red flags for customs. Onion gave Socas €2200 for expenses, and scribbled down his phone number on a piece of paper. Luiz gave him the air tickets and wrote his number on a piece of paper too. Onion then waved them off and went back to his apartment block and downstairs to Lenzi's flat. Together they sniffed, got high, and started making frivolous calls to the travellers, recklessly creating a trail.

Luiz and Golden drove the horses for four hours through the night to Curitiba airport, safer than Florianópolis – one precaution they did take. The convoy arrived before sunrise, and Socas and Nucci checked in for their 7.20 am flight via São Paulo and Frankfurt to Amsterdam.

From there, the plan was typically simple. The horses would clear customs in Frankfurt and fly on to Amsterdam, arriving at Schiphol's domestic terminal. Once out, Socas would phone Onion at home to get Leo's number. As the man on the ground in Amsterdam, Leo didn't want horses flying in with his number in their pocket..

But Socas and Nucci didn't make it.

You, sir, entered the Federal Republic of Germany on flight LH503 together with Nucci Avilla from São Paulo, Brazil, through the airport of Frankfurt. 3000 grams of narcotics was found hidden inside the surfboards you brought as luggage.

– Frankfurt police interrogation of Eduardo Socas da Silva

Customs officers found 6.9 kilos of pure blow inside seven boards. Investors lost cash, horses were going to jail, and Socas turned snitch. He named people, including his sometimes boss,

Jorge, wrongly implicating him in his bust run, and exposing details of the game.

How did you come to transport the narcotics?

Some associates of mine started to make these trips. An associate of mine, Thiago, introduced me to two men named Jorge Break and Onion. I already knew Jorge by sight.

Can you give me the first and last names of the associates of yours who have already transported cocaine in the past?

Yes. Onion and Jorge Break. They fly every month. These two travelled as narcotics transporters. Now they send transporters to make the trips for them.

Do you know the exact addresses and phone numbers for Onion and Jorge?

Jorge is a fugitive of the Brazilian police and from the people he owes money to.

You didn't answer the first question!

I have telephone numbers in my pocket. (Observation: the accused takes out two papers with two numbers on them.) Onion's home number is: 30952893 in Florianópolis, Brazil – his cell is 98245332. On the other paper is the number 9199533 – this belongs to Luiz, who is a friend of Onion's.

If you travelled with these people on your trip to Europe in March, according to your passport stamp, then I assume that

you also brought cocaine with you on that trip, maybe also in surfboards. Is that correct?

I had a surfboard with me, but I didn't know if it had cocaine inside, since the real motive of my travels was bringing money from Amsterdam to Florianópolis.

Your answers seem credible until now. What doesn't seem to add up is you not knowing if there was cocaine in the surfboard. Surfing on the Dutch coast in March must bring certain difficulties.

Yes, I suspected there was cocaine inside the board but I didn't know how much.

You mentioned that on your trip in March you transported money for Onion from Amsterdam to São Paulo. How much money was it?

€50,000. I transported part of it in my shoes, on my body and in various bags.

   – Frankfurt police interrogation of Eduardo Socas da Silva

It wouldn't be long before a copy of this statement landed on Fernando Caieron's desk.

Jorge was unaware Socas was snitching on him. He was busy fighting another war. He was in Amsterdam, waiting to fly to Bali to collect the cash for the kilos from the condo deal weeks earlier. But Rafael was having his own problems. The bent cop was reneging on the deal Rafael had made, arguing Jorge did nothing and should get Brazil price, not Bali price, for his kilo.

He was complaining that I didn't do anything! I supplied the fucking blow.
   – Jorge

Jorge's hopes of seeing the cash were fading. He had no plans to summon his superpowers to overthrow forces against him this time – and on Bali turf he wouldn't stand a chance anyway – but Rafael finally called with good news. 'I have your money, man.'

The police guy says, 'Why you gonna pay him – he's a playboy, fuck him.'

Didn't he like Jorge?

No, he was kind of jealous because Break was in very good shape, and he was a success. He was the one that have the stuff there, good shit, makes it happen, have the horse. Success. I say, 'No way, I'm going to pay the guy.'

– Rafael

Rafael stood up for me. He was like a hero to me.

– Jorge

Two days later, Jorge walked out of the Bali surf after his long flight from Amsterdam. With his China White board under his arm, he crossed the road to his beach hotel and sitting out the front, on a kids' swing, was Rafael. A smile split his face, the sun glinting off the diamond in his tooth. Jorge saw the magic-like sparkle, and the familiar backpack at his feet. 'Hey, brother,' he said, giving Rafael a warm hug. Inside Jorge's hotel room, they had a beer, counted the cash, and then spent many of the next ten days hitting the surf together.

It was much better for both of them to keep the friendship and the business relationship healthy. They liked each other, and it was safer. Ex-friends made mortal enemies by harbouring a perilous mix of bad blood and good intel. Marco had already given Rafael's name to the cops to try to help save his own arse, triggering a police raid on his Bali beachfront house, although they found nothing because Rafael was scrupulously careful these days. Bali was hot.

As was Brazil for Jorge. He flew back to São Paulo and stashed his cash into various bank accounts, juggling work and partying, always moving from villa to villa, switching five-stars, dogged with paranoia.

Jorge knew Luiz was now obsessed with him. Frustrated and impotent to do anything while Jorge was overseas, Luiz had resorted to making a barrage of menacing calls.

All these people were telling me, 'Be careful of Luiz, he's going to get revenge, he's going to kill you.' He was telling everyone in our circle that I was fucked, I'd be dead soon.

Rufino was saying, 'He is always asking about you, he is obsessed with you.'

He even called my mum saying, 'You tell your son I'm going to kill him.' I worried a little bit that he could do something to my mum, just for revenge.

– Jorge

Jorge imagined Luiz's shifty dark eyes blazing with fury, his agitated fingers twitching on the trigger of one of his guns. It was now more about ego than money, as everyone was having a good laugh at the board-swipe story. Being back on home soil where Luiz had cartel connections, Jorge wasn't feeling quite so cocky or untouchable.

I was a bit afraid of what Luiz could do because he threatened me bad on the phone that day in Amsterdam. He said, 'I work with Alemão, and he isn't going to be happy with what you've done to me.'

I met Alemão two or three times and you could see in his eyes he was a killer – he could order to kill anyone, anytime. He was a heavy guy, and he's got bodyguards. They weren't the playboys I was used to dealing with but people who kill for little. I thought these people were upset with me too, and I knew Luiz was quite crazy. He's always got a gun, and he was very, very angry. So, I was quite worried.

– Jorge

Jorge was avoiding Florianópolis, but even in other parts of Brazil he was on high alert. At his regular haunts, restaurants, bars, clubs and hotels, he was always watching to see who was around. If he saw the same face in two different places in the same day, he'd assume the worst and flee.

At his newly rented villa at Maresias beach on São Paulo's coast, he felt exposed. A moving target was harder to hit but he was regularly staying there every Friday, Saturday and Sunday night when in Brazil, and this fixed address made him vulnerable. Whenever he walked out the security gates, he glanced up and down the street for a lurking car, or a motorbike with a pillion rider who might be Luiz's hired assassin, as drive-by style hits were popular in Brazil.

Across the road from his villa, Jorge and his landlord, São Paulo playboy dealer Martino, were building a beach club together, to be called Ombak bar. Whenever he was on site, Jorge practically had eyes in the back of his head, acutely aware of exactly who was around him at all times.

His paranoia often wasn't rational, but blow-induced. Partying hard, some nights he'd return to his villa and feel sure one of Luiz's hitmen was skulking outside the window. The complex was securely gated with patrolling armed guards – like almost all upmarket properties in Brazil – but he'd peek out a crack in the curtains, just to make sure.

I was a bit paranoid, day and night, but especially when I was very high and just bad thoughts come to my mind; the threats of Luiz on the phone – the messages he sent through people – I start to think about the image of Luiz in my mind and if he could pay someone to come to me and kill me.

– Jorge

Jorge also knew the civil cops were still furious with him. Jorge's ex-brother-in-law was a cop, and warned him not to come home. So as much as Jorge's world was expanding – with a new luxury apartment in Amsterdam, shared with Dimitrius and Ryan, a golf course villa among the elite rich in Paraguay and the one at São Paulo's party beach, Maresias – it was also shrinking. He could no longer go home to Florianópolis and in Brazil he was always looking over his shoulder. This menacing veil of paranoia was not just about Luiz and the civil cops, but things he'd suppressed like busted horses, outstanding payments to various people and Marco's possible death sentence, all magnified by his continuous sniffing.

Sometimes this veil descended fast, out of the blue in the dead of night. He'd hurl things into bags, check out and race off in a taxi to another hotel. When he had girls or hookers with him, they'd come along, bemused by his behaviour. He never felt the need to explain. He'd just check into a new five-star suite, crack open a bottle of champagne, sniff lines of blow and get back in bed with the girls.

Fleeing from hotels was quite a habit for me – doesn't matter the time or with who I was – I just vanish in the night.

– Jorge

This paranoia and adrenalin was as addictive as any drug. It gave life a knife-edged excitement, living minute to minute. It fuelled him to play and work harder. He had more scams going on than ever and more than anyone else. He relied on trusty soldier Timi in Florianópolis to help move cash, organise the shapers to build more and more boards, or do any other jobs that came up. Timi often drove Jorge on long trips, whether to the border of Paraguay to buy blow or up to Maresias, because Jorge didn't have a licence. He had never been able to bring himself to go into an office full of cops to get it. For short trips, he used his expired Californian licence, as the English word 'expired' meant nothing to most Brazilian highway cops. It'd worked several times during road checks, but for long trips Timi was a safer bet.

Timi, and a bunch of Jorge's clients around Brazil who were keen for a finger in the lucrative blow pot, were also continuing to find fresh new horses.

I created a net of people looking for horses all over Brazil. Every one of my clients wants a piece of the business, and the opportunity was to find a good horse.

– Jorge

Jorge was doing castings, not on the couch – although many of his pretty horses did end up there – but on the phone. A sporty, tanned, fit guy would carry surfboards or paragliders, skinny and pale guys like Cafiero took backpacks. Hookers often carried blow in their long leather boots. Jorge always matched the horse with packing that visually complemented who they were and where they were going. He'd also learnt to ensure horses were well briefed after once sending a horse to Amsterdam with a paraglider sail full of blow. The horse had told customs he was going to glide off cliffs in Holland, a famously flat country.

Incredibly, the horse still got through because customs couldn't find the blow bricks perfectly packed in the paraglider seat.

Jorge was often using female horses and hit the jackpot after one of his clients introduced him to Madam Vivienne, who ran a whorehouse in Curitiba. She did one run to pay off some debts, and then opened up her books.

In Holland, I treated Vivienne like a queen. I put her in a nice four-star hotel, I gave her money in advance to buy clothes, I took her to restaurants, I even fucked her. She was so happy that when she returned to Brazil, she made me a proposition; she would find good-looking girls to run for me if I gave her a commission. I agreed right away and we began to work together.

I was treating not just the girls, but every single horse very well, making them feel special during the trips. So the news spreads, and everyone wants to run for me. I had horses everywhere in Brazil. I was doing castings, matching the route and equipment according to the horse I was using. I have many horses standing by, and this was one of the reasons I have so many scams running at the same time, because the horses I was not using, instead of keeping them waiting, I was lending to other guys, with one condition . . . to give me space in the bag to smuggle my drugs as well. They were investing the money and taking the risk, I was getting money or drugs taken as rent payment. I was lending horses to Rafael, Ryan, Oscar, Martino, Dimitri. So, I had my runs and also a piece of other people's business. But even having horses everywhere in Brazil, Florianópolis was still the place where most of my horses were coming from, for reasons I can't really explain.

– Jorge

CHAPTER TWENTY-SIX

ONCE, TWICE . . .

Despite Tizzy's two 'get out of jail free' cards in Amsterdam, and one of his best friends, Darcy, now busted in Lisbon, the smart lawyer was roaring down the highway to Florianópolis with two blow bricks under his seat.

He and a friend, Jaco, another surfer and dealer, had earlier driven 300 kilometers from Florianópolis to Curitiba with cash and a paraglider, for a new run organised by Oscar. Oscar was a hubristic Rio guy, with a very wealthy family and a model girlfriend, now living in Florianópolis. He was also the guy who'd sent Darcy on his bust run.

Tizzy and Jaco had met him at a hotel where he'd announced a change of scam: instead of the three of them sending a few kilos, it was a bunch of investors sending 15 kilos.

I thought, that's too big, too risky.

– Tizzy

Tizzy and Jaco had opted out, but decided not to waste the trip and bought two kilos from Oscar's Paraguayan supplier. They tested a sample of the pure Bolivian blow in the Blue Tree hotel room. 'Very nice stuff.' Tizzy and Jaco were happy, agreeing to the supplier's terms: $10,000 for two one-kilo bricks, meet on the street in their cars in the dark of night to make the switch.

But at the handover, Tizzy felt uneasy.

'What the fuck are you doing, man? You're crazy, you stand in the street. Let's go,' Tizzy said, watching the clown count the cash in the lights of the car. 'Oh I need to check it.' 'I don't check yours, I'm leaving, you leave too.' 'No, I have to count this money, I have to check.' The argument escalated. Tizzy refused to wait, exposed on the road with a two-kilo bomb in his car, and drove off, leaving the Paraguayan angry.

He was just an Indian like all the Paraguayans – a skinny motherfucker.

– Tizzy

Tizzy was still uneasy. The guy had seen their car and licence plate. He didn't trust him. 'Jaco, let's check into a hotel, leave the shit in the room, go out with the girls, sleep, and tomorrow we'll find somebody who can take this shit on a bus.' 'No, let's take the shit now,' Jaco countered. Ignoring his churning gut, Tizzy acquiesced and they organised a safety plan. Lucas was in town too, investing in Oscar's big deal, and driving home tonight. He agreed to go ten minutes ahead and call them if cops were working any of the highway checkpoints.

They got no warning call from Lucas, no chance to divert. The lights at the highway checkpoint in front were suddenly blazing like the sun. 'Fuck, man. Drive, drive fast, man,' Tizzy implored Jaco. 'No, we'll die. If I try that, we will die.' They saw six snipers lining the sides of the two southbound lanes, pointing automatic rifles. It was 2 am. The road was empty except for them.

As Jaco slowed down, Tizzy thrust his arms under the seat and grabbed the two kilo bricks, then shoved them inside his jacket. They pulled up, and saw the cops keeping a safe distance back with their guns poised. It was Brazil, anyone could be in this car. Guns were common in a country with over 40,000 gunshot deaths a year – locals calling it a constant civil war. They could be drug dealers with heavy artillery, maybe machine guns. The cops didn't know what to expect. They had to be careful. But Tizzy's only weapon was his Jiu-Jitsu moves, and the heaviest thing Jaco had was his Burberry coat.

'Open the door slowly,' a cop yelled. 'Get out of the car, out of the car, slowly, hands up, hands up . . . slowly, slowly, hands up.' Two cops stood a metre away with guns cocked. Covering them were four more cops, further away, shielded behind police cars, pointing their rifles, tense, waiting. Regular procedure at highway checkpoints was a quick document check and search of the car. But this was not routine. Tizzy and Jaco got out of the car, squinting in the glare of the lights, putting their hands in the air.

One of the closer cops gestured with his gun at Tizzy's jacket. 'You're looking a little fat, eh? . . . Open your jacket, use your left hand.'

Tizzy gingerly lowered his hand, unbuttoning his jacket. The two bricks fell heavily to the ground. Tizzy was now sure the Paraguayan had snitched on them.

These guys knew, they knew everything.

– Tizzy

The cops ushered them with their rifles across to a little roadside hut. 'Why didn't you try to escape?' one cop asked. 'Because we would die,' Jaco replied, still with his hands in the air. 'Have you ever shot anyone dead?' Tizzy asked soberly. 'Yes, I have killed two people here on this road. I'm a good shot.' 'Do you like killing people?' Tizzy asked. 'Yeah, I do.' 'Okay, let's make a deal, I will run, and you shoot me in my back.' Two cops lunged at Tizzy, grabbing his neck and propelling him to the ground. They didn't plan on letting him run tonight, and cuffed him to a metal bench.

> *I wanted to die. My life is finished in this moment. I will go to jail; my family will know about this. Shit, I'm a stupid guy.*
>
> – Tizzy

Jaco wasn't giving up hopes of escape, just yet. 'I will pay you guys R $30,000. You can take my car too, and you have the coke. Cash, my car and the coke, if you let us go.' What the cop said next didn't surprise them. 'The federal police are on your back. If I let you go, it's bad for me.' The guys had known they were hot in Florianópolis, but still suspected that the Paraguayan had tipped these cops off as they hadn't been visible when Lucas drove past ten minutes earlier.

Jaco and Tizzy were taken inside the hut and searched.

> *We go inside, take off the clothes, humiliate. Naked, bend over – body cavity search. Put your clothes on. The guys find my weed and one tells me, 'Oh, very nice stuff, eh. Good for me,' and put it in his pocket. I have one 500 euro note, and he takes it for himself.*
>
> – Tizzy

Tizzy's son was now six months old, his daughter nine years old, his father a lawyer, his workplace the Tribunal of Justice.

He'd gambled everything, again, and this time he'd lost – third time unlucky. There'd be no Hollywood ending, no reprieve or magic fairy dust this time. No way to keep it secret and discreetly slip back into his charmed life. He would lose his job, and family – and he knew it.

In prison, Tizzy slumped into a dark hole. He shaved off his long dark curly hair and big moustache, which had earned him the nickname Viking, and started starving himself. He went for entire weeks without eating a morsel of food, then after having a few mouthfuls of beans and rice, he'd eat nothing again for days. He hated himself, hated this life, aware he'd brought it all on himself. He wanted to die.

His status as a rich guy, a lawyer from the justice department, high class, educated, won Tizzy favours and caused him hell. By Brazilian law, he was to be treated as special, entitled to a good cell, like all inmates with university degrees, and his friends from the justice department could visit regularly.

Listen, we are third world . . . how many people like Tizzy – lives at the beachfront, a lawyer – goes to jail in Brazil? Nobody, nobody. If you go to jails in Brazil you will see there is nobody like that inside. So, Tizzy arrives, 'Look, his father is a DA, prosecutor . . . a lawyer, he works in the Tribunal of Justice.'

– Friend of Tizzy's

When Tizzy asked the prison secretary about his special cell, it backfired spectacularly.

She went into the pavilion where all 200 prisoners are – and said, 'His dad is a DA and since he's graduated, he wants your bed,' and she closed the gates.

– Friend of Tizzy's

Suddenly, Tizzy was surrounded by 200 glaring faces, 200 enemies wanting to fight him. Even as a black belt in Jiu-Jitsu, he couldn't fend off that many. One mean-looking guy emerged from the pack and went to attack. The guy didn't know what hit him when Tizzy made his deadly moves.

Well, he got badly beaten. He was the leader, so if the leader is beaten up in front of everybody – there's a new leader in town.

– Friend of Tizzy's

Despite acting in self-defence, Tizzy was put in the penalty cell for four days.

Tizzy also felt his perks singled him out for jealousy by the guards, who were constantly escorting him to see his unusually high number of visitors. His lawyer friends from the justice department were allowed to freely visit, but every time, Tizzy was subjected to a cavity search before and after visits.

'Take off your clothes, bend over'– the guards make me bend over naked many times . . . 'Let me see your ass' – many times, just to humiliate.

– Tizzy

One afternoon, Tizzy and his two cellmates smoked a joint. The guards got a whiff and came in, demolishing the cell. They found nothing, as the butt had already been flushed, but the smell, under prison justice, was enough. Tizzy again got special treatment.

While his two cellmates were moved into another cell, Tizzy was locked in the initiation cell – a tiny two by two and a half metre concrete room – with 12 prisoners. Now 13. It was freezing cold, but Tizzy was ordered to strip, and left naked among the 12 other men, for seven days.

I don't have clothes. Naked, naked, nothing. Don't have nothing to sleep on, nothing, not a blanket, nothing, not a mattress, nothing. Only I was naked, other 12 guys have clothes. No one gave me any, because everybody only has one shirt and shorts, don't have nothing to give. Have one guy inside the cell . . . a rapist, and the guards told me all the time, 'Hey, Tizzy, if you kill this guy, you come to your cell,' or 'Tizzy, if you snitch on your two cellmates, you can come to your cell.' All the time make these proposals.

– Tizzy

Tizzy and Jaco were each sentenced to four and a half years in jail.

CHAPTER TWENTY-SEVEN

366

'Pray, dude. Just pray not to go to Caxias.' The words spun nonstop in Darcy's brain as he sat, cramped, in the back of a police van bumping along the Lisbon streets. Just like his close friend, Tizzy, he was living on the flip side. Today, he was being moved from the police cells to jail with eight others, all in the dark about their destination and destiny. The van jerked to a stop, the back doors flung open and a guard pointed, 'You, you and you, out.' Darcy grabbed his plastic bag and jumped out.

'Where am I?' he asked.

'Welcome to Caxias.'

I was, 'Oh my god.' I just entered and I was looking, looking at everyone.

– Darcy

He was checked in and given a prisoner number, his new name: 366. He instantly saw the irony; it was a leap year, and he'd be spending not 365 days here but 366 in his first year, if he got a long sentence. It was only one extra day but symbolic.

The guards walked him along the wide corridors to his new home, a cell shared with two skinny Portuguese junkies and a bloated African. It was a catastrophic fall from glamour, but Darcy hoped he'd soon be back enjoying some sushi, a glass of wine and waking up in a soft bed with pretty hookers. 'I was still thinking I am going to get out.'

On day three, he got his first death threat.

This big black guy put his Creole music very loud and went to the toilet. I was already sick and tired of that music, so I turned it off.

– Darcy

'Who the fuck did that?' he yelled, charging out of the toilet. 'I did. There are three other guys here, and I don't want to listen to your music,' Darcy asserted. 'Fuck you, I'm going to kill you.' 'Okay, do it now, what's it going to be?' Darcy stood, ready, waiting for an attack, aware he needed to stand his ground early. 'I'm going to kill you.' 'Okay, fuck you, let's do it now. Right now.' Darcy wasn't big, but strong with Jiu-Jitsu moves up his sleeve. The other guy retreated.

It wasn't over. Darcy went to bed on high alert and didn't sleep. As soon as the doors were unlocked at sunrise, he walked out and asked to be moved.

I said, 'Somebody's going to be dead. I don't know if it's me or him, but there's going to be a fight if I stay in that cell, so please move me. Put me in Vietnam, my friends are there.'

The nine guys I met on the first day in the police cells were my fans — all those Africans from Angola, they were like, 'You are with us, man.' They loved me from the first day for some reason.

— Darcy

So Darcy was transferred upstairs to one of the most notoriously violent jail blocks in Europe, dubbed Vietnam.

It was radical. I stayed in probably the worst place in Europe. It was known as Vietnam because of the wars that go on inside. There were blacks from Mozambique, Angola and Cape Verde, from tribes — they all have knives. And on the other side — the Russians. Those guys are bad, they're mean, the roughest guys on the planet — they kill for nothing. When there were clashes between the blacks and the Russians, they finish it — there were usually deaths or people getting really severely injured. The guards lock the doors, they don't want to take part, and after everything is solved, they come and take the bodies and whatever is left. I saw big fights. It was bad shit in my block. Basically, there is no law in Caxias.

— Darcy

The prison fast exorcised the ghost of Jorge. Darcy no longer had time for agonising over his belief that this dark fate was all down to his friend snitching. He now had real ghosts, lurking with knives and anger issues in every corner.

I had some confrontations inside with Africans, even Brazilians, many people telling me, 'I'm going to kill you' . . . 'Okay, what's it going to be, let's do it now, here, just do it now, man.' 'Not tonight, tomorrow.' 'No now, man, you said you are going to kill me, do it.' In the patio, in the corridors, guys threatened to kill me, some guys tried to hold me. There is a Jiu-Jitsu move . . . you boom, put someone down on the floor, and then move around and get his neck. So they tried to hurt me, they said they would kill me, but they never accomplished it. But I had to sometimes fight just to make sure I wouldn't be killed. I had to keep my eyes open all the time just to live, just to survive. I didn't have time to think about Jorge Break.

– Darcy

Darcy hadn't heard a word from any of the playboys. No cash, no call, no card from his boss, Oscar. His siblings and mother were furious with him. His dad was working like crazy to get him out, trying to assert some influence that casually worked in Brazil, but not here.

My mother would say, 'Your dad, every day, he wakes up, he goes downtown, he talks to his friends. He talks to the governor, he wants to go to Brasília to speak to the President.' There was nothing he can do but he spoke to everyone, his friends, his cousins who were federal judges. He comes from a nice family.

– Darcy

Darcy's hopes of walking free were fading as his court date loomed. Other prisoners told him Portugal wasn't Holland: no fairy dust here. He was dreaming if he thought he was going home after being busted with 3.5 kilos of blow. Darcy got a copy of the police report and did a double-take. The amount of blow had shrunk by almost half – 1.6 kilos were missing.

They profited from me. They took a bunch and they sold it. But I couldn't say anything – it would be even worse, because I was inside the system.

– Darcy

Darcy's only chance of a lenient sentence was to snitch.

When I went to trial, my father hoped that I'd be released if I said something because there was a Colombian who snitched on everyone, and they sent him home. But his friends told me he was killed a month later when he got back. That's how it works.

— Darcy

Snitching was never a possibility. The only person he'd be ratting out was Pineapple, his fantasy friend.

It's not in my blood to snitch. I knew what I was doing, so I took responsibility for my mistakes. Retaining composure for whatever crap lands around you is worth its weight in gold. It's all about attitude. Act like a man, take it — that's what I did.

— Darcy

Darcy sat in the courtroom, daydreaming, hoping beyond all advice to the contrary that the judge would say, 'Okay, Darcy, you're not a truly bad guy. Go home, go enjoy your life, your soft bed, your pretty view — you've done your time here.' But reality obliterated that fantasy.

When I heard that hammer go down, it was bad. I went, fuck, it's happening right now . . . my whole life is going down the drain. I took four and a half years, that was my sentence, the judge — boom went with the hammer — 'Four and a half years, plus ten years expulsion from Portugal.'

— Darcy

Darcy sat there shattered. It was the beginning of hell all over again.

When he got back to his cell, his mind was spinning. 'Dude, your life is ruined, it's over, finished, done.' The last few months of this shithole had only been a taster. Severely depressed, he asked his cellmate for a pill to sleep then passed out. The pain in his heart was only growing.

I woke up two or three hours later and I felt like shit, this heavy hangover . . . and everything started to sink in. I'm in jail, now I have to go over and call my dad. When I called my dad it was like . . . I feel so sad for that.

– Darcy

But Darcy couldn't wallow in self-pity – staying alive meant staying alert. The brutality was constant. He walked around attentive, psyched to fight, his eyes sharply focused on his surrounds. With so many savage criminals packed in so tightly, fuses were short, and it took little to trigger an explosion.

One day, Darcy watched an African, who claimed to be the Angolan President's nephew, shouting at another African about making too much noise in the toilet at night. Suddenly, there was a blood-curdling scream.

I was just looking and I thought, 'Oh my god, I can't believe it – he stabbed the guy in the chest in front of me with the TV antenna.' It was quick. The guy had a hole, you could see the blood. He went downstairs, and I didn't see him again.

– Darcy

One of the most violent inmates was Jerome, a Brazilian who'd risen like a phoenix from a broken mess on arrival to the self-appointed jail president, feared for his terrorising ways.

Jerome was in jail for a 24-hour crack cocaine-fuelled rampage, attacking and robbing 17 taxi drivers, slicing off their ears and stabbing them. He then bashed the arresting policewoman. Her colleagues exacted revenge by beating him senseless. The Caxias guards knew of his violent past and feared him. Fortunately for Darcy, Jerome had taken a shine to him, and particularly loved his story about trafficking blow in boards.

Since day one, he was pulling me in. 'Oh, Brazilian, tell me your story.' So I tell him. He was like, 'Oh, man, don't worry, you're with us.' He was always around me.

He was the leader of the whole 600 inmates; he was the guy who cut the drugs, who would sell everything – he had coke, hash, heroin, telephone cards, cigarettes. Everything was coming to the Brazilian, every week. The blacks would bring him a block of hash because their wives or girlfriends would bring the shit from outside. I saw black ladies there, the girlfriends – they were huge, very fat ladies . . . that's how drugs entered, inside their vaginas. They would bring drugs, cellphones – the chargers for the cellphones too.

– Darcy

When Jerome invited Darcy to move into his cell, he accepted. They often spent hours cutting blocks of hash into small, saleable bits, smoking as they worked. One night, the guards burst in, pushing Darcy, Jerome and the other two cellmates out and forcing them to strip in the corridor while they raided the cell.

They started taking everything from our cell, the alcohol, the little bit of hash, and then they had a knife, then a bigger knife, the chief was asking, 'Whose knife?' – we're all standing naked – the Brazilian says, 'That's mine,' the second huge knife . . . 'Whose is this?' He goes, 'Mine.'

He used the knives for controlling, fighting . . . this guy was nuts. The big one was an iron bar from the bed, he took it off and sharpened it. That thing was old and rusted and thick and could do some damage; it was like a sword from the war. So when that third knife came out the chief said, 'Don't tell me this one is yours too?' He said, 'Yes it is.' And I thought, good on you, Brazilian, you're taking responsibility for your shit. Well, they tore the cell apart — it was demolished.

The next morning, we started rebuilding and then the Brazilian found out, ah, it was the fucking Bulgarian snitch. So, he called his group — the little blacks from Cape Verde — and gave them all two little pieces of hash and a blanket. They went down the hall, got the Bulgarian, put him inside a cell, put the blanket over him, and kicked the shit out of him. Later, he was taken out of the corridor by the police. They closed all the cells, and this guy was never again seen in Caxias.

— Darcy

After the shock of his sentence abated, Darcy started using his time to get fit. He woke at 6.30 each morning to stretch and meditate while looking out the barred window, thinking about his life back home.

I could see the Tagus River wall, I could see the Vasco da Gama Bridge. I had a great view from that window. I would wake up and watch the sunrise right by the Christ statue, so I would stretch every morning overlooking that, looking through bars, and just meditating, thinking about my parents, my family, my life — where I lived, how I had everything, so I thought, 'Forget about it. Work out, get fit.' The only thing I want to do is to leave this place, hug my parents before they die. If they die before I get out of here, then things are going to be very bad — I am going to be an angry man.

— Darcy

CHAPTER TWENTY-EIGHT
GLOBAL MASTER PLAN

Fernando Caieron sat in the wire-tap room in Florianópolis, hatching an ambitious master plan. He wanted to bust and bang up more playboys like Darcy across the globe – with the help of a ghost. The voice he was listening to was soft, high-pitched. He'd assumed it was a woman, who was smart, cryptic and cutting in and out of conversations fast.

He'd first heard the voice talking to a dealer from Rio and soon realised two things: this was an effeminate-voiced man, named Olaf, and he was a VIP travel agent to the playboys – making him a VIP target.

I heard a guy who was too clever, very sharp. That's the thing that most caught my attention, thinks fast. He came like a ghost – not even a minute talking – seconds, too fast, a woman's voice and he never said the same thing twice.

— Chief Caieron

His cryptic tactics should have kept him invisible but the VIP travel agent was unlucky – Caieron had glimpsed his shadowy presence as he had lots of time on his hands. He rarely listened to intercepts under normal circumstances, leaving it to his agents, but right now, they were on a nation-wide federal police strike, so there was little else for Caieron to do, with no agents to send out on cases.

I was there for two and a half months all by myself, all alone, hearing lots of intel, lots of intel – lots.

– Chief Caieron

He listened, took notes and got to know the playboys. He sat through hours of boring chatter, everything from chitchat about soap operas to guys booking hookers. Then, suddenly, a hot bit of intel would drop, making it all worthwhile – like Luiz Alberto Dias' girlfriend telling her mum that Luiz wanted to kill Jorge Break for robbing him of $200,000. Caieron didn't know this was about the Schiphol surfboard swipe but he tucked the ace up his sleeve.

Caieron regularly heard his own name mentioned. He once heard Lenzi complaining they couldn't get the horses' passports, because the feds who issued them were out on strike. And he heard a lot of talk about sex – even when his agents were working, as they'd call him in for a laugh to give their stressful days a bit of levity at the playboys' expense.

Those guys sometimes do some ridiculous things like . . . go to the nightclubs after a goal, hire hookers to celebrate their victories, and 'Man, last night we spent R $10,000 with four hookers, good champagne, it was crazy, I was so doped I didn't fuck any' . . . I mean, *it's insane, they are risking their lives and this is the moment, 'Let's celebrate,' and then . . . nothing. So it's funny for us, we start to laugh because it's a fun side of the bad guys.*

– Chief Caieron

But it was the effeminate voice that Caieron was keenest to catch – his ears pricked up the second it floated onto the airwaves. But then the voice would vanish, appearing one or two days later on a new number. Unlike the playboys, Olaf changed numbers frequently and kept Caieron playing chasey – dashing in and out of the judge's office, requesting a new warrant to tap every new number. Eventually, he got a warrant for the phone company to release all numbers registered to the name. It was a lot of effort, but Caieron felt this guy would be worth it.

He saw Olaf as the dynamite to blow open the playboys' global operations. His master plan was simple; bust Olaf covertly, cut a deal fast and drop him back into play within hours, untarnished. His playboy clients would have no clue he'd been busted. Olaf could keep working as their VIP travel agent while spying for Caieron and disclosing who was flying for whom, when, where and with what. It would give the cops a crystal ball-like ability to bust them all.

Olaf was the guy I always dream about to have in my pocket. I could see clearly which way I'm going to take it – an international operation.

They will hire a guy here – put a ticket in his hand, 'Okay, man, go to Amsterdam.' We will know in advance and put two agents on the same flight or we could go first. Once he got to Amsterdam, we would be there with the Dutch police, follow the guy wherever he goes to see the connections they have abroad. We don't need to show ourselves, in order not to put suspicions on Olaf. We give the arrest to the Dutch.

They will do the statement and send it to us and we could use that against the guys here. If I could put my hands on Olaf, I would do the perfect operation.

– Chief Caieron

Caieron was imagining busts going off like landmines: Zurich, Frankfurt, Lisbon, Paris. It would make a global impact, world headlines. But his plan was on ice while he did an eight-week English course in Canada. Caieron felt sure he had time on his hands – the playboys wouldn't stop any time soon.

Out of the blue in Canada, he got a call from his right-hand man, agent Jair. He'd heard in the intercepts that two horses were trafficking 35,000 ecstasy pills from Amsterdam to Rio. Olaf had booked the tickets. Could they pass this intel to the Rio feds? Caieron was dead against it. 'No, Jair, it's not the right time. I will be back in 15, 20 days. Don't do anything. You don't have all the information I have.'

Jair didn't take no for an answer. They bounced calls and emails back and forth: 'Please let's do this, chief?' – 'No no no, it's not the time, it's not the time.' – 'But listen, we've never made any kind of seizure of this size.' – 'Listen, don't worry, we are going to do that but it's not the time.'

It was a big seizure but small in terms of what we could achieve. It's our chance to appear to the world, show to the world we are good. There were a lot of people involved in Florianópolis. It won't be a smart move to come and get only two guys. We had an open view of everybody who was involved – we knew everybody who was playing in that scenario.

– Chief Caieron

But while still in Canada, Caieron capitulated.

With my heart broke, I said, 'Okay, you old crying guys, you can pass to Rio as long as Rio stays in Rio. Don't come to Florianópolis, don't touch Olaf. Let's make those guys think this is a thing from Rio. On these terms, we have a deal.'

– Chief Caieron

The Rio feds broke the deal. They busted the horses in Rio, discovered they'd bought their tickets from Olaf, and came to Florianópolis. Nothing was done covertly; everything was exposed. They got an arrest warrant for Olaf and sent two of Caieron's men to bring him in.

Typical for a bust, they went early. Olaf appeared at the door. 'Morning, Olaf. You have to come with us,' Agent Bernardo stated. Olaf looked upset. 'Why? What did I do? I didn't do anything.' 'Ah, you're going to learn why. Come with us,' Bernardo said, still yet to do one bust where he didn't hear the mock cry of innocence.

He's a complete pussy. He almost cried when we arrested him.

– Federal agent Bernardo

Back at the office, no one saw the explosive potential of this pudgy, emotionally fragile felon. They had no idea of Caieron's lofty ambitions for him, or the integral part Olaf played in the playboy matrix. They weren't interested in the cache of secrets he claimed to hold when he offered, 'I can give you a lot of information if you set me free.'

Olaf had just sold tickets to Onion for a horse running with four kilos to Amsterdam. He knew Big House had half a million euros stashed in his house. He knew more – much more – but his plea was rejected. 'I don't give a shit about what you think you know, man. You're talking bullshit. It's too late. You're fucked.'

An agent rifled through Olaf's pockets and wallet, emptying them onto the desk. 'I'm lost,' Olaf thought, looking at the bits of paper scribbled with playboys' names and numbers. Then he got a gift: all the cops left the room. With his hands cuffed behind, the incriminating notes in front, he took his chance. He bent his face down to the table and ate the scraps of paper.

'Man, where are all those notes?' an agent asked moments later. The smart, dumb-looking guy rattled his hands behind his back. 'I'm handcuffed. What could I do?' The window had just slammed shut for Olaf to talk. He realised these cops were clueless about his key role, so decided he'd simply deny everything.

When Caieron got the news in Canada, he was furious.

The Rio police messed up. It was not the time, it was not the deal. They did bad work because they tainted a real good source. Olaf had connections with everybody, everybody, everybody. Andre, Big House, Jorge Break, Luiz Alberto Dias, Timi, everybody ... we had the cards in our hands and on the table and we could choose the day, the time, the hour to do the job with no risk, like easy, easy.

Olaf was very smart because he never touches the dope or puts a fingerprint. But I was following him for two and a half months, all day, every day. So I knew his life from top to bottom. I knew if I sat with this guy, he would play with me.

– Chief Caieron

But he was a compromised asset – scorching hot. The playboys wouldn't want to go near him anymore. The Rio cops had cooked Caieron's golden goose and sent his master plan up in smoke.

But it only made him more determined to catch the playboys.

CHAPTER TWENTY-NINE

ON A WHIM AND
A PRAYER

'He is guilty of importing a type one narcotic, cocaine, and the court punishes the defendant with the death penalty.'
— Judge, Tangerang court, Jakarta, Indonesia

Marco lifted his head at the pronouncement and turned to look at Danilo, his Brazilian photographer friend, to give him the money shot, as promised — but a Reuters photographer got in the way and snapped it. Marco looked solemn, but not crushed. Although facing a firing squad, he had two appeals, plus a clemency bid left and he knew the Indonesians had never executed a westerner.

A week later on the other side of the globe, a bunch of his ex-protégés were buzzing after a Lenny Kravitz concert at Amsterdam ArenA. Jorge, Dimitrius and Ryan were at their new apartment, behind Vondelpark, listening to music, sniffing blow, and drinking whisky. Ryan's mum, on holidays from Rio, had already gone to bed, after sipping water laced with LSD and falling in love with the world. Rodrigo, their horse, was also partying with them after flying in with three kilos of coke. With the exception of Marco's death sentence, life was great. Business was booming, and in their shared safe was half a million dollars which Jorge had counted that afternoon with their new bank-style note-counting machine.

We'd been smashing it for almost 40 days, just receiving the horses full of blow that we previously prepared in Brazil – and we had a lot of plans to invest this money. Rodrigo was staying in our apartment because he was a friend, but he was a horse still, and not in the same position as us. He was waiting to run back to Brazil for Ryan and Dimi, and I had two horses waiting in a hotel to do the trip for me.

– Jorge

They were all high, laughing, joking and tossing around ideas for a new scam, freely talking in front of Rodrigo. They liked him. He was gentle, softly spoken and a good surfer – usually first in the water and last out. Jorge often caught waves with him in Bali. The crew there had nicknamed him Fraldinha – 'little nappy' – because 'he complained like a baby'. His addictions had started early, as a solvent-sniffing teen, and now he was badly hooked on blow. His rich mother, Clarisse, had tried everything to get him working, investing in various enterprises including the latest, a pizzeria in Florianópolis. Nothing got traction – except trafficking. He was a good horse, ran often, investing a bit in his own bags. Tonight, he threw in an idea.

I have two guys, two perfect guys, top horses in Brazil waiting to work. They're ready to go but I don't want to bring them to Amsterdam, only to Bali so I can invest a little, make some cash and stay there surfing for the rest of the season.

– Rodrigo

Rodrigo had carried blow to Bali many times, two or three runs a season for the last three years, something that even the bosses thought was crazy. But right now, black clouds hung over paradise. It was only eight days since Marco was handed a death sentence. 'Death to drug traffickers' wasn't just a scary airport sign anymore – it was their close friend's reality. They pointed this out to Rodrigo, but he batted it off. He'd done a run to Bali only two months after Marco's bust. 'Marco was fucked up on the plane, he was high, he made mistakes. I know how to do it. I've done this many times. Nothing is going to happen if we do things correctly,' Rodrigo said. He'd take responsibility for the horses, and chaperone them to Bali.

The room filled with excited talk as they all pitched their thoughts and debated the pros and cons.

On one side, we had enough horses, the trips to Holland were relatively safe, and Marco was in a very difficult position, encapsulated in an Indonesian prison. On the other side, one kilogram in Indonesia was worth $80,000 to $90,000; in Holland, a good price was $30,000. Was a big difference. So to make the same profit in Holland we would need a bigger investment, more horses, and more effort. And, Rodrigo had two quality horses ready to go.

Ryan was very close to Marco, one of his best friends. He'd been saying 'never Bali again'. But in one second of drinking and partying, moved by alcohol, pure cocaine and rushes of adrenalin, we just – 'Ah, okay then, let's do to Bali again.' Everyone agreed. It was the feeling, the atmosphere, everyone high and feeling powerful and stuff . . . and

*in one second we just boom — we make this fucking decision to send
Rodrigo to Bali. It's the nature of our environment, to take risks to
have adrenalin rushes. It's like to catch a huge perfect wave, with a
gold pot in the end.*

– Jorge

They drank to it, and in that hedonistic moment, made a decision
that would haunt them all.

They grabbed the phone and called Timi in Florianópolis,
telling him to start organising the blow boards. Timi wasn't so
upbeat. He warned them that the shaper, Gaspar, a friend of his
and the third guy they were now using, wasn't happy. Dimi and
Ryan still hadn't paid him for the last batch of boards, and he
was refusing to make any more until he got his money.

*Gaspar made, I don't know, 20 boards, 25 boards by that time – three,
four, five at a time, but they didn't pay the last three or four boards.
I talk to him all the time, on the phone, at his house . . . and he told
me about the payment. Gaspar was crazy with those guys, and with
me also. These guys were in Europe . . . they are always travelling . . .
they don't care, for them it doesn't matter. They stay there and people
are working here. They were in Amsterdam, 'No, no, no, send more,
send more, send more.' It turns into a conflict situation cos those guys
at this time have a lot of money, but don't pay people. I try to manage
this, but it was not good. I was in the middle of the confusion, of
all this shit.*

– Timi

Oscar, Dimitrius and Jorge told Timi to convince Gaspar to
make these new boards, to tell him he would get what he was
owed when they got cash from the new boards.

Model Maryeva Oliveira was a *Playboy* cover girl and dated tennis super star Guga Kuerten. Her brother Bernardo was a horse who the drugs bosses feared could bring a blowtorch of media scrutiny if he got busted.

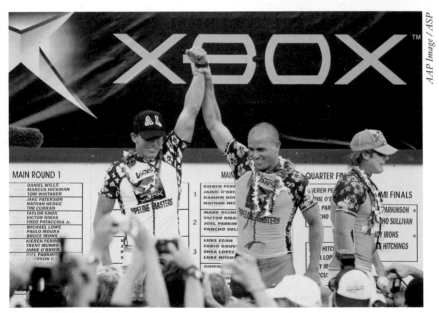

After Kelly Slater was chauffeured by Darcy around Brazil and won the event there, Kelly's bid to reclaim a world title moved to Hawaii. Here Kelly puts on a brave face after losing the title race to Andy Irons at the final event of the year.

Federal police chief Fernando Caieron is smart, confident and tenacious – and became the playboys' nemesis.

Chief Caieron is a straight cop in a bent legal system who became a master of mental techniques to break criminal codes of silence.

I always like to watch the mafia, mob films . . . to see how the bad guys think; to see how they see the world. 'Cos if you have to deal with them, you have to know them.

– Chief Caieron

Brasília civil police boss Chief Fernando Cesar on the cycling holiday, across the mountain tops of Chile and Argentina, which he had to cut short to go home and bust playboys.

Chief Cesar started an operation to catch one local Brasília guy, only to discover a much wider network. His surveillance included surfing anonymously beside a target at Joaquina beach.

Polícia faz maior apreensão de ecstasy do RS

A Brazilian newspaper report on the bust of journalism student Bica, a horse who became a cliché.

We had created a monster. – Andre

Chief Caieron, second from the left in a white t-shirt, with some of his team on the day they stormed Andre's luxury beachfront home in Garopaba.

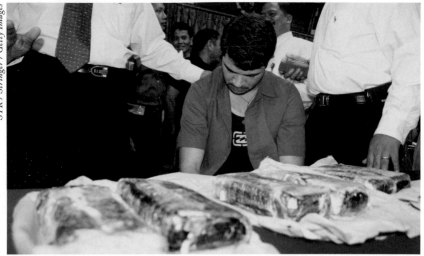

Showtime in Jakarta. Rodrigo Gularte is put on display with the large bricks of blow that had been extracted from the surfboards he was carrying to Bali.

Indonesian authorities reveal the surfboards which put Rodrigo Gularte on death row. The playboy bosses who have seen this photo are shocked at how badly hidden the bricks of cocaine were.

The worst job I see in my life. – Rafael

Chief Caieron escorts Dimitrius, who is forced to wear a flak jacket and handcuffs, off the plane in Florianópolis in front of a throng of media waiting to see the high-profile playboy.

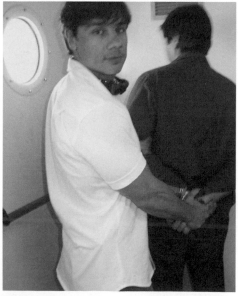

This celebratory photo was taken by one of Chief Caieron's agents as he cuffed Dimitrius seconds after he walked off a flight from Europe.

A nun holds up a photo of Rodrigo Gularte next to portraits of seven other condemned men, including Australians Andrew Chan and Myuran Sukumaran, who were all executed in a clearing on Nusakambangan Island in Indonesia.

Rodrigo Gularte's playboy life ended in an open coffin in Indonesia.

Marco turns to the camera immediately after the judge announces his death sentence in Tangerang court, Jakarta.

Marco's body is taken away after he was shot through the heart by a 12-man firing squad. He was the first westerner ever to be executed in Indonesia.

Timi wasn't having fun anymore. He'd never been chiefly motivated by cash, but now they weren't paying him what they promised. And Marco's death sentence in Indonesia, his close friend Bernardo's bust in Frankfurt, and Darcy's in Lisbon had really upset him. The game was losing its lustre, but for now he was still playing. Somehow, he needed to sort this out. He drove across to Gaspar's house to put him on the phone to Amsterdam and let them all spar directly.

'No, I will not make more boards. You must pay me first,' Gaspar told them. They replied exactly as Timi had conveyed.

'We must pay you, okay . . . So help us send more boards, make these for Timi . . . then we pay all we owe you. But if you don't make these boards, we cannot pay you. The horse is already waiting, we are waiting. So, just make these boards.'

They make that pressure on Gaspar.

– Timi

A week later, Jorge flew to Brazil, dropping off some grass and pills in Maresias, checking on his beach club's progress, and partying at one of his favourite nightclubs, Sirena. He then flew to São Paulo to enjoy some nights at a friend's exclusive luxury brothel, filled with cover girls and soap stars, where both the B-list models and A-list power clients were guaranteed privacy. Jorge supplied the brothel's party drugs so always got very nicely looked after. Back at his hotel, he was ordering hookers online as often as room service, two or three at a time.

Jorge flew on to Rio to meet Dimitrius, who was organising logistics for the Bali run.

In black Dior boots, Gucci black leather jacket, crisp white Philipp Plein shirt casually unbuttoned to frame a 24-carat gold

Bulgari necklace, and a matching gold ring on his finger, Jorge strode across the foyer of Rio's InterContinental Hotel. His sharp style, combined with his designer stubble, long blond ponytail and armful of tattoos, turned heads – as always.

My look was a mix of sophistication and Hell's Angel and I called lots of attention, everywhere I was.

– Jorge

At check-in, he did his usual trick of flaunting his wealth. Placing his Hermès man bag on the counter and ensuring his left sleeve was pushed up to show his Cartier watch, he pulled a cash-bloated Montblanc wallet out and ask for the top suite.

Just hanging on my body, counting shoes, clothes, bags, watches, chain and ring, I had 20 to 25 grand on me – not counting the money I was always carrying in my bag. I used to make jokes about that – but those things gave me a very powerful look and feeling as well.

– Jorge

Jorge swung open the balcony doors to breathe in the salty breeze coming off the sea and take in the spectacular view. This was his favourite Rio hotel. His little show downstairs worked to allow him to check in without a credit card and just pay a hefty cash deposit. Only twice had it ever failed anywhere in the world.

Soon, Dimitrius arrived and after a quick hug and catch-up, they got down to business. Dimitrius, who still had his bowl-cut hairdo, was less flash than Jorge, preferring to invest in his pizzeria and a new house rather than Gucci and Cartier. He was more practical, with natural business acumen like

Andre: good with numbers and logistics. He also had a good nose for relevant news, like baggage handler strikes, or heavy snowfall delaying flights. It combined to make him highly adept at organising operations.

Now, he was pacing, serious. His business head on, he read out calculations scratched on his notepad: this deal being done in dollars. Jorge owed him US $10,000 – broken down as $6000 for the kilo of blow and $4000 for the horses' hotels and airfares. The $15,000 carry fee for each horse would be paid in Bali. The other five kilos were being split between Dimitrius, Ryan and Rufino, who'd organised the blow, plus Rodrigo was getting half a kilo as a bonus.

Jorge grabbed a bunch of dollars from the bag he'd just put in the safe, sat down at the desk and counted it with nimble fingers. Then he slid the $10,000 pile across to Dimitrius. As the pair worked in sync on their latest run, they didn't think about the significance of where they were. For anyone superstitious, it would have been a bad omen. The InterContinental sat at the base of Rio's most famous hang-gliding cliffs – a view Jorge could see from his pillow. São Conrado had been Marco's launching pad since his teens. Hundreds of times, he'd swooped off the edges, soaring above Rio's beautiful beaches, often high on lemon juice, with the wind in his hair, the world and its problems far, far below – gliding as free as a bird. Now, with wings brutally clipped and stuck in a prison cage awaiting a firing squad, these majestic cliffs could have been a poignant symbol of reckoning. But in the shadows of these cliffs, Jorge and Dimitrius were too busy organising the new Bali run, using the same route as Marco via Jakarta, to notice.

Several days later in São Paulo, Jorge was having a drink with horse and friend Psychopath, and found out he was about to run to Bali for bent cop Claudio and Rafael. Within a whisky shot, Jorge was investing in a kilo, his third Bali scam for the season.

I had no plans to send anything to Bali, but in this business, things go very crazy and change very fast – both things came at the same time. I said, 'Well, Psychopath, if there's a space for me in this, I'm going as well,' so I put in the money – was very fast.

— Jorge

CHAPTER THIRTY
THE MATRIX

Caieron flew back from Canada to Florianópolis, aimed straight for the VIP travel agent, Olaf. Putting a face to the ghost and getting him to spill all he knew was his top priority. It was no longer the perfect global plan, not the crystal-ball effect he'd dreamed of, but still, no one had the same level of access to the playboy bosses' intel.

Olaf was running like hell with those guys.

– Chief Caieron

Caieron's own boss was dismissive, wanting to transfer Olaf out of the police cells before Caieron even got back.

I said, 'No way, I have to talk to him,' and my boss, who didn't know shit about what's going on, says, 'Ah, the guy's already in jail, what's the difference if you talk or not talk?'

– Chief Caieron

All the playboys would have been a lot safer without Caieron's tenacity and ambition. Olaf would have been taking their secrets to his cell. Caieron wasn't about to let that happen. He sat in his office, reading the pack of lies that made up Olaf's statement. Caieron imagined Olaf had quickly sussed out that the cops knew nothing about him and felt lies would set him free. He was in for a shock.

I need to shake down Olaf, take him from the relaxed position to 'I'm still in danger; if I don't play, they're going to fuck me.' I felt that he would talk, but you have to motivate.

– Chief Caieron

Two agents brought Olaf into Caieron's office, leaving him cuffed and standing. Caieron stood in front of him and belligerently began. 'I am the guy who should have put handcuffs on you because I am the guy who knows everything about your life. But for your good luck or bad luck, I was abroad. Now I am back and I just took a look at your statement and man, you are full of shit.' Caieron ripped the statement in half. 'We're never going to use this statement because you told us a lot of bullshit. You have a second chance. A last chance. If you fuck this up, man, you're fucked. So, if you want, you can tell me all the lies again, but if I was you, I wouldn't do that.'

Caieron was still ripping up the statement. It was a photocopy; he couldn't lawfully destroy the original, but to give his little display more impact, he made it appear so. It was working. Olaf looked scared, gravitating backwards, away from the crazy cop.

'Man, I'm going to throw this in the garbage, then we'll do a new statement. And listen, I won't put down any lies you tell me, because I know you. I know your life and I will know if you're lying.

So it's better that you tell me the truth because you are fucked, but guess what? I can make your life more fucked. I can prove to the judge all your connections with previous travels.

'But I don't want to fuck your life, man. I want to know everything you know, that's what's important to me. You made mistakes but they don't matter to me. I mean, if I get a 50-year sentence for you, it won't change anything. And if you help me, I can help you.'

Olaf wanted to talk to his lawyer, Gastao Snr, to confirm the chief could cut a deal. Gastao's custom was to flounce in, flamboyantly friendly. Caieron knew he'd tell Olaf to talk, because more busts equalled more clients. Caieron warned Olaf that Gastao was notoriously loose-lipped, so if he spoke in front of him, he couldn't guarantee confidentiality.

Olaf was contemplating the offer – and Caieron knew he'd won the first round.

You move a little bit, then you relax, then you go a little further, then you relax. You can't push all the time. You have to push, then easy, man, then okay, let's do this.

– Chief Caieron

As the pudgy travel agent sipped coffee, waiting for his lawyer, Caieron played his next card. His tone was less badass, but the content brutal.

'Listen, man, are you aware of the riots in Bangu prison in Rio recently? Did you see what they did with the drug traffickers? A psycho gang boss cut their heads off – he took a rod and skewered it through their ears – in one, out the other. And then burnt them.

'Well, man, I can send you to Bangu. I don't want to. I can talk to the judge and have you sent to Rio because you're responsible for trafficking pills to Rio. You're a young guy, how long do you think you'll last in there?'

Tears rolled down Olaf's chubby cheeks. 'Chief, I've lost my grandmother since coming in here three weeks ago,' he sobbed. 'Well, you have a grandfather, you have another grandmother, you can turn this around. I can help you if you talk to me. Listen, I'm going to show you another thing.'

Caieron felt no sympathy, the opposite in fact. He was relishing the moment and was about to exploit Olaf's vulnerability.

'Listen, man, you're already arrested, you're already fucked, but I can fuck you worse – you know why? Take a look at this.'

Caieron was holding pages of phone records.

'Man, this is why I know you've been telling us a lot of lies. These phone records show those numbers were being used in trafficking activities – they're calling Onion, calling Lenzi. A lot of calls with these guys. And guess what? Those numbers are in the name of your girlfriend, Pamela. It's her name on all these chips making calls to Amsterdam. Take a look.'

Olaf leant forward to inspect the page.

'You were using her name to do this, so I can fuck her life too. I can bring Pamela in here easily, it's a piece of cake to arrest her. Or I can leave her out of it – up to you, man.'

That was the final card, the final card.

– Chief Caieron

Olaf was still staring at the numbers when his lawyer pranced in, advising Olaf to talk, and waiting for him to agree. But Olaf declined to cut a deal. He was escorted back to the cells, the lawyer briefly gossiped to Caieron and then left, dismayed. Caieron sat at his desk, excited. Minutes later Olaf was brought back up. He'd given Caieron a wink behind the lawyer's back, smart enough to see it was wise to cut Gastao out of the loop. But, thanks to the Rio feds, Olaf had lost his wings to make Caieron's global master plan fly.

He is the big trophy. But it could be a lot better, a lot lot lot better.
                                                            – Chief Caieron

They cut a deal: Olaf would spill his cache of secrets and assist Caieron in the future in exchange for two months in jail and no conviction. The playboys had ignored the risks of bringing the travel agents into the game, and the consequences were about to be played out.

Olaf put some bare details and names in an official statement, basic stuff like: 'Jorge Break and cronies had already ordered and financed air tickets for Lucas, Darcy Santos, Luis Alberto Cafiero and others.' Off the record, he gave Caieron a tsunami of intel, even doing a scenic tour of the island, pointing out the playboys' homes, and where the drugs were stored. Caieron could now put names to most of the faces pinned to his wall, photos that his agents had accrued over months of covert surveillance as they quietly tailed the playboys, building intel, while keeping Operation Playboy top secret.

Tadashi had told me how it all works but Olaf filled the blanks with the names. He brought me boxes of flight tickets and he has a fantastic memory; this trip was made by Onion, this was made by . . . he sold tickets for those guys for years. I mean, Olaf knew everything.
                                                            – Chief Caieron

Olaf had just lit up the playboy matrix like a Christmas tree.

CHAPTER THIRTY-ONE

BLOW BOARDS

Paradise was bliss. Jorge clubbed all night and surfed all day, splashing some of the $80,000 he'd picked up on Psychopath's blow run to Bali. In another few days, Rodrigo was arriving with his two horses, and he'd get another $80,000.

In Florianópolis, Timi was driving across to Gaspar's house to collect the blow boards for the Bali run. Under pressure, Gaspar had agreed to do the job so he could get all the money he was owed. He'd warned he was cutting costs, only laying the expensive carbon fibre over the areas of blow, not the entire boards. In an X-ray, patches of carbon fibre would look odd, although the horse could possibly argue they were foot grips. To help camouflage the blow and carbon fibre, Gaspar had spray painted the boards with chaotic, dark coloured patterns.

When Gaspar told us he didn't put the carbon all over ... we thought that, you know, it should not be a problem. And Gaspar says, 'I don't know who will travel with these boards, I wash my hands. I don't care.

I just make them to receive what I'm owed.' Those guys also, they don't care. Even Rodrigo don't care. They think, 'Ah, put other boards together in the bag, clean boards that don't have stuff inside.'

– Timi

These boards had a second problem; the bricks of cocaine Timi had given Gaspar were large. The blow was usually machine-compressed into lean, marble-like bricks, with smooth, straight edges, making them easy to slot into slim holes, but these were loosely pressed boulders. Gaspar had to make bigger holes and thicker boards.

Gaspar made very heavy, very large boards, like a boat – they were not well made.

– Timi

Timi took the boards from Gaspar, drove to Rodrigo's apartment and carried them up in the lift. He'd done this many times, so he knew Rodrigo liked to inspect the equipment the day before a run.

I arrive with the boards, and he was waiting for me. I put those boards in his hands and he looked at them, one by one. And they're very coloured, heavy dark colour, not clear boards. He got very content, because he made goals with Gaspar's boards before. Gaspar's boards got success in Indonesia, in Europe. So, he was confident when he sees those boards. He liked the boards, he was happy.

He showed me some photos of the other trips – himself surfing in Bali. He was very excited to go – his head was already in Bali. I'm feeling sure that he would make the goal, but always there's a big tension, you know, when these guys try to go to Indonesia, everybody knows that risk of that country. I wish him a good travel, a successful trip. Was ten minutes, quick.

– Timi

It was now 51 days since Marco's death sentence.

*

Jorge and Dimitrius were having dinner at Made's Warung in Seminyak, the place where they'd had lunch on Jorge's first trip to Bali. Tonight, they were anxious. Rodrigo should have already messaged that magic word, 'goal'. It was after 7 pm and he'd been due to arrive in Jakarta at 3 pm. The message still hadn't come by the time they finished, so they split up. Dimitrius went back to his villa and Jorge on to Ku De Ta, agreeing to call each other with any news.

At Ku De Ta, Jorge was soon partying with a Russian babe, splashing out on cocktails, sharing generous lines of blow in the bathroom and sitting on lounges perched on the beachfront, where the club cast out lights that made the water glow. Jorge loved this stylish bar, but tonight he was edgy, constantly checking his watch, looking at his phone and trying to get through to Rufino or Timi in Florianópolis. Around 3 am, walking out of the toilets with the Russian babe after sharing some more blow, his phone rang.

'We're fucked, we're fucked. We're all fucked,' yelled Rufino.

As music blared around him, Jorge tried calming him down so he could find out what was going on. He needed facts, not hysteria, despite his own rising panic.

'Cool down. Tell me what's going on.'

'They've busted Rodrigo and the two kids at Jakarta airport.'

Jorge was high and drunk and now seized by gut-wrenching terror. He'd been suppressing fear about Marco's fate, but now it compounded the panic tearing through his body. He had one instinct. He said goodbye to the Russian babe and some friends, raced out of Ku De Ta, and fled to his nearby villa. He grabbed his passport, threw essentials into a bag, left cash for the bike, car and villa rentals, scrawled a note for two friends staying with him, then grabbed a cab to Denpasar airport.

I was very scared. I thought that Rodrigo could talk, I didn't know. I felt that he wouldn't tell my name, but you never know.

– Jorge

It was 5 am by the time he arrived at the airport, still high and drunk, dressed in head to toe black Gucci, and a pair of black D&B aviator sunglasses to mask his eyes. He quickly bought a ticket to Singapore. From there, he'd book a flight to Amsterdam to break his trail. The airport was ghostly, and he was facing six hours here as he'd just missed a flight. This was the last place he wanted to be, but he had to get out – if Rodrigo talked, he'd be a sitting duck in Bali. With his long blond ponytail, dark glasses and the usual bling, he was hardly invisible, but he was trying to blend in and appear calm. Attracting attention could be fatal. He skulked in and out of shops, occasionally sitting down. His heart was pounding, a mix of blow and adrenalin rushing through his veins, the blow exacerbating his paranoia. He was in constant fear of the clutching dark hand of an Indonesian cop coming from the shadows and nabbing him.

It was terrifying. I didn't even call Dimitrius. I got so scared. I switched off all my phones. I was sweating, and hiding my paranoid eyes with my aviator sunglasses. Waiting to get into the fucking plane was the longest six hours ever.

– Jorge

Finally, the flight was boarding and he slunk on and sank into his KLM business-class seat. But he wouldn't relax until the plane was in the air and out of Indonesia. He buckled up and waited. The plane didn't move. 'What's going on?' he asked the flight attendant as she offered him a drink. 'Technical problems,' she replied. He was unsure whether to believe that, watching now for any odd signs. She put the drinks tray down and walked into the cockpit. He stared at the door, waiting for her to come back out. She did, two minutes later. His eyes trailed her as she walked across to another flight attendant. They both looked over at him, a suspicious look, he felt sure. Fear gripped him tighter. He started looking at his Rolex Submariner, 20 minutes, 30 minutes, 40 minutes. Why wasn't the plane moving? He checked his watch again: 60 minutes. Then, finally, the plane was taking off.

It blasted along the Bali tarmac and up into the heavens. The lift-off also lifted the blanket of terror from his shoulders. Jorge was ravaged and exhausted after hours of staring into the abyss. He soon fell asleep, waking two hours later as the plane began its descent into Changi airport.

As he stood in the immigration queue, dark thoughts started flooding his mind again. What if Rodrigo had talked? What if the cops tracked him to Singapore? He was in his own surreal bubble as he handed over his Brazilian passport, scrutinising the guy's face. He saw nothing. The guy stamped his passport and handed it back. Jorge walked through into Singapore, and immediately bought a ticket to Amsterdam. The curtain on his tropical playground had just closed. The Bali show was over.

When he was safely back in Amsterdam, he was still anxious. It took a couple of days for him to calm down a bit, but even after the shock abated and the drugs wore off, the sober reality was no better. He was sure his friend Rodrigo and the two horses were now dead men walking – just like Marco.

> *I was devastated. I knew that Rodrigo was gone, I knew it as a fact. I thought that the two kids were gone also. I thought that I was guilty of putting three people to their deaths.*
>
> – Jorge

Jorge also felt guilty about fleeing without calling Dimitrius. Unsure where he was, he sent him an email, using their security trick. The pair shared an email address and password, so they could write and save a message in drafts. The other would read, delete and reply in drafts, never actually sending a message through cyberspace, so they'd vanish without trace.

I'm in Amsterdam. Where are you? What are you doing?

I'm still in Bali, everything is fine. Rodrigo hasn't talked. Come back.

No, it's too hot, you should leave.

No, it's fine.

In Florianópolis, Rufino broke the bad news to Timi. It blew to smithereens any lingering allure of the game.

> *I felt like I have Rodrigo's blood on my hands. I give to Rodrigo's hands those boards. I was very down. In that moment, I was with a heavy culpability for Rodrigo. I didn't excuse myself. I knew he was dead, I've been to Indonesia, I know their laws.*
>
> *I knew that I would never see him again. I knew that we would get hard consequences. For me, was the finish; the end. I lose the funny moment – no more funny. No more smiling. No more joke after that.*

I'm afraid, very scared in that moment. I thought that really, I would answer for that — that I will go to jail too. That's the last time I saw him, when I gave those boards to him. I was in a bad moment when he got arrested — with a lot of culpability.

But he chose to do it?

He chose, yeah, but I was there. I promote . . . I was — how can I say . . . incentive. It was not my drugs with Rodrigo, but was me who give those boards in his hands and in that moment, I was impulsion, I was incenting him, I was part of that — we are like a team. He was going, but I was working the boards, the guy makes the boards, other guy buys the tickets, other gets the drugs, all guys who have part participation, to me he's responsible too. I don't know if these guys are feeling something — I don't think so.

And they make that pressure on Gaspar. And so he made those boards — those shit boards. But these guys, no no, didn't feel nothing. I'm sure . . . they never feel nothing — after Rodrigo's bust or other busts — especially Rodrigo, we had a relationship. He's a dear guy, you know, a good guy, everybody likes him but nobody felt nothing.

— Timi

In Bali, Rafael wasn't too upset or surprised, but he was worried — another Brazilian busted with blow in Indonesia was bad news, putting a spotlight on them all.

There was a big shit. Someone come and say, 'Fuck, they catch Fraldinha with six kilos in Jakarta.' I say, 'What, how?' 'In the boards.' I say, 'Fuck, man.' Everybody was like, 'fuck, man'. But people talk about Rodrigo like crazy addicted, lost, not respectful, people don't give a shit, because he was super addicted, would do anything for a line, and he was 'I wanna bring, I wanna bring, give me something to bring to Bali.' People were, 'whoa'. And it came to this.

— Rafael

Rodrigo's bust was headline news in newspapers and on TV. He was put on display in Indonesia's bizarre catwalk show of traffickers. With a cop clutching him either side, they paraded Rodrigo, wearing handcuffs, a bright orange police issue shirt and a grim expression, to a room full of journalists. He bowed his head as they made him pose for photos sitting behind a table covered with his blow bricks. The showpiece was the surfboards, standing upright in a row with the tops peeled down, exposing the holes in the foam for the media to photograph. It was easy to see Gaspar's patch of carbon fibre and the gaping holes for the bloated blow bricks.

> *Those boards are the worst job I see in my life. I think they were so crazy because there was no way it's good – no chance to make it.*
>
> – Rafael

The press confirmed that the blow was exposed in an X-ray.

> *Rodrigo Gularte was arrested along with Fred Silva Magueta and Emerson Vieira Guimarães . . . According to local authorities, they were very nervous, which drew attention of the police. The boards were analysed by X-ray, which showed the drug.*
>
> – Terra.com

The *Jakarta Post* ran a story pointing out the fact that the three busted Brazilians had insouciantly ignored the glaring warning of Marco's fate weeks before.

> *The death penalty handed down to Brazilian Marco Archer Cardoso Moreira on 8 June for attempting to smuggle 13.7 kilos of cocaine from Peru apparently failed to deter three of his countrymen from*

*attempting the same thing last week ... On Saturday, officers of the
Interdiction Task Force at Soekarno-Hatta International Airport
arrested the three Brazilians for trying to smuggle 6 kilos of cocaine
from São Paulo in six out of eight surfboards they were carrying ...
As with Moreira, the three suspects have been charged under Article
82 of Law No. 22/1997 on narcotics, which carries the death penalty.*

— Jakarta Post

Rodrigo admitted guilt so convincingly, taking the rap for
carrying those boards, that the Indonesian police incredibly let
the other two Brazilians fly home.

*I don't know how these two guys get away without problem, and
Rodrigo pay the bill.*

— Rafael

Jorge felt abashed that he'd ever suspected that Rodrigo might
snitch on him.

*I flew from Bali with a selfish feeling that he could snitch and not even
a word he spoke. The only thing he did was kept his word, setting his
friends free with a hero statement, taking the responsibility all alone
over the apprehended drugs.*

— Jorge

Jorge was surprised Rodrigo had actually been carrying the
blow boards, as that wasn't the plan.

*Rodrigo was not supposed to carry anything. He was going to Bali
to coordinate. He proposed the kids for the trip, but he got a little bit
greedy, he thought, well, I'm going to get $15,000 for each guy plus*

my half kilo, so I'm going to make like $80,000, get all the profit and just pay for these kids to have the holiday of their dreams and they're happy with that, everyone's happy. He didn't tell us the truth – he lied to us.

– Jorge

*

Dimitrius stayed in Bali. He was so audaciously confident he'd escaped any ties to the bust that he later flew to Jakarta to visit Rodrigo and Marco in their shared jail. He took cash and food but Marco mostly wanted lemon juice. He was sick of smoking the cheap local stuff that flooded the jail, and he knew Dimitrius could work his magic. For a global trafficker, figuring out a way to get grams of skunk into an Indonesian jail was kids' play.

Marco gave me an address of a guard's house and I sent a box full of clothes, toothbrush, toothpaste, deodorant, and a bag of bubble gums.

– Dimitrius

It was a treasure hunt, but Marco quickly sniffed out the skunk.

Marco called me and says, 'Eh I got 22 . . . this number is right?' I say, 'Yessss!'

– Dimitrius

Dimitrius had opened the bag of Hubba Bubba gum, unwrapped half the individually wrapped pieces, switched them for skunk, then rewrapped each perfectly, and resealed the top of the bag with glue.

*

Rodrigo's wealthy mother Clarisse had screamed when she got the call about her son's arrest. Within two weeks, she flew to Indonesia to see him after hiring a lawyer in Brazil, who denied to journalists that Rodrigo was an 'international drug trafficker'.

> *César Augusto de Carvalho – who coordinates actions to defend the surfer, said the hope of the family is trying to prove to the Indonesian courts that Rodrigo is innocent. 'Despite the mistake he may have made, he is not an international drug trafficker.'*
>
> *– Folha news*

*

Police Chief Caieron had learnt about Rodrigo's bust while drinking a coffee and reading the morning paper at his desk. This was the first he'd ever heard of Rodrigo Gularte, but his bust would add rocket fuel to Operation Playboy.

> *When I saw the news, I said 'motherfucker' because there's a lot of places you could go, and you decide to go to Indonesia where you're going to be killed. That was my first impression when I saw the news. It was very important what happened, very important. I mean, it's hard that news . . . I mean, it's bad, bad, bad news, and I was, 'Man, those guys are crazy.' One thing is to take 1, 2, 3, 4, 5 kilos to Amsterdam, it's almost okay when you compare to taking 5 kilos to Indonesia. It's crazy to get killed for this. It was bad news, bad moment. Not for us – I mean, we only started the Operation Playboy because it was absolutely necessary. But when we started, we never had any idea that those guys were taking cocaine to Indonesia where they can be killed.*

I mean, doing the traffic activities was already bad enough, doing it to a country where there is a death penalty is far, far worse. I mean, after Curumim was caught they're all, 'Man, that's a shit, fuck man, they're going to kill him, they're going to kill' – but even after this, Rodrigo Gularte went to Indonesia. I mean, it's insane, insane. Those guys are psycho, psycho.

– Chief Caieron

Caieron was sure the Florianópolis playboys were behind this run, but had no clue as to which ones, and with Olaf still banged up, he had no lead on who sold the tickets. The bust confirmed to him that Operation Playboy needed to be his focus, that the slave-like hours he and his agents were working were imperative to catch the hands-free bosses who were sending young horses to their possible execution.

We've got to stop this – that is our priority. We are digging, we are doing the operation, getting pieces of the puzzle. We didn't have any suspects but we felt it would be some of those guys under investigation. Deep down I knew, if we keep going on our investigation, someone, someday in the future will be arrested and will tell us who is behind this.

– Chief Caieron

Caieron got arrest warrants for the two guys who'd been sent back from Jakarta, but only managed to get Emerson, who'd been Rodrigo's flatmate. His statement to Caieron said nothing much: '. . . that the purpose of the trip was to know the place; that he doesn't know the name of the travel agency where his ticket was bought; that the trip to Bali was his first and only trip overseas; that he'd surfed for ten years, but did not take any surfboards to Bali.'

Caieron squeezed out what little intel he could, then released him.

*

Jorge, whose angst after a month was finally fading, was busy in Amsterdam organising new runs to Europe.

I carry on with my life and activities. It was just the business, it's a gamble, and when you gamble, you know you can lose or you can win, but you can't stop. You're just addicted and you keep putting your money on the table, and let's go, let's go. It's something that it doesn't matter how many times it goes wrong, and how many people get caught and fucked, you keep playing, you keep gambling, it's crazy. This addiction of betting something and the money multiplies so fast, is like an addiction in the casino. Different in we have much more risk, but it's pretty much the same addiction.

– Jorge

CHAPTER THIRTY-TWO

BREAKING BAD

After Rodrigo's bust, I was sending people to Europe as if nothing had happened. I was carrying on with Dimitrius and Ryan as well, but we didn't talk too much about Rodrigo. We tried to be very discreet so people didn't notice we were behind that story. And we kind of tried to avoid the subject to not feel more guilty. Was kind of cold blood, not much emotion, I just kept going and going and going. I was doing things when the world was falling down . . . I couldn't stop sending people.

– Jorge

Jorge shut out the ghosts. But they were always lurking and, this time, not just in his head.

Luiz Dias was driving to Taió, a city about 290 kilometres north-west of Florianópolis, to pick up blow. Despite still nurturing a soul-stinging hatred of Jorge, he was unwittingly working for him via Rufino. Jorge was taking five of the 15-kilo load. He never wanted to see Luiz again but he wanted his blow.

The lingering fears over the death threats had faded, coming to nothing over the months.

Luiz arrived in Taió and met Pedro, his blow contact, who got in the car, took over the wheel and drove to a country-side bus stop. Luiz knew the routine and jumped out. Fifty-four kilos of Bolivian blow had been tossed from a narco plane onto an unfurled bed sheet in a forest clearing and two guys had collected and buried it. All 54 kilos were for Luiz, but he was buying it in three instalments. Pedro was driving to the hiding spot alone – his trust of Luiz didn't extend to sharing its location.

Fifteen minutes later, Luiz was back behind the wheel and driving towards Florianópolis with the 15 kilos stashed in a stereo.

He'd done this many times, but today, he glimpsed a tail in his rear-view mirror. Following his instincts, he turned off the highway to a busy city. He stopped and called a friend to come and collect him, meeting at a garage. Luiz, quick as a flash, transferred the loaded stereo from his car into his friend's boot. It was futile. His intuition was correct; the cops had been in his rear-view. They ambushed him, guns pointed, and searched the cars. Spotting the stereo in the boot, they smashed it open and found the blow. Luiz was cuffed and taken to Itajaí police cells.

Two weeks later, he was in the back of a police car flying down the highway to Florianópolis. One of the agents, who'd made the 200-kilometre round trip, walked into Caieron's office, shaking his head. 'Boss, he won't talk.' 'Why not?' 'Cos, he's a real badass motherfucker.'

Caieron smirked, sure he had the cards to make this 'badass' squeal. 'Okay, let's see. Bring him up.'

Two agents escorted a handcuffed Luiz into the office and sat him down at a table. Caieron pulled out a chair and sat down opposite. 'Good morning, Luiz. I'm Chief Fernando Caieron. You are here because of me. The good news is I can help you, as long as you play ball with me.'

Caieron was behind Luiz's bust, but had stayed invisible to preserve the secrecy of Operation Playboy. He'd passed the intel to the feds in Itajaí, making it look like an incidental bust, in no way connected to Florianópolis police, so as not to scare the other playboys out of their usual habits.

Caieron looked at Luiz. He knew more about this man's life than Luiz himself. For months, his agents had been tailing Luiz's VW Santana, spying on him and taking surveillance shots. During the police strike, Caieron had sat for hours, listening into Luiz's conversations, as well as his girlfriend's and those of several family members. Now he was about to dust him up without laying a finger on him.

Luiz glowered in fury. He leant forward in the chair, banged his handcuffs noisily on the table, and rolled his dark bulging eyes up to meet Caieron's, locking on them with a murderous stare.

For me, it's like two guys, or two animals; who's going to be in charge of that place? It was a heavy look from him; confronting, intense. I got angry because I'm talking to him very polite. I was thinking, who is he trying to impress here? And I already knew what I'm going to do if he says no. I was thinking, I'm going to eat this guy. Okay, let's do this.
       – Chief Caieron

Caieron placed his elbows on the table, mirroring Luiz, and engaged his cold, hard look.

I didn't say a word. I just kept my eyes on his eyes.
       – Chief Caieron

Caieron's métier was mind games, and he didn't like to lose.

They sat, a nose apart, staring in stony silence. Ten seconds stretched to 20 seconds, to 30 seconds, then bang – Luiz snapped back in the chair like a rubber band, the loser, but not yet losing his tough guy act. He looked sourly at the floor.

'I don't give a shit about you' – this was the message.

– Chief Caieron

Luiz spat his first words at the ground. 'I don't want to be here. I won't talk to you and I want my lawyer.' 'Well, man, let me tell you three things,' Caieron countered. 'If you're gonna talk to me or not is not your decision, because every day at 7 am, you're going to be here in my office waiting for me, and you're going to be here with me until I leave at 7 pm. I have a judge's warrant so I can keep you here. If I want to send you to motherfucker's hell, I will. You're going to have to face me every day, and one day you're going to get very sick of it and you're going to talk to me. And the third thing. Give me your lawyer's phone number and I'm gonna make the call.'

Caieron needed time to play his hand. He didn't want Luiz's lawyer to come in just yet.

I may have dialled the wrong number because I showed him, 'Look, it's out of service, there's no answer.' It's time to shake him, unbalance his confidence.

– Chief Caieron

Caieron then dialled the coffee lady, while asking Luiz if he wanted one, using a tone that dared him to refuse. 'No,' Luiz snarled. 'Two coffees please,' he told the lady. 'I don't want one,'

Luiz spat. 'It's not for you, man. I have two.' The air was heavy when the sweet old lady wheeled in her coffee cart, singing out brightly, 'Good morning, Chief.' 'Good morning, Mrs Alba,' Caieron sang back. She offered a cup to Luiz who said 'Yes.' 'No, you didn't want one, you don't get one. They're both for me,' Caieron said, reverting to his biting tone, feeling sure acting in such a bizarre way was putting Luiz off balance.

Caieron sat back, sipping his coffee. 'So, Luiz. Does your father know you're here?' he asked. 'No.' 'Well, would you like to talk to him?' Luiz looked across at Caieron in his first civil moment. 'Yes, I'd like to talk to him, Doctor.' Caieron felt a small win – in Brazil, 'Doctor' is a sign of respect. He dialled Luiz's dad's number, introduced himself, telling him, 'Your son was caught with a lot of cocaine, he's not in a good situation, but we can help him. His part in the organisation isn't so big.' This was for Luiz's ears, so he could realise Caieron might be able to help and drop the gangster act. He then put the phone to Luiz's ear and stood out of sight in his doorway, listening. About ten minutes later, Caieron took back the phone and saw Luiz's dark eyes were glistening and tears were spilling down his face. *Perfect*, Caieron thought happily, but offered some vague sympathy. 'I know, man, it's difficult.'

He was crying, crying crying crying . . . that was kind of funny, because they're all tough guys, but once they sit in front of us, they're like lambs; away from us they're like wolves; near us, like lambs.

– Chief Caieron

Caieron was using his push, relax, push technique, quickly pushing again. 'Does Kelly Ferreira still use this number – 9976 5874?' he asked, reciting it from memory. It was out of left field; he was keeping Luiz on his toes, unsettling him with how much he actually knew. It worked. Luiz looked shocked.

'You know my girlfriend?'

'Man, I know every little thing about your life. I know your life better than you do. And I can help you if you help me. Otherwise, no one can help you.'

'If you know my life, then you know I am not so bad,' he replied.

Now Caieron was ready for his big moment, set to rip out the ace he'd tucked up his sleeve in the wire-tap room.

'Listen, Luiz. You're only here because of Jorge Break.' The lie hit its mark. Luiz's face contorted with fury.

Caieron wanted Luiz badly because his job in the matrix made him another big catch. Jorge was on Caieron's hit list. He knew from Bernardo's statement and from Olaf, as well as chatter about him on the wires, that Jorge was a big player. But Caieron had never caught him on wire-taps, or in undercover surveillance in Florianópolis, nor did he have a clue that the civil police were chasing him. Right now, Jorge was just snitch bait. Caieron knew the playboys were always having fallouts over cash, and the bitter feud between Jorge and Luiz was sweet for him. He started rubbing it in.

'Jorge Break was our target, not you. We were following him and became aware of you because you were working with him. When we lost track of him, we kept watching you, hoping to find him again. Man, Jorge Break is the only reason you're here.'

Caieron watched Luiz spasm with apoplectic rage. He'd been feeling this for months and was still threatening to kill Jorge. It still stung that Jorge mocked him on the phone from Amsterdam, in front of the horse, while he sat like a lame duck in Florianópolis. He'd become the laughing-stock of the surf-board swipe story and lost cash – with his heavy cartel suppliers wanting payment for the kilos he'd taken on credit.

Caieron didn't know these details but sat silently, watching flames of fury burning in Luiz's dark eyes as the words sank in. 'Okay,' he hissed. 'I'll tell you anything you want to know about that motherfucker.'

Within 40 minutes, Caieron had him and was acutely aware that Luiz couldn't talk about Jorge without implicating plenty of others.

I broke the guy. I got into his mind and it was easy from then, he starts to sing like a bird.

– Chief Caieron

For Caieron, this was better than Christmas.

He sat at the table with a notepad, asking questions and scribbling down Luiz's answers. He knew jumping behind the computer could spook him back to badass, and right now his focus was to squeeze out as much intel as possible. Afterwards, he'd call Luiz's lawyer so he could get it all on the record. Caieron knew the lawyer, and his habit of immediately telling his clients to zip it.

I couldn't let this happen because what he was saying was too important. After he talked about Jorge, he talked about whoever else I ask him.

– Chief Caieron

Three hours later, Caieron had a notepad full of names, runs, dates and even home addresses. Luiz admitted the 15 kilos in the stereo had been for Rufino. Caieron offered to try calling his lawyer again, dialling the correct number this time. The guy soon showed up, predictably telling Luiz to shut up.

Caieron wasn't out of cards, though. He put on his poker face. 'Well, man, if you don't talk on the record, this is what I'm going to do. I'm going to put you away for an extra ten years. I have enough proof to arrest you on two counts of international trafficking. I have the evidence and testimony of one guy arrested in Frankfurt. Man, I don't want to fuck your whole life, but I can. I'm offering you a chance to rebuild your life in one or two years from now. Otherwise –'

'Okay,' the lawyer interjected. 'Let's see your proof.'

'I have an Interpol letter but I can't show you until I get the okay from my boss.'

'No deal unless we see it,' the lawyer stated.

It was after 7 pm, late enough to claim his boss had left, so they agreed to meet in the morning. Luiz was taken down to the cells, his lawyer left and Caieron got busy. Working with his secretary, they doctored up a fake Interpol letter. He knew that Luiz was the supplier and driver in Eduardo Socas da Silva's and Achylles Nucci's fateful run to Frankfurt, but he didn't have the proof needed to take him down. Caieron wasn't going to let that get in his way.

That's my play. I could perfectly screw him in a different procedure because I had the evidence. Then I made up the Interpol letter; everything I wrote was true.

– Chief Caieron

'Are you ready to talk?' he asked Luiz in the morning.

'We need to see the Interpol document,' his lawyer replied.

Caieron began his show. 'My boss has refused to give me the green light.'

'Well, no deal,' the lawyer snapped.

Caieron shut the door. 'Listen, I'll give you a quick look but keep this quiet, okay?'

'Okay.'

Caieron took the Interpol letter out of his top drawer, cast his eyes over it, then handed it across to Luiz. 'It's confidential, so make this quick.'

Caieron watched Luiz's face contort with increasing angst as he read down the page. 'Man, I'm fucked. I'm totally fucked,' he said, passing it to his lawyer. Within minutes, they agreed to cut a deal. Luiz would give an official statement to reduce his sentence and to exact revenge on Jorge, whose name had just got hotter.

Luiz decided to play with us because I use the Interpol letter, I use the Eduardo Socas da Silva statement, and I use his anger against Jorge Break. I said to him, 'If you want to make a deal with us, you have to fully disclose all the things you've done. So, let's say you sold cocaine, like, 30 times, then you tell me about every sale you made because once you make a deal, no one's going to touch you for these. But all the things you leave out of our agreement, you can be responsible for in the future.'

So he told us a lot, everything I ask about this guy, that guy, the other guy. I always asked, 'How do you know?' 'Because I was the man who gave the coke.' Some names he told me just off the record. Big guys. So Luiz gave us a lot of big information and a lot of names – Jorge Break, Rufino, Dimitrius, Onion.

– Chief Caieron

Luiz also gave Caieron an icing-on-the-cake tip. In coming days, there were operations planned to traffic blow in sports equipment, departing from São Paulo airport to Europe. Caieron alerted the airport police, who in turn advised airlines to get all passengers to collect and recheck any transiting sports equipment, and to scrupulously search any being checked in.

This would be very bad for Andre.

Rufino broke the news of Luiz's bust to Jorge. He was busy in Maresias beach and barely gave it any thought. He felt sure Luiz wouldn't talk and that the bitterness between them was no match for their pathological contempt for cops.

I was not relieved or happy because I hate it when anyone is busted by the cops. I would prefer him to be killed, then I will be happy. But not when the cops win and bust people. I hate that.

And there was so much going on, was so many people busted at that time; Curumim, Cafiero, Bernardo, Tizzy, Darcy, then Rodrigo – all these people. Maybe I just make a comment about them, 'Oh, he got arrested, how sad,' but in this next second, I was already talking about business.

So Luiz was just another one. I didn't really pay attention how dangerous he was for me. I was acting as if nothing was happening. I was so on the skies [on top of the world], *so full of money and I didn't see all this mess. I was moving stuff like crazy. It never passed through my mind that Luiz would grass me up.*

– Jorge

CHAPTER THIRTY-THREE

BABYLON

Jorge had reached the stars.

> *My clients were very rich and influential; Maserati car dealers,*
> *owners of famous nightclubs, lawyers, models, pimps of luxury whore-*
> *houses, sons and daughters of millionaires of São Paulo society,*
> *actresses, singers.*
>
> — Jorge

Jorge was now orbiting in an unparalleled world, living out of his
Louis Vuitton suitcase in a fleeting succession of five-star hotel
suites in the biggest city in the southern hemisphere, São Paulo.

> *São Paulo is a Babylon. You can get anything you want if you've*
> *got money. Prostitutes drive Mercedes-Benz cars, have expensive*
> *bags and jewels, studying in private universities. You are not able to*
> *recognise who is the whore, who is not. Corrupt cops hang together*
> *with millionaires, playboys, pimps, dealers, prostitutes, celebrities.*
> *I was not just hanging with dealers, but good people from high society.*

And they are different from people from my city, different mentality, they're open-minded, so I felt more connected with them.

— Jorge

Jorge only snuck back to Florianópolis to see his mum, driving 100 kilometres south from Navegantes airport at night and straight into her underground car park. Using the internal lift, he'd shoot up to her apartment and spend a few hours there. He still had no idea about Operation Playboy and Caieron's sharpening sights on him. He felt he was hot right across Brazil, trafficking drugs like crazy and partying like a maniac. He stayed a moving target; home was wherever he lay his Louis Vuitton suitcase.

For safety, I decided to live in five-star hotels, moving every week to make it difficult to find me. To check in, I was using names of friends, sometimes they give me a form to fill in and didn't even ask for ID. I was checking in and out of all the five-star hotels of São Paulo; the Hyatt, Marriott, Hilton and Unique, spending a fortune, always cash, so the crew of those hotels treated me like a king.

— Jorge

He was playing in the heart of the rich São Paulo set where decadent parties, wild sex, drugs, vast cash, luxury cars, yachts and choppers were a part of daily life.

Owners of the hottest São Paulo clubs and whorehouses were his customers, giving him VIP tables and hookers on tap, perfectly blending business and pleasure; friends and clients, one and the same.

Rogerio ran an exclusive 'private list' whorehouse, a mansion in the most prestigious part of São Paulo, Morumbi. Clients included a world-famous Brazilian footballer and some of the country's richest businessmen. They were able to discreetly use beautiful whores, mostly B-list working models and actresses who also wanted secrecy. Rogerio did all the negotiations, so the clients only had to wander around chatting to the girls, picking the ones they wanted. It was like being at an elegant party, where the hottest girls were a sure thing.

Rogerio the pimp was a fat, ironic, tough man with this magnificent mansion, a thousand square metres with indoor swimming pool, sauna, Jacuzzi, decorated in a Victorian style. Had its own nightclub, eight suite bedrooms and a beautiful garden – and with high quality drugs I supply.

– Jorge

Jorge sold in bulk to Rogerio, who kept a smorgasbord of drugs for his houseguests. He paid Jorge in cash, as well as giving him access to his mansion and an array of gorgeous hookers.

I was sometimes in bed with five girls and it was more friendly atmosphere than business. Doesn't mean I wasn't spending money on the girls; the payment could be gifts of flight tickets to Europe, expensive watches, jewellery or sometimes cash. I was always taking pure MDMA, sniffing blow, drinking champagne, dancing and fucking as many of those birds as I could. I was taking Cialis, a generic of Viagra, very powerful, that helps me in those sex marathons; nice cocktail of blow, MDMA, weed, tobacco, alcohol, Viagra was on top.

More than once I met those chicks out with their respective boyfriends at social events, and the guys had no idea how hard those birds work and party with me. Every time those girls were free, they were always calling me to have fun with me.

– Jorge

Jorge didn't discriminate between girls he paid and society girls he laid. He loved diversity, he loved women, and they flocked to him. Rafael jokingly called him gay, mockingly imitating him sitting cross-legged, holding a champagne flute, earnestly discussing the latest Prada bag. It was partly Jorge's penchant for fashion and fine things that attracted the girls. Through his latest girlfriend, Ana, a high society babe, he met three rich girls who were always inviting him to parties at their mansions.

I was dating a lot of birds but I was having an affair with Ana, daughter of a very powerful businessman, and hanging with her high society friends – Renata, Constancia and Isabella. Beautiful daughters of millionaires who were studying fashion design in one of São Paulo's most expensive universities. They loved to hang with me.

– Jorge

Returning at least once a month from trips to Europe, always with just-off-the-catwalk bags, shoes, watches and jackets, turned him into a living sartorial lesson for the three fashionistas, who were now always hanging out with the funny, charismatic and surprisingly well-read, drug lord.

I was bringing new clothes from Paris that no one yet had in Brazil – my clothes were the cutting edge of fashion – and I hang in the most sophisticated hotels, restaurants and clubs and I had lots of free time, so my three friends were always around me. Renata was so rich that she used to go places by her father's brand-new chopper, and more than once I was going to Maresias by air, or on trips by 80-foot boat of Constancia's father. Those three girls were always together, and I was calling them the three musketeers.

– Jorge

The girls were invariably among the guests at Jorge's marathon parties in his Maresias beach villa, or the São Paulo hotels where he often booked suites next to close friend and business partner Martino, the guy who'd paid off the judge after Caieron had busted him in Florianópolis with Clay and Pedro a couple of years earlier.

Martino was very famous in our underworld. He was also this mega-lomaniac; staying in five-star hotels, hang with gorgeous models, going to these Michelin-starred restaurants, so we identify.

– Jorge

Sometimes, they'd book all the suites to take over the entire top floor, then party for days, sharing big bags of blow and magnums of champagne with their fantastically eclectic mix of guests. Almost no one was off limits, except cops, bent ones exempted. He even lured an employee from the Hyatt spa into his bubble of debauchery.

The presidential suite of Hyatt was on the top floor, together with the spa club and I was always high, walking around the corridors, wearing a robe, semi-naked, going from my room to the spa as if it was my own house. One day I got into the massage room, completely high and drunk, and we started to flirt and when I realise I was kissing her, I try to fuck her in the room but she refused, so I told her to pass by my suite after her shift and she agreed.

– Jorge

Later that night, she knocked on Jorge's door, and met the three musketeers, Martino and his girlfriend. They all went for dinner at Nakombi, a top Japanese restaurant, followed by a wild night of clubbing. By 6 am, it was only the spa girl and one of the musketeers, Renata, who were still out with Jorge at the club, Love Story.

I was kissing the spa girl, who I'll call Priscilla – because I can't remember her name – and Renata was looking at me with a wild stare, and taking lines with me like never before. We were just friends, but on this day, she was ready to rock. I went to the toilet to take a line with her. Priscilla stayed on the dance floor, talking to a very tall blonde girl who I figured out later was a prostitute. I locked myself in the toilet with Renata and was getting the blow out of my pocket, when she became wild; took off her top, started to grab my hand and touch her breast, telling me she was horny and wants to fuck. I was quite shocked because she was very discreet and sensible and had a boyfriend, but with my blood contaminated with drugs and desire, I kissed her and she gave me a blow job in the toilet.

– Jorge

As the sun was rising, the spa girl, the hooker and the society girl were back at Jorge's Hyatt suite, naked in his Jacuzzi.

Me and Renata begin having sex in the Jacuzzi, the other two girls started to kiss and to play with us. I lead them to my king-sized bed, opened another champagne bottle, got the silver tray, put a bag of pure blow on it – went to the living room and took a 30 milligram Cialis to improve my performance – and back to the bed where Renata was having fun with the girls. I contemplated that image; a high society girl in my bed playing with a prostitute and a middle-class worker girl. Then I sink deep into those desirable bodies.

So, there I was for another two days. I was sniffing, drinking and fucking Renata and the prostitute. Priscilla made a big drama that she was partying in the place of her job and left, but during the two weeks I stayed at the Hyatt, she visited me every night after her shift, and I like her so much that I almost remember her name. I was partying every day, preparing scams, focusing on drugs, parties and girls.

– Jorge

Business was crazier than ever. Jorge was setting up more scams and, now that Luiz was out of action, regularly flying around South America to buy blow. He'd fly with Rufino to their golf course villa in Paraguay, where his neighbour was a supplier, or with Martino to meet contacts in Peru or Columbia. No matter how hard Jorge partied, he was always weaving work into the days and nights: taking calls, casting, hiring and organising horses, first to bring blow to Brazil, then unpacking, repacking and sending it to Europe to sell, buy skunk and pills, pack, send and sell in Brazil.

It was a business and it required a lot of work, but his contacts constantly grew and so did his profits. He was now using a client's condominium in Alphaville, an exclusive, heavily guarded gated enclave 15 minutes from São Paulo city, to stash his kilos. Packing was sophisticated too. Martino had introduced him to 'the magician', a Lebanese guy who had a factory, making bags. Jorge could just take him kilos of blow, often with some fake Louis Vuitton or Gucci fabric that he'd bought at a market, and a few days later pick up the knock-off designer bags with built-in blow.

His new party network was absorbing most of his drugs in the blink of an eye. Although most of his horses were still returning to Florianópolis, Jorge had them deliver to São Paulo, where a hungry market could devour a load of 10,000 pills and 20 kilos of skunk in a week. 'Everyone wants, was never enough, everything disappears.'

His biggest client was Hugo – the ultimate Brazilian playboy. He'd originally bought kilos of lemon juice from Marco, then moved on to Dimitrius, and now also bought from Jorge, who'd become a close friend.

Hugo was the king of the playboys in São Paulo – big playboys just living from family money. They have the best cars, choppers, jets, boats. They are rich, and in Brazil, rich are very, very, very rich, just top five percent – and Hugo was this guy who was commanding these people – selling drugs to these playboys.

I pretty much used to give everything to him for a good price, and he was selling for absurd prices, like crazy crazy money and we didn't understand why people are buying so expensive, but Hugo's got his aura, this thing; everybody just wants to know him, to buy drugs from him.

– Jorge

Jorge rented Hugo's luxury villa at Maresias beach, the weekend hotspot for São Paulo's wealthiest. Coming to this party beach was the only predictable stop in Jorge's unpredictable life. When in Brazil, he was there every weekend; checking the progress of his Ombak beach bar, partying in the private villas and sitting at a VIP table every Saturday night at the beach's famous Sirena nightclub. He'd sniff blow and watch other people partying on his drugs, never admitting he was a dealer or selling directly – he knew that was suicide.

His weekend routine made him visible, but he loved being at Maresias beach. The place combined his old and new lives; partying with Timi, Rufino, Dimitrius and Oscar as well as his newer friends and partners, Martino and Mich and Rocco, guys from Brasília, Brazil's political capital and, like Florianópolis, a capital of rave parties. Jorge regularly partnered up with these guys, who usually moved part of their drugs to Brasília, and who were on the radar of Brasília's police.

Jorge continued to suppress any thoughts of his fallen friends – he was living in the hedonistic moment of this rock-star life he'd dreamt of as a kid. But a constant subliminal paranoia – the malignant sense that his star could explode at any time – manifested in a worsening habit of fleeing hotels, especially when he was high on blow, which was most of the time.

I start to have hallucinations when I was too high, about being surrounded by cops, or having nightmares of running and bust.

Often, I was getting haunted by this feeling of chase, persecution, and my first reaction was to move hotels. Doesn't matter the time or who I was with. I was rapid to put my belongings together in a suitcase and vanish in the night. This started to happen often; it could be São Paulo, Rio, Brasília or any other city in Brazil – in Europe, I was usually relaxed because I believed I was clean and unknown to European authorities. I did move hotels there, but not as often as Brazil. I knew I was hot in my country. I just didn't know how much.

– Jorge

Sitting in a bar in São Paulo's Hyatt Hotel one night with Martino and his girlfriend, Kate, he noticed two men in suits walk in and sit at a table in front of them. One of the guys was staring at him. Jorge glanced at Martino; their thoughts were synced. Undercover cops.

Jorge tried to relax. A friend of Kate's arrived and they all ate dinner in the hotel restaurant, then adjourned to his suite for a drink and sniff. After an hour or so, they got in the lift to go out to party. On the way down, the lift stopped. The two suited men from the bar got in. Jorge tensed and shot Martino a look.

I knew he was thinking the same as me: 'We are being followed by cops, they know our movements, we're surrounded.' We'd just received ten kilos of blow from Paraguay a day before to make suitcases with the Lebanese guy. We'd stashed it in our friend's place in Alphaville. We thought the cops are after us, they know we will transport the gear from Alphaville to the bag factory. I tried not to panic – we left the lift and walked to the bar and noticed the two men going outside. Instead of getting a taxi or using valet parking, a car with another man in a suit was already waiting for them.

I told Martino I was going up to get my things and check out – he agreed. In less than 20 minutes, I was at reception, finishing my check-out. We got into Martino's Audi to start looking for a hotel on the other side of the city.

After 40 minutes of turns and going round in circles to check no one was following us, I decide to stop at Blue Tree Towers. Kate did the check-in in her name, and I decide not to go out. Kate was used to our lifestyle and behaviour, but her friend was in shock. She didn't understand why these two crazy guys suddenly start talking in codes and changing hotels in the middle of the night.

Those situations happened very often. Could be night or day, if I start to think about the events around me, my scams, my horses and friends in jail and the raids in Florianópolis, I would almost for sure start to pack my things and move on.

– Jorge

CHAPTER THIRTY-FOUR

COLD CASE

Several of Caieron's agents were working undercover, staking out a guy at his house after a tip-off. After waiting all morning, they saw him leave just after midday in a black VW Parati and tailed him to a restaurant, and then with a blond guy onto busy Itaguaçu shopping mall. On foot, the cops lurked behind, watching as the pair went to the second floor and met with another two guys in front of McDonald's. All four then walked back to the car park, clueless they were being shadowed.

The agents pounced. Their target went ballistic, hurling a grey folder from his hands, screaming, hitting out at the cops. With his limbs violently flailing, the agents pushed him to the ground and cuffed him. A cop retrieved the folder and found a plastic bag of 1000 ecstasy pills inside. He was gone; busted red-handed. The other three were cuffed and frisked. The feds found a loaded handgun on the blond guy and US $11,430 in a Black and Decker box on the back seat of the other pair's car.

It was another bust. Caieron's agents were making a lot of them these days as Florianópolis was still the major transit point for ecstasy tablets. Caieron was now paying cash for tips, and club bosses were also feeding him intel. Small dealers were falling fast, but today's bust was going to be different. Their target was just another dealer, but his blond friend would turn out to be collateral gold.

All four would be interrogated, but Caieron's eye was now on the tall blue-eyed blond guy. He sat nervously in front of Caieron, who was flicking through his passport, seized in a house search after the bust. A boarding pass stub fell out for a flight from Amsterdam. Caieron looked at the name: Alex Conte. He'd never heard of him before, but this guy was obviously a horse, and Caieron was ready to ride him for intel.

'Man, ten, eleven stamps in your passport for trips to Amsterdam, Paris, Frankfurt in the last 12 months. Are you going to tell the judge you were taking a holiday? "I love Europe, I go every month as a tourist." You really think he will believe you?'

The guy looked scared. Caieron pushed harder.

'Man, no one will believe your story. I'm telling you, the judge knows a lot about this type of activity. He's sent more than 20 people to jail already, and I'm going to tell him that every single stamp represents a trip you did to bring in ecstasy, because there's no other plausible explanation for this number of trips. Which means you're fucked. Truly fucked. You're going to be charged for all these trips, every single one.'

Caieron watched the guy absorb his bluff.

You can have 100 stamps, it's not a crime.

— Chief Caieron

Caieron then targeted the guy's wife, Fabrícia whose passport was also full of stamps from Europe. He told Alex he could charge her for every trip too. Then he swung from a new angle. 'You had a loaded gun in your hand today, so we will charge you — beyond international trafficking — with illegal possession. You are going to jail for 15, 20 years.'

Caieron had him.

In less than ten minutes, he was flipping, like roll easy, a piece of cake. He said with a bit of jealousy, 'Man, I'm a small guy, why should I go to jail? There are a lot of bigger guys than me.' Then I instigate: 'Well, if you give me a big fish, I can give you the benefits. But listen, man, your situation is bad, fucking bad, unless you have something truly important to tell me, we can't do a deal. So give me your best, and I can give you the best as well.'

— Chief Caieron

Caieron wasn't expecting what came next.

'Do you know about those three guys arrested in Indonesia?'

'Yes, why?'

'I sold the tickets.'

Caieron's pulse quickened. 'To who?'

'Have you heard of Dimitrius Christopoulos — the Greek?'

Caieron felt a shiver. He nodded. 'Yes, I know the name.'

'Well, Dimitrius sent those guys to Indonesia. I have the proof. I sold the tickets.'

Caieron had not just lassoed a horse; he had a playboy travel agent.

'Do you have the copy of those tickets?' Caieron asked.

'Yes, I do.'

'Okay, let's go to your office and get those tickets now, okay?'

'Okay.'

It was 44 days since the global story of Rodrigo's bust, and now Caieron had the name of the elusive, faceless boss.

I mean, fuck, I got goose bumps. I was truly happy, excited, satisfied – this was the goal, my target. Some part of me knew that some day, in the future, I would know who sent those guys. And that day just came without any notice. It was a great moment.

– Chief Caieron

Caieron's agents took Alex to his home office and collected copies of those fateful tickets. Now Caieron needed the prosecutor's nod to officially offer 'the benefits' – a soft sentence for strong intel. He hit a snag: the prosecutor was not amenable. Alex Conte was involved with the sale of 1000 pills and was carrying a loaded, unregistered gun in a crowded shopping centre. No deal for this guy.

In Caieron's hands, Conte quickly succumbed to confessing everything. He'd brought 10,000 ecstasy pills from Amsterdam the previous week and the boss, another dealer, asked him to take 1000 pills across town to the small dealer. Alex then went with him to the shopping mall, taking the gun just in case the buyers tried to rob them.

Alex's arrest was exactly why Andre had always warned horses never to sell drugs – if they got busted, they had too much intel. Travel agents Alex and Fabrícia were as lethal as assassins with what they knew. They could shoot everyone down with their fully loaded intel. They knew the game and all its players. Timi had warned the guys about Alex's threats – *'If I go to jail, everybody goes to jail.'* Caieron had seen that jealous streak in him and used it. Now, for the price of a light sentence, Alex was ready to pull the trigger. Caieron argued his best case to the reluctant prosecutor.

'Man, listen. He can give us the guy who sent those other guys to Bali, Indonesia. One of them will be killed, so we can talk about murder as well. Which situation is more important? Giving Alex Conte ten years or stopping other guys from sending more people to the death penalty?

'I know I will bust those guys but I'm going to take like one year, two years without Alex Conte's statement. With it, I can get to those guys fast. If you don't give him the benefits, other guys can be sent to Indonesia. That's why it's so important.'

'Okay,' the prosecutor capitulated, convinced by Caieron's argument and passion, and more open to future deals as well.

He saw I was interested in stopping the bad, bad, bad, nasty things going on.

– Chief Caieron

Caieron called one of his agents, asking for the Cafiero file, the surfer without a tan. Caieron had remembered this case as soon as Alex Conte had said 'Dimitrius Christopoulos'. It was an unusual name and he'd seen it once before, in the statement by Cafiero, busted at São Paulo airport en route to Bali with blow in his surfboard bag. 'I remember once I read Dimitrius Christopoulos, I thought to myself, who has that name?' The Cafiero file had been put on ice. Now, it was hot – a top-priority file.

Caieron re-read Cafiero's statement, written up by the feds at São Paulo airport straight after his bust a year earlier:

Who offered him the trip was an individual named Dimitrius Christopoulos . . . whose nickname is 'The Greek' . . . he has a Greek and a Brazilian passport . . . Dimitrius was the one who gave him the plane tickets and instructions for the trip, particularly through his email christopoulosdimitrius@hotmail.com.

– Luis Cafiero, police statement, São Paulo

Cafiero's words backed up Conte's. Caieron now had two unrelated sources stating on the record that Dimitrius sent horses to Bali. No one had chased up the phone numbers in the statement, so Caieron ordered the records. One number stood out for the high volume of calls to Cafiero, from days prior to his bust right up to just before it. It was registered to a 'Timi'. Another name in the statement was 'Zeta'. Caieron had heard of neither Timi or Zeta until now.

Caieron phoned his best intel source – his other busted travel agent, effeminate-voiced Olaf. He'd just walked free and was now indebted to Caieron as part of the 'benefits' deal. Olaf filled in the blanks – he knew Zeta, he knew Timi, and he knew their roles. Caieron didn't tell his agents why Olaf was coming to his office as he'd promised to keep their deal secret, but a sudden flurry of tête-à-têtes didn't go unnoticed.

All the guys made a nickname for him, 'little tit', because he was kind of jelly, not a muscle guy, and they made some jokes, 'Hey, Chief, are you on a date with Olaf because it's the third time he's coming this week.'
– Chief Caieron

Caieron's mission now was to hunt down Dimitrius Christopoulos – the Greek. He sent two agents to Rio as they now had his home address, and he told other agents to keep a keen ear on the wire-taps.

But Dimitrius was gone.

CHAPTER THIRTY-FIVE

UNMASKING
A DRUG LORD

While his agents chased Dimitrius in Rio, Caieron jumped on a plane to São Paulo. His icing-on-the-cake tip from the shifty-eyed blow supplier, Luiz Alberto Dias, had paid off. A horse had been busted in São Paulo with eight kilos of blow inside windsurf booms.

For the horse, Diego Fonyat Duarte do Amaral, a 24-year-old law student, it had been an unusual request to collect his sports equipment at Guarulhos airport and recheck it. Only eight weeks earlier, he'd done a run for Andre and sent his luggage all the way from Porto Alegre to Europe. This time, he'd rechecked the bag, got the all-clear and gone to the gate.

He never made it onto the plane.

A federal cop had called Caieron with news that his intel had snared a guy, but he was oscillating between wanting to sing like a bird and hostile silence. 'He's bipolar,' the cop told Caieron. With 35,000 passengers a day coming through, they didn't have the time to nurture intel out of him. He would sink into the legal system without a trace, taking the information on his bosses with him. Caieron refused to let this happen. 'Man, I'll come and sit with this motherfucker for as long as I need,' he told the cop.

Caieron and agent Jair were soon sitting opposite a very highly strung horse.

'Easy, man, easy. Are you okay?' Caieron soothed. 'I'm okay.' 'I'm here to see if I can help you, man. Is anyone treating you badly?' 'No.' 'Is there anything I can do for you? Contact your parents, your friends? Would you like a glass of water? A coffee? Anyone come to see you, to see if you need anything?' 'No.' 'Not even the guys who hired you?' 'No, no one.'

Perfect, Caieron thought.

'Listen, you're here because those guys think they're smarter than you. They say, "Man, I have a deal for you. You will travel, you will get rich, nothing will happen to you," but now you know that's bullshit. You're charged with international drug trafficking, facing ten, 15 years in jail, maybe more. But I'm here to help you.'

He had Diego's attention.

'Man, you're not the only one. There are lots of guys like you. The sad thing is that the guys who hired you are free and out hiring more young guys full of life, just like you.

'So, think this over. You can rescue your life back, or you can fuck yourself forever. Do you think you'll survive in jail? You are fresh meat. You're gonna wash the dirty underwear of bad guys – that's what's in your future – would you like to wash underwear of bad guys, Diego?' 'No,' he replied.

'Have those guys who hired you organised a lawyer for you?' 'No.'

'See, that's what I mean, man. They've turned their backs, you're alone now, do you think they care?

'Those guys are out enjoying life, surfing waves, drinking champagne. They're smart, they never touch the drugs, they find a young guy like you to do the dirty work. Man, you're a kind of victim and right now you're fucked. But I can help you, if you help me. It's up to you, it's your life. My life will be the same tomorrow – I'll catch a plane back to Florianópolis, go wherever I want, whenever I want . . . You won't. Your life is going to be fucked, unless you talk to me.'

It took Caieron just 25 minutes to get a talking horse. 'Okay, I'm going to tell you everything I know.'

Caieron grabbed a pen and paper. 'Okay, if you don't mind, I'm going to take a few notes. Who hired you for this job?'

Diego looked directly at Caieron. 'Andre Mendes.'

Caieron turned, giving agent Jair a quizzical look. 'I know that name?'

'Yes, remember, man, that dossier of the guy in Garopaba from the civil police,' Jair prompted. For 18 months, Andre's file had sat in a low priority stack. Garopaba was an hour from Florianópolis and Caieron hadn't had the spare manpower to start digging. There were so many files, too many names. A big part of his job was prioritising who to chase. Andre's file may never have seen the light of day, but for Diego catapulting it into the spotlight and setting a ticking time bomb under Andre's beautiful life.

I say, 'Okay, tell me more about the guy,' and Diego tells me details, details, details; how many trips, the dates, the places, how they work. He starts to talk, talk, talk, talk, talk. Once I was satisfied, I said, 'Okay, we're going to do this officially after lunch, if you want? I've already set free other guys like you, carrying coke. I can try to do this for you, but you have to play with me.' He said, 'Yes, I want to do this.'

– Chief Caieron

During the break, Caieron made a quick call to informant Olaf. 'Is Andre Mendes a big fish?' he asked. 'Yes, I've sold him many tickets,' he replied, verifying Diego's intel.

After lunch, Caieron called Diego's lawyer, his aunty Vera Fonyat in Porto Alegre, outlining the deal. 'If Diego's intel is accurate, and if it leads to the bust of Andre Mendes, he will spend no more than one year in prison for eight kilos of cocaine.' She agreed and Diego divulged all.

Eight weeks earlier, he'd done a run to Amsterdam with three kilos of cocaine inside windsurf booms. Andre had delivered these to his house in Porto Alegra in a green VW Gol with Florianópolis number plates. Diego had then phoned Andre on safe arrival, and he'd arrived the next day. Diego spent two hours helping Andre to saw open the booms, remove the blow, and stash it into plastic zip-lock bags with a green stripe. Diego later sat in the hotel room with Andre, counting the €66,000 payment. Diego did a sweet return home with 2.2 kilograms of skunk and 10,000 ecstasy pills hidden inside a paraglider sail squashed into a blue wheelie bag with yellow Quiksilver logos.

Diego explained that on the bust run, Andre had set things up for him to deal with Claudio, the bent cop. This time, Claudio had driven the booms to Diego's home in Porto Alegre. Two days before he ran, Diego got a call from Andre saying he was in Waikiki and waiting for him to come for a surf.

Caieron took down every word. This horse had just lifted the veil on Andre's life, unmasking him as a drug lord.

Andre was still in Hawaii, playing golf and staying at a friend's luxury resort. He'd made a dash several weeks earlier for the clear blue skies of Bali, then to Waikiki. He was enjoying an escape from those dark clouds gathering in Brazil. Bust after bust had made him nervous, and the latest one was very, very bad news.

I felt shocked. I knew the problems will be close to me now.

– Andre

The irony was that Diego's bust run wasn't Andre's run. He was tangled in it but just for helping out bent cop Claudio. He'd called, asking if Andre had a spare horse to carry eight kilos of blow that had been confiscated in a São Paulo bust. Also, could Andre book the horse's flights through his usual girls? Claudio would pay him a kilo commission, so €30,000 for two phone calls. It was a no-brainer. Andre had set it up, then gone surfing, with no clue he'd just lit a fuse to his door until he got the call about Diego's bust. Now the million-dollar question was: was Diego talking?

Andre hoped not. Three weeks later, he sat in first class with his girlfriend, Gisele, jetting back to Florianópolis to attend his best friend's wedding at his beachfront restaurant, Oriental Mormaii. He knew he needed to be careful and had no plans to touch any drugs.

He and Gisele went straight to the restaurant, spent two hours at the wedding, then drove home to his Silveira beach house. The landline rang. Andre glanced at Gisele. 'Did you tell your mum we're back?' 'No.' It was odd. Only those at the wedding knew they were here. He snatched up the phone.

'Hello!' 'Hey, you need to send money to my son. He needs your help.' Andre's pulse quickened. 'Sorry, you have the wrong number. I don't know you, I don't know what you're talking about.' She hit back. 'I know who you are, Andre.' He hung up. It was Diego's mum; a set-up for sure. The cops were onto him, using her as bait to catch a confession.

Andre's brain worked fast. He told Gisele to go to her mum's house, then turned on the lights as a decoy. Grabbing a bag he ran out through his garden and across three kilo-metres of jungled mountains to reach the house of a friend and client, who took him to the airport. He flew straight back to Hawaii.

At the federal police office, Caieron's agents were wire-tapping Andre's phones. They didn't set up the call from Diego's mum, but were listening in for his next operation to catch him red-handed. They heard him talk in code to a guy named 'Renato' and immediately got a warrant to tap his phone too. The chase for Andre hit full force: Caieron sent three of his surfer cops to Garopaba. They took their boards and rented a beach house – surfing was now surveillance.

It was great for me because I took all my surfboards and kept them there.

– Bernardo, federal agent and surfer

Their dream job wouldn't last long. Andre's childhood friend, horse and waiter, Renato Pinheiro, was already organising to bring 6000 pills from São Paulo to Garopaba for Andre. Renato talked on the phone, setting up the domestic trip with the agents listening in. He was hiring a girl, Christiane Ferreira Lira, to fly to Florianópolis with the pills and check into the Ibis hotel. Renato would later meet her there, then the next morning, they'd drive to Garopaba.

After three more weeks in Hawaii, time had partially defused Andre's paranoia, and he decided to come home for the summer season and Christmas, and because his gorgeous girl Gisele was missing him. He rationalised that if he worked in his restaurant, acted the businessman and kept his hands free of drugs, the cops couldn't pin anything on him. Renato was bringing the pills down but they'd go directly to his storage house and be sold to one buyer, so he'd be fine.

Andre couldn't have anticipated Caieron's tenacity, and the conga line of snitches leading right to him.

CHAPTER THIRTY-SIX

CHASING ANDRE

Caieron and his blonde wife were drinking beers in the foyer bar of Florianópolis' Ibis hotel. 'Now I know why you like your job so much,' she laughed. His wife was a psychologist, not a cop, but with no women on Caieron's team, he'd asked her to come along as a couple looked less suspicious than two men. Two more agents sat unobtrusively further away. Caieron's back was turned to the glass front doors, his wife's eyes were his mirror.

Everything was going to plan. The feds at São Paulo airport had called their counterparts at Florianópolis airport, reporting Christiane Ferreira Lira had boarded the flight, just as the wire-taps had foretold. When she landed in Florianópolis, Caieron's agents watched her collect her bag off the tiny carousel then called their boss. 'She's in a cab on her way. White pants, blue shirt.' That was 25 minutes ago.

'I think she's here,' Caieron's wife said. Caieron felt a rush. A moment like this was big, crystallising all their hard work, making the abstract tangible. He kept his back to the door, watching his wife's eyes. She was faking nonchalance, casually watching the door as Christiane walked inside. Caieron took a sip of beer, staying cool, but feeling a thrill as he glimpsed a wheelie bag roll right by his leg. It was exactly the bag Diego had said Andre gave to his horses to use: a blue Quiksilver bag with yellow details. He couldn't believe it.

I was like ... ahhh – it's exciting, the scenario is perfect. Everything you imagined before in order to make an arrest is fitting. 'Man, I was right, she's here,' you really get happy. It's amazing, it's amazing, like, man, we are doing this. It was crazy, because I knew the pills were there, I smell the thing is here but I have to be patient because we want to arrest the real owner.

– Chief Caieron

This was big fish stuff. She was a minnow.

As soon as she checked in, walked across to the lift, and vanished behind the closing doors, Caieron sprang into action. He went to reception and showed his federal police ID to the manager, explaining that the woman who'd just checked in was a drug trafficker with a bag full of ecstasy pills. He said they'd need a room near hers. 'They'll be staying here tonight,' he said, pointing over at the two agents in the bar. 'Whatever you need,' the manager said, assured by Caieron that there'd be no busts in his hotel.

Caieron and his wife went back to their apartment a few blocks away, and the two agents ordered another beer, waiting for Renato. He turned up around 11 pm, and went straight up.

First thing in the morning, Caieron and one of his agents, Cintra, were in one car, tailing a green VW Gol on the highway to Garopaba. It was the exact car Diego said that Andre had used to deliver the booms of blow. Two more agents were in other cars, and more of the team were already near Andre's house in Garopaba, waiting.

As they got close, their so-far perfect operation was thrown into jeopardy. Renato suddenly turned off the main road and was circling small back streets. Cintra slowed, dropping right back, scared they'd been spotted. They watched the green VW Gol vanish around a corner. It was a balancing act: don't let him get too far away, but stay out of his rear-view mirror. But when Cintra turned the corner, the green Gol was gone.

'We've lost him,' Caieron alerted the rest of the team.

They cruised the streets, hoping the green car would flash into view again. If Renato had glimpsed a tail, he might abort. Every minute now seemed like an eternity. All agents were on high alert. Ten minutes passed and Caieron's phone rang. 'Boss, we've found Renato's car. It's at a house down the hill from Andre's.'

Now Caieron needed to decide; wait until Renato goes to Andre's house and catch Andre red-handed, or bust them both now in separate places. Caieron was thinking fast. He wanted the pills in Andre's hands, to give him no chance of slipping through his fingers in court. But he had the wire-taps, Diego's statement, and hopefully Renato would snitch. He needed to make the call fast. 'Man, we've already lost him once,' Cintra opined. 'Okay, let's arrest them now,' Caieron ordered.

Andre was glad to be home and up early for a morning kitesurf. He had no plans to meet Renato – somehow the cops had misconstrued that. He knew he was hot. He was never going to give them any chance of catching him red-handed. He had no sense of foreboding as he put his kiteboard in the back of his car until he glimpsed two men lurking outside his front gates.

His heart began pounding – cops, for sure. Andre left the car and walked briskly around the side of the house towards the beach, dropping two joints out of his pocket as he went. He felt panic; he had to run.

It was too late.

His garden exploded with action. 'Stop, stop! Don't move.' Cops came from all directions, pointing guns, surrounding him and shouting, 'On the ground, don't move or we'll shoot.' Andre dropped to his knees and put his hands up. 'On the ground, get on the ground.' Andre fell flat on his stomach, turning his head to the side. Gun muzzles came in close, voices still shouting, 'Hands behind your head.' He clasped his hands at the nape of his neck, as a boot smashed down on them. 'Don't move or I'll blow your head off,' a cop shouted.

Andre had long-feared this day, and frantic thoughts rushed his brain – call a lawyer, bribe the cops. He started shouting, 'I've got money. You don't need to use violence.' A businessman would think these guys were robbers, so he acted the part. 'My money is in the safety deposit box. I'll just open the safety box, and you can go.'

'We're not thieves, Andre. We're federal police.' It was Caieron. He flashed his badge low to the ground for Andre to see. 'I'm the narcotics police chief and I've been watching you, Andre.'

Caieron ordered his agent to remove his boot from Andre's neck. Another cop cuffed him. 'Get up,' Caieron ordered, grabbing his shirt and yanking him up. Andre saw he was surrounded by cops pointing guns. It was his waking nightmare, one he'd run from all year. They took him inside and searched the house, finding 76 plastic zip-lock bags with a green stripe across the top – exactly the same bags Diego had described using for pills. They also found around €2000, and US $2000, but no drugs, missing Andre's skunk stash, and his three guns.

Caieron then went to see Renato, who'd been arrested simultaneously at the other house, Andre's storage place. As soon as Caieron arrived, he knew exactly what to do – use the waves as a weapon. He told his agents to lay some surfboards on the grass outside. Then he led Renato, now in handcuffs, to a little bench perched on the hillside, overlooking the ocean. He sat next to him in silence, letting the view and sea breeze do the talking. The surfboard props lay on the grass. 'I need to show what he is going to miss for too long, too fucking long.'

For a surfer, this was heaven; Silveira beach, a crisp sunny morning, good waves – and Renato was about to swap it for a dank cell. Caieron was about to rub it in. 'Man, I know you like to surf, so take a good look at those waves, and try to save this beautiful image in your mind. It's the last time you're going to see it for a long time.

'You're going to jail. Your life's done, finished. Take one last look at this view, man. How long before you see this view again is up to you. It's your life, your decision, if you want to talk or not. It's not my life. I can come here tomorrow, stay here all day. You can't.'

Caieron played his usual cards, telling Renato that he was being used by Andre, who was already singing like a bird, telling them everything. Caieron taunted Renato that they knew a lot about him – that he and Christiane flew in last night, stayed at the Ibis hotel, and that he was an international trafficker. Renato was in a spin. Caieron could see he was getting to him.

'Renato, the only reason you're being arrested is because Andre is using you. Man, he's already admitted the pills belong to him, he's already said you're working for him, and he would like to have the benefits of collaboration. Would you like to have those benefits too, Renato?'

I know how they think, but they don't know how I think. I turn one against another. I gave him a reality shock and with him, it worked.
— Chief Caieron

Right there on the hill, Renato agreed to snitch on his childhood friend.

Andre wasn't snitching; Caieron couldn't break him. Showing him Diego's detailed statement back at police headquarters only made him angrier. He loathed snitches. When he walked past an office and caught Renato's eye, he slashed a finger across his throat. In the police cells, they shared time in the communal area, and Andre convinced Renato to only confess to domestic trafficking, not to implicate him and a bigger global network. When Andre got out, he would pay for the best lawyer for Renato. He'd be out in 18 months. 'Deal?' 'Deal,' Renato agreed. But, once back in Caieron's clutches, he flipped again.

Andre was furious. His childhood friend was obliterating his facade as a successful restaurateur, blowing away his life, all because he'd done him a favour. Renato had instigated this run, calling Andre, crying poor — again. For years, he'd given Renato work whenever he called up desperate for money. He was the waiter who refreshed beach towels filled with ecstasy pills, as well as a regularly running horse. This time, Andre had proposed the pill run to give Renato some fast cash. He gave him the ticket to Amsterdam and a hotel voucher. His middleman in Amsterdam passed him 10,000 pills. Renato's fee was half the pills. He'd been unable to sell his last 1000 in São Paulo, so had brought them to Garopaba with Andre's half to sell to the bulk buyer. Andre couldn't believe he was now snitching, and saw his betrayal as demoniac treachery.

Renato and his lawyer asked to see Caieron one afternoon. They told him Andre was threatening him and had sent a note to his cell. Agents retrieved it. It called Renato a 'traitor' and a 'coward'. Caieron immediately moved Andre to a prison, sabotaging his efforts to muzzle Renato.

Andre had already hired an expensive lawyer, Rolex-wearing Claudio Gastao Da Rosa, famous for his 'connections' to judges in the Brasília appeal courts. With his help, Andre didn't plan to stay locked up for long – money talked and his could say plenty. Caieron had other ideas.

The guy is psycho, absolutely. He thinks he's doing the right thing and no one has the right to stop him doing this kind of activity.

– Chief Caieron

CHAPTER THIRTY-SEVEN

OPERATION CONNECTION NETHERLANDS

Caieron didn't know it yet, but another cop was hunting playboys in Florianópolis. This cop was physically the opposite of Caieron – fair-haired, blue-eyed and sinewy from long distance cycling, in contrast to Caieron's darker, pumped-up, gym look. He had a quieter, more relaxed confidence compared to Caieron's flash and swagger. However, their shared traits made them lethal to their prey. They were straight cops negotiating a bent judiciary, both passionate, young and hungry. They liked to win, and put their hearts and souls into operations, wanting to make a difference to the future of Brazil. And they shared the first name: Fernando.

Despite this, when Chief Fernando Cesar, a Brasília civil police boss in the Organised Crime Division, dropped in to see Caieron to potentially share intel between Operation Playboy and Cesar's Operation Connection Netherlands, it didn't go well.

Not a good meeting. He was very silent about his operation, not very friendly. I understood.

– Chief Cesar

Cops didn't trust cops – and civil police across Brazil were notoriously corrupt. For Caieron, there was still blood in the water from two years earlier when a Brasília civil cop had flown in and interfered with his case, greasing the palm of the judge to free Clay, Pedro and Martino. Caieron didn't forget. Now, another civil cop from Brasília was in his office, asking questions about Martino and other playboys. Caieron was hostile, protective of Operation Playboy. He was so close to making big, impactful busts. Sharing hard-gotten intel with the Brasília civil police was not on the cards.

Cesar was just as hungry. He'd come to Caieron because, after six months of investigating playboys trafficking drugs to and from Amsterdam, he saw a likely crossover in targets. Despite knowing little about Caieron's secret operation, he saw the playboys were all connected. They moved in the same circles, partying, surfing and partnering up on runs, often coming to Florianópolis.

Cesar had initially started his Operation Connection Netherlands to catch a local guy, Mich Tocci, dubbed the baron of ecstasy in Brasília, but he was untouchable. A year earlier, Brasília police had aborted an operation targeting him after Tocci found out about it from friends in 'high society'.

High society in Brazil means supreme court judges, superior court judges and politicians. We have a lot of judges, prosecutors and police officers who knew Mich very well and also some, especially prosecutors, bought some good stuff from him.

– Chief Rodrigo Bonacci (Brasília civil police)

They were his customers?

Yes.

– Chief Cesar

Tocci's connections gave him a protective shield – if anyone was chasing him, he'd find out – but Cesar was smart, shrewd and acutely aware of the machinations of corruption. He knew contorting like a gymnast through the tricky maze of corrupt cops, prosecutors and judges was the only way to make an operation fly. He was keen to try to do what others failed to do – catch Tocci – as well as investigate possible collusion with bent cops. Several ecstasy-related deaths at Brasília's ubiquitous rave parties provided a catalyst for Operation Connection Netherlands.

The first thing Cesar did was wait for a notoriously corrupt judge to go on holidays. Then he asked another judge for a warrant to tap Tocci's phone, and for the investigation to be sent to another court to avoid future phone-tap requests going to the dirty judge. This was approved. 'By luck the other judge was straight – a very good judge.' Cesar had no doubt the corrupt judge would have instantly tipped off Tocci, so all trace of the operation was wiped from his courtroom by the time he returned. Cesar was free to fly.

Cesar named his chase Operation Connection Netherlands after pulling back the curtain on a much bigger stage than Tocci. He and his agents discovered the broad network of playboys trafficking blow to Europe, bringing back pills and skunk and sending them around Brazil. They had seen that Florianópolis was a hotspot.

I couldn't imagine the size of the operation. We knew that it was very important, but we thought it was just local in Brasília, people from here who were going to Europe, but in the middle of the operation, we realised it was very big. A lot of people involved.

– Chief Cesar

Cesar's operation widened, and his targets now included Tocci's close partners. One of them was Rocco, who'd got his start in the drugs game years earlier by trafficking for lemon juice king Marco. Rocco's father was friendly with top judges, something Cesar discovered by listening in to their home phones in his extensive wire-tapping. He had up to 100 phones tapped at any one time.

Another of Tocci's partners became the most important target for Cesar: Martino, Jorge's friend. Cesar had done a background check and seen Caieron had once arrested him, which was one of the reasons he wanted to share intel. Listening in to the playboys' calls, Cesar had quickly realised that Martino was more powerful than Tocci.

Martino was the guy who had the connections in South America to buy pure cocaine, and to get the best synthetic drugs in Amsterdam. He was the guy who knew everybody – who has the knowledge, the contacts in the police in São Paulo.

In fact, we realised that he was the boss, and he started to collect money from a small group of people. This was just one operation. We know that on other occasions, probably this group operated with other people. In fact they all knew each other, everybody. It was dynamic, very dynamic, depending on the opportunity. Somebody has the money, somebody was in Brasília, somebody has the equipment, and they start to plan.

– Chief Cesar

Cesar was also chasing a surfer, Marc, who now lived in Florianópolis. On his trip to see Caieron, Cesar would call his 'listening team' in Brasília to find out from the wire-taps which beach Marc was hitting, and started surfing right beside him each morning. In the water, Cesar sat on his board, anonymous among the other surfers waiting for waves, and listened and watched who Marc talked to, mostly wanting to know where he hung out for potential future busts.

Cesar and one of his agents also spent several days spying on the playboys in the lake area of Florianópolis. The house belonged to Rafa, a prolific drug user from a rich family, who was a close friend and client of Jorge's. He wasn't in the game but Rafa loved to party and opened his house to all his trafficker friends. Cesar and his agent poked binoculars through venetian blinds from a house opposite, watching the action day and night and dubbing it the 'Big Brother house'.

> *They didn't sleep in that house. It was 24 hours of party, loud music, only doing cocaine and drugs from Europe. A lot of people in transit there, coming and going, coming and going.*
>
> – Agent

They found out who they were by using a local cop to do seemingly random licence checks up the road.

> *Every time we check someone coming from the house they had been arrested, or were somehow connected to drugs, but these people in the house were high class and educated.*
>
> – Agent

By the time Cesar flew back to Brasília, he felt sure it wouldn't be long before his main targets, Martino, Tocci and Rocco, hatched another plan he could focus on. They were constantly busy on their phones, talking cryptically about paying, picking things up, depositing cash. Cesar just needed an operation with all their fingerprints on it so he could bust the unlucky random horse flying in from Europe with drugs. He would use that as the centrepiece to take them all down.

The two Fernandos wouldn't meet again, but, very soon, their operations would.

CHAPTER THIRTY-EIGHT

WAR PLAN PLAYBOY

It was two days before Christmas. Caieron had promised his agents time off, but had forgotten until his agent Jair jokingly reminded him as they went on some raids. Caieron was pumped; there was no time to relax. Bust after bust, snitch after snitch, were lighting up his targets like a pinball machine. There was barely enough time in the day to chase the flashing ones.

Today their target was Big House, the guy who'd first taken Jorge to meet the bosses in the Amsterdam attic on his inaugural run. Big House's name was pinging on the radar after Caieron's latest catch, 'snitch on the hill' Renato Pinheiro, exposed the scam of switching pills for cars. Big House and Andre were sometimes partners in these transactions.

In one of their regular tête-à-têtes, travel agent snitch Olaf had also told Caieron that Big House had just finished a couple of runs. Caieron was chasing drugs, unsourced cash and intel, to get an arrest warrant for Big House.

Caieron's men were split into two teams. Jair and his guys were going to raid Big House's home, and Caieron's team were going to shake down the customer who allegedly paid cars for pills.

Using all his mind tricks for two gruelling hours, Caieron procured nothing. 'If you want me to say I exchanged the car for the pills, I will,' he'd said. Caieron didn't even bother to write it down.

He was kind of a weak guy and I knew in the future if some of those playboys pressured him, he'd say, 'They forced me to say that.' It's hard being police in Brazil, you have to be careful, because judges rather accept as true what the bad guys say rather than what the police say. It's insane, it's insane.

– Chief Caieron

Jair's team found no drugs and only US $20,000 and €7000. The big win of the day was a treasure trove of photos. They showed Big House in Bali with friends, including Curumim, Jorge and Timi, as well as drinking by the pool in Garopaba with Andre. Caieron put names to faces, thanks to Olaf. 'We took those photos and called our number-one informant asking, "Who's that? Who's that?"'

Caieron loved photos, not for their memories but their power of truth. When two drug bosses denied knowing each other – as Andre and Big House did – he'd whip out the trump-card photo. Caieron could also use these photos and the unsourced cash as evidence in his application for Big House's arrest warrant. He'd pin the photos on his wall to use when he surely caught Jorge, Dimitrius, Timi, Zeta and Rufino.

He'd just successfully got arrest warrants for the Florianópolis four and Dimitrius, using the many corroborating statements from the various snitches: the pale surfer, the travel agents, the shifty-eyed blow supplier and the 'snitch on the hill'.

That group, with Break, Dimitrius, Rufino, Timi and Zeta, was a strong cell in Florianópolis and we could prove this to the judge, so the judge gave us the warrant.

– Chief Caieron

The two guys Caieron wanted the most, who would be the star pin-ups of his playboy operation, were Dimitrius the Greek, who he was sure had sent Rodrigo to Bali, and Jorge Break, whose name was on every snitch's lips and all through wire-tap chatter. This proved to Caieron he was a dynamic, pervasive force, working with everyone. Caieron was planning a blitzkrieg of busts; the moment he had Dimitrius and Jorge, he'd flick the switch to the others.

The one flaw in his war plan was that he had absolutely no idea where Jorge and Dimitrius were. 'I got the warrants. Now let's find out where these motherfuckers are.'

It was fortunate for Jorge that the two tenacious Fernandos weren't sharing intel, because he was now on Cesar's radar too. Cesar was listening in to Martino and the Brasília guys and had caught Jorge in crosstalk, as he was working on a new operation with them. Jorge was often a partner in blow runs with these guys now. They'd even rented an apartment together in Amsterdam.

As Jorge rarely spoke on phones, Cesar saw him as a bit player on the periphery, a horse who he knew only by the nicknames Cabelo and Cabeludo. Caieron knew these nicknames too, aware they belonged to Jorge Break, no bit player, but his prime target who was playing a leading role in trafficking cells across Brazil, Europe and Bali.

So, while one Fernando knew exactly *who* Cabeludo, aka Cabelo, aka Jorge Break, actually was, the other Fernando knew generally *where* he was. Luckily for Jorge, the two cops were failing to splice together their potentially explosive information.

Cesar was continuing to listen to his targets, particularly Martino who was organising the money, waiting to bust them all in one beautifully synchronised sweep. During Jorge's hotel vanishing acts in São Paulo, his biggest danger was ironically right beside him in the reflective heat from Martino.

But that changed in a flash.

Caieron got a hot tip from Olaf that Jorge was partying regularly at Sirena nightclub at the party beach Maresias.

Simultaneously, he got a hit on Dimitrius. Caieron had learnt he was in Bali and had a warrant to track his emails. Now, he'd just seen a message from Dimitrius to some girlfriend saying, 'I'm coming back to Rio right after Carnival.' He didn't say when or to which international airport, so Caieron decided to hit Brazil's busiest, São Paulo's Guarulhos airport, and start asking the airlines about their bookings.

His plan was to first go to Maresias beach and find Jorge, tail him and photograph him, then as soon as Dimitrius flew in, bust both their globetrotting arses, taking down the two lords of the playboy traffickers. It was coming together. Caieron got set to go hunting for Jorge, to end his days of freedom and turn his dreams into nightmares. He was excited; after more than a year of trying to track down Jorge Break, finally he had him. Almost.

It took a long time. Every guy who we arrested, I used to ask about Break: 'What do you know? Do you know where he is?' 'No, I heard he is in Spain, I heard he's abroad . . .' No one knew, no one ever said to me where Break was – until Olaf finally said he's in Maresias. Now I have a place to look, it doesn't matter if he was carrying drugs or not. The moment I saw Jorge Break, I could handcuff him.

– Chief Caieron

CHAPTER THIRTY-NINE

UNIQUE RUN

It was like a horror film; the police bursting into the suite with guns, shouting, 'Get down on the ground, on the ground.' The guests were screaming, collapsing to the floor, hands behind their heads. Naked bodies in the spa and beds untangled fast, tumbling indecorously to the floor. Jorge frantically looked around, but there was no escape; mountains of blow were piled high and little packets of pills strewn everywhere. A gun was pointed directly at his head. He put his hands up and fell to his knees. It was over.

MINUTES EARLIER

The party on the top floor of São Paulo's sophisticated Hotel Unique was rolling into its third night, the usual eclectic mix of guests coming and going in the private lift; the stayers, a little bedraggled, drifting around in the corridor and sumptuous suites, high, drunk and happy. Little cliques sat on swanky couches, sniffing blow and drinking champagne. Others were having sex on the beds and in the Jacuzzis. The drugs, booze and glamour always turned Jorge's rolling parties into orgies. Jorge, Martino and their pimp friend, Rogerio, had booked out several rooms as usual, with private elevator access. Around 3 am, Jorge was in the presidential suite with just two girls, giving himself a bit of space from the hordes of guests after partying for days.

> *I was with a beautiful, blonde 20-year-old girl with deep blue eyes and a voluptuous ass, and my girlfriend, Ana. I was trying to convince Ana to have a trio. She was against it but with a bit more MDMA in her champagne, and Sade playing, I was on my way to manipulating her.*
> – Jorge

A sudden sharp knock on the door interrupted them. It was Rufino, calling out that Jorge needed to take this call. 'I couldn't believe he was disturbing me, but his voice was concerned, so I opened the door.'

Jorge grabbed the phone. It was Florianópolis DJ and drug dealer, Persiana. Jorge listened as the guy warned that he'd just got a tip-off from a lawyer friend that the feds were doing an operation to bust a bunch of playboy traffickers. Jorge's name was top of the list. Jorge hung up, shocked. A silent shriek of terror tore through his body.

Rufino stood in front of him, asking questions, but the room had gone mute, his senses hijacked by his paranoia.

> *I could see his mouth moving but I couldn't hear anything. My mind was running from reality – a film of the police busting into my presidential suite and arresting me and my friends was invading my imagination.*
> – Jorge

Jorge's hallucination was terrifyingly real. He felt it, smelt it and saw the vivid details, the cops shouting, holding a gun to his head, guests collapsing to the floor.

Ana running into the room in her underwear with a bottle of champagne, laughing, snapped him out of his trance and back to reality, but he was badly shaken. 'Ana, please give me a moment with Rufino,' he said, then called Martino and Rogerio into the suite. He told them about Persiana's call, that they needed to alert all their partners. Momentarily, the guys were concerned – news like this was heavy – but they fast dismissed it, laughing at Jorge's paranoia.

They were kind of making fun of me and laughing, because they said this Persiana is a liar. As if the federal police are going to let information escape for him to tell us they're searching for us, they are investigating us. This is not real, this is just another fantasy because Persiana is quite a liar. They didn't give any credibility to this information, they were all trying to convince me to stay. But police had been orbiting my life for a year, there were many busts, too many people in jail – Cafiero, Rodrigo – a lot of publicity, and I just felt in my bones that something was wrong.

I had a quick conversation with Ana and told her the truth. She knew my story, my past, my life, so even in shock, perplexed, she understood my fears and supported my decision to leave the party. She wanted to go with me, but I told her I had no idea how long it would take for me to show up again. She was a very sweet girl, she held my hands and kissed me. Then she helped me to pack my suitcase.

– Jorge

Jorge took US $5000 from the safe and gave it to Rufino for his share of the party expenses, and put the rest of his cash in his

Louis Vuitton bag. He told Rufino his spontaneous escape plan: he'd take the bus from São Paulo to their jointly rented villa in Paraguay. He didn't share the rest of his moves with Rufino, but he planned to finish a blow deal there, then fly to Europe from Buenos Aires, which he often did now. He'd expedite the operation in Amsterdam with the Brasília guys, unwittingly running from one Fernando straight into the hands of the other.

Rufino, who usually jumped at his own shadow, was more concerned than Martino and Rogerio, but still thought Jorge was overreacting. They all refused to drive Jorge to the bus station, saying they were too high and drunk, and urged him to stay. But the acute sense of persecution dogging him ever since the civil police's first failed raid on Jéssica's apartment now engulfed him. He wouldn't hang around the Unique to see if his latest hallucination was a premonition. He said goodbye and discreetly left with Ana, taking the private lift down to grab a taxi.

Ana was sad. Her eyes reflected her fears and frustration to be a girl-friend of who I was – an international drug dealer. Her eyes were full of tears. I told her not to worry, I would be in touch soon and we would be together again. Even trying to be strong, the untold message in her eyes was begging me to stay. We kissed and I got into the taxi.
– Jorge

After waiting for about two hours, Jorge departed São Paulo's Tietê bus terminal for the 16-hour journey to the border city Foz do Iguaçu. He felt a world of pressure bearing down on him. Yet, despite the unrelenting tension and anxiety, he was unsure what, exactly, he was escaping.

It wasn't the first time I was panicked and decided to move, but this time I was feeling in my bones something new, like a pressure in my chest, something inside me was telling me to run. But from what? I was scared by the information, but something else; I was running from the unbearable guilt I was experiencing in the last two years. A lot of friends and horses in jail. I think the ghost of Rodrigo's bust was haunting me. Marco on death row, two escapes from the civil police, and a promiscuous life was affecting my reality, making me run from the truth my life had become. A tsunami of emotions, conflicts and doubts, and there I was running again. I was leaving behind my family, my girls, my friends, my loved ones. I knew something was about to happen, I could feel it in my bones. I just didn't know what or when. My escape was pure instinct.

– Jorge

As the bus hurtled along, the hours dragged. He was thinking about life, how he could easily leave, and set up in Europe. 'I was always a kind of pirate. If I have my clothes and money, I can go anywhere and adapt myself. My life was pretty much suitcases.'

As life whizzed by outside his bus window, the passing time and distance wore the edge off his anxiety. By the time the bus pulled up in Foz do Iguaçu, Jorge felt quite relaxed. He grabbed a taxi to take him to his luxury villa just across the Paraguayan border in Ciudad del Este, but the driver stopped on the Brazilian side of the bridge, refusing to go into dangerous Paraguay late at night. Jorge flashed some dollars, but even that didn't convince the driver, so he got out, slung his Louis Vuitton bag over his shoulder and started walking half a kilometre across the famous Friendship Bridge spanning the Parana River.

In the balmy night, Jorge turned around, taking a nostalgic look back at the twinkling lights of Foz do Iguaçu, wondering when he'd be able to return home to Brazil. Then he turned back to face the future, looking ahead at two Paraguayan immigration agents standing at the end of the bridge. They usually didn't bother asking questions, as during the day the bridge was full of people crossing, thousands on foot and 40,000 vehicles, mostly Brazilians going to buy counterfeit and tax-free goods. But tonight Jorge was a lone walker, so they asked to see his passport, then started asking questions. He answered by whipping out a crisp US $20 bill. They waved him through with big smiles. He jumped in a Paraguayan cab, his sense of paranoia almost gone.

> *By the time I cross the border, I was starting to think I had panicked unnecessarily, but I decide to carry on my Plan B and move my trip to Amsterdam forward.*
>
> – Jorge

At his golf course villa, he grabbed a bag of Bolivian blow from his stash and sniffed several generous lines, then rolled a joint and drank a whisky. Refreshed, he went next door to see Jack, his partner and good friend. Jack was surprised to see him, but listened to his story, then suggested they go clubbing. After a few hours, they were back in Jorge's villa garden with a bunch of girls, drinking and doing blow by the pool, looking out across the golf course and the Iguaçu River. When the going gets tough, party – that was Jorge's credo.

The next day, he finished up some business with Jack, who was sending two kilos of blow to São Paulo for the new run, then continued his journey. He took a taxi to a hotel near a bus terminal in Asunción, Paraguay, stayed overnight and caught a morning bus to Buenos Aires. He flew, business-class, on Aerolíneas Argentinas to Paris and was then on a three and a half hour train ride to Amsterdam.

I was on my way to the city of my heart, the place where I always feel safe, the city that gave me all I had and was. I was not thinking too much about Persiana and that hypothetical investigation that he told me was going on.

— Jorge

Jorge walked into the huge, brand-new three-bedroom apartment, built in the centre of a park, with white marble floors, Persian rugs and expensive art hanging on the walls. He'd rented the apartment with Martino and Tocci with great excitement three months earlier, but now, as he slumped onto one of the large black leather couches, the capacious rooms made him feel alone.

I was feeling alone in that apartment, unsure of my decision. I was in Amsterdam in the wintertime, while the Carnival was just a few days ahead.

— Jorge

Jorge decided to go back to Brazil after the job and booked a flight home.

CHAPTER FORTY

FUCK FUCK FUCK

Jorge's global hopscotch on buses, planes and trains was in complete contrast to Caieron's forced inertia. He was still stuck in Florianópolis – and pissed off.

His boss had put the kybosh on travel plans to hunt Jorge in Maresias, worried about image. 'My boss said, "Man, you can't go, it's almost Carnival. There's a lot of parties, how can I let you go there with public money? How can I justify you are working in Carnival? Who's going to believe you?"'

Brasília civil police didn't have the same issue. Cesar's agents had been darting between Maresias beach and São Paulo city for the past two weeks, doing surveillance on Martino, Rocco, Tocci and anyone they met. Their Operation Connection Netherlands was close to reaching its crescendo. On the first day of Carnival, the curtains had opened on its final act when they'd heard the horse, Sandra, on the wire-taps saying, 'I've checked in.' She was their unlucky target, departing São Paulo on an Air France flight to Amsterdam. The clock was now ticking on her freedom.

For us, the important thing was to arrest somebody coming from Europe with drugs, and connected to our guys. She was the perfect situation for us.

— Chief Cesar

Day two of Carnival, a Sunday, Caieron was at home when, out of the blue, he got a green light to fly to São Paulo.

My big boss, top level in Brasília, calls me and says, 'Man, you have to go to São Paulo,' and I say, 'Why?' 'Because I was contacted by civil police, they want to exchange intel. They're solid, they don't want to fuck your operation. They want to share.' I say, 'Yeah okay, but my boss here says I must wait for Carnival to finish.' He says, 'Man, buy the ticket and go. Fuck your boss, let's work as real cops.'

— Chief Caieron

It took no arm twisting. Caieron flew straight to São Paulo with an agent. On Monday, he went to meet Cesar's agents in a shopping centre. Caieron was finally ready to share some intel – these guys had got him here, and his top boss had given them the thumbs up. Tomorrow, he'd do what he really wanted to do: hunt for Jorge.

They started to tell me about their operations. They are asking me a lot of questions, 'Listen, we have a guy nicknamed . . .' and I said, 'This guy does this, this guy does that.'

— Chief Caieron

Caieron opened up a little about Operation Playboy, revealing 'I'm here to arrest Cabelo.' 'Ah man, you've missed him. Cabelo took a flight to Amsterdam, he's gone,' one of the agents said, unaware of the torment he was unleashing. He quickly found out.

334

'Fuck, I can't believe this! Fuck, no way, man, you are fucking kidding? Fuck!' Caieron was furious. 'It was too intense for me.'

Until this moment, Cesar's agents had no idea Jorge was anything more than a bit player.

Fernando Caieron becomes crazy when he discovered Cabelo was already gone. After that, we realised he was a very important target. For us, in our investigation, Cabelo was just a horse who went to Amsterdam. The fact is, if Caieron had not been so arrogant and had shared his intel with us, he'd have arrested Cabelo with our help.

— Chief Cesar

Caieron didn't see it as arrogance; he didn't share intel with police he didn't know or trust and had simply been protective of Operation Playboy. It had cost him. The two bits of intel had been plugged in, but it was too late. He proposed a change of tactics. If he could find out when Jorge was coming back, he'd bust him at the airport. But he was hit with more bad news. 'He's not coming back,' an agent said. 'What? Fuck, fuck, fuck.'

In the days since Jorge had fled the Unique to Amsterdam and flopped into the big leather couch, feeling lonely and starting to wonder if it had all been a needless panic, he'd learnt in a brief call with Martino that it had been a timely escape and his instincts had been razor-sharp. A lawyer had shown Rufino the statement by shifty-eyed blow supplier Luiz Dias, and the trove of photos confiscated from Big House's home.

The coded warning by Rufino to Martino had been intercepted by Cesar's agents.

WIRE-TAP [translated from Portuguese]

Rufino: *Man, the grill is heating up. Tell Jorge that his photo, bro, everything is there, bro.*

Martino: *Excuse me?*

Rufino: *Tell him that his photo . . . tell him, brother, tell him to pack his bags 'cos things are really hot around here, brother. He's totally fried, bro.*

Martino: *What happened?*

Rufino: *Fuck! There's a photo of him there. They have everything . . .*

Martino: *Photo of what?*

Rufino: *There's a photo of him with Big House in Indonesia . . . Luizinho* [Luiz Dias] *screwed him over. Tell him that Luizinho . . . he better take care of that guy for good . . . because the guy fucked him over bad.*

Martino: *Really?*

Rufino: *Yeah, he fucked him over. His full name is there. I saw it, tell him.*

Martino: *Yeah, but . . . but . . . but he's in the same photo as Big House?*

Rufino: *Yes, he's in the photo, it looks like Jorge is one of the god-fathers, understand?*

Martino: *With Big House?*

Rufino: *Yes, yes, they just busted Big House, they entered his house and took his photos, everything, you understand?*

Martino: *Shit!*

It was one of a flurry of calls between the playboys who'd been leaked information about Operation Playboy, and eavesdropped on in the wiretaps.

Persiana, the DJ dealer who'd warned Jorge at the Unique, also called Martino, saying that Caieron had a *Prision Preventiva* for Jorge, a type of arrest warrant that gave Caieron authority to arrest him on sight, even if no drugs were present. Cesar's agents had listened to this call too.

Thirty minutes later Martino was talking to Jorge.

WIRE-TAP

Martino: *Hello?*

Jorge: *Yo, brother.*

Martino: *What's up?*

Jorge: *You asked me to call you?*

Martino: *Yeah! But you did not call me, man.*

Jorge: *But what do you want me to say, brother?*

Martino: *Because it's a big deal what's happening.*

Jorge: *It's serious?*

. . .

Martino: *Rufino called me, and Persiana called me, they said that it's going to be bad.*

Jorge: *Yeah?*

Martino: *Swear to God.*

Jorge: *Why, what did he say, man?*

Martino: *I don't know, man; it seems that 'T' arrived at the hotel* [police station] *there today.*

Jorge: *T?*

Martino: *Yeah.*

Jorge: *What T?*

Martino: *Timi.*

Jorge: *He arrived at the hotel?*

Martino: *Yes.*

Jorge: *No way.*

Martino: *Yeah, looks like he went into the spa today.*

. . .

Jorge: *But what does that have to do with me?*
Martino: *What does it have to do? Looks like they have photos of you with Big House . . . in Bali. They went to the guy's house, found lots of photos, you with the guy . . . in Bali.*

For Jorge, these photos exposed what he had been hiding for six months.

We lived with this fear of being related to Rodrigo's bust, haunted by this ghost, and pictures of us in Bali during the same year was suspicious. Knowing the facts as we did, this was a very bad omen.

– Jorge

News that Timi had been to the 'hotel' or 'spa', both code for police station, was also ominous. Jorge felt sure Timi wouldn't snitch, but the cops were getting closer to those close to him. Timi was released without charge, but this only exacerbated Jorge's fears.

WIRE-TAP

Jorge: *Do you think things will blow up if I leave?*
Martino: *No, no, I think you need a new plan, understood?*
Jorge: *Sooner? For me to leave sooner?*
Martino: *No, I mean other plans . . . you want me to send your things to you now . . . that little coffin that's here, you want me to send it to you now?*
Jorge: *Yes.*
Martino: *It's better, man.*
Jorge: *What?*
Martino: *To stay longer there.*
Jorge: *Okay.*

Martino: *Your trip is going to be longer.*

Jorge: *Okay, who's coming to bring it?*

Martino: *What else is here?*

Jorge: *No, just the green bag, and that other bag.*

Martino: *Okay, call me in an hour.*

Jorge: *Okay. Bye.*

Cesar's agents had heard every word, but the cryptic dialogue, and missed conversations on untapped phones, meant they didn't always get the full picture. They'd deduced from these calls that Jorge was still in Brazil and was soon leaving with a 'green bag', which they assumed was a special bag for carrying drugs, confirming their belief Jorge was a horse. In fact, Jorge was waiting for a horse, the green bag was his cash, the coffin his suitcase of clothes.

Two days after the call between Jorge and Martino, Jorge had called Rocco.

WIRE-TAP

Rocco: *Hello.*

Jorge: *Hi brother.*

Rocco: *Hi brother, all sound?*

Jorge: *Sound, I've orgasmed, this is what's going on . . . hello . . . hello* [call cuts out].

The agents translated this as Jorge's 'goal' with the green bag, but he'd actually been saying that a horse had arrived with blow.

Even though Cesar's agents had made a few miscalculations based on the intercepts, they'd caught up by the time they were talking to Caieron at the shopping centre. They correctly told him Jorge had gone to Amsterdam and wasn't coming back.

While Martino was concerned about his friend Jorge's fate, ironically, he was closer to the precipice.

At the meeting in the shopping centre, Cesar's agents showed their surveillance photos to Caieron. For the past couple of weeks, they'd been following Martino and the Brasília guys in Maresias, and São Paulo, like covert paparazzi. They'd scrutinised them through camera lenses, sat near them in cafés and hotels, watching who they met and listening in on their chats. The agents often knew where their targets were going before they went, thanks to the crystal-ball effect of wire-taps and the team back in Brasília feeding them updates.

Cesar's agents also informed Caieron about Sandra, the horse who'd flown out two days before. She had a return seat booked on Air France in one week's time, and they'd bust her red-handed on arrival at São Paulo airport, then take down her bosses, or so it was planned.

Caieron asked the agents to delay their bust and not arrest Sandra at São Paulo airport but wait for her to fly to Brasília, otherwise they could scare off his new top target, Dimitrius, who was due back around the same day. Their curt reply was 'no'. They would give their Operation Connection Netherlands priority over his Operation Playboy.

The only problem was that Cesar was pedalling across the mountain tops of Argentina and Chile. He'd gone away on his cycling trip, confident the playboys were still some weeks off executing their operation. He'd been correct at the time. Then Jorge had fled the Unique and expedited the new scam with Sandra to a time that was smack-bang in the middle of Cesar's holiday. The agents were now phoning to alert him, but their calls went straight to voicemail. Cesar was out of range, cycling hard and soaking up the fresh Chilean mountain air.

Caieron was exasperated about missing Jorge and would now put everything into catching Dimitrius. 'Fuck. Fifty percent lost, which means all my energy was on Dimi. I'm going to catch at least Dimi. I need to achieve at least 50 percent.' He was on a mission, and was going to do whatever it took to find out what flight Dimitrius was coming home on. At Guarulhos airport that afternoon, he and an agent spent two hours traipsing from one airline desk to the next, scouring passenger manifests to check if Dimitrius had a booking, aware it was likely to be made at the last minute. He would do this twice a day until he had him.

In an eerie coincidence, Caieron was starting this airport search for Dimitrius, the guy he was certain had sent Rodrigo Gularte to Bali, on exactly the same day, 7 February, that Rodrigo sat in a courtroom, 16,000 kilometres away in Tangerang, Indonesia, listening to his verdict. The judge had just put a target on his heart. He was sentenced to execution by a 12-man firing squad.

Dimitrius was in Bali, spending the sunny days pedalling along-side rice paddies, often with Rafael or his daughter, trying to get fit and lose a bit of weight. Rafael was trying to convince him not to go home. It was too dangerous, too many people were getting busted, but Dimitrius was adamant he'd be fine. Rafael asked him to carry €3000 to give to a contact for a new operation, and for Dimi to pack the blow in Florianópolis. Dimitrius agreed. His confidence was unshaken by the fate of others – he was planning on doing the biggest coke deal of his life, coordinating the shipment of 50 kilos from Paraguay to Bali by boat for some Rio guys he'd just met. He'd use his Greek passport to slip into Brazil undetected, and he wouldn't have any drugs on him anyway.

He wasn't counting on a very pissed-off, ambitious and hungry chief of narcotics who had a *Prision Preventiva* warrant for him, and who wanted to bust him like crazy.

CHAPTER FORTY-ONE

WAITING FOR SANDRA

Dimitrius was hopping on a plane in Bali.

Caieron was running back and forth at Guarulhos airport, hunting for Dimitrius' name on the passenger manifests.

Cesar was in Santiago, waiting for a flight to Brazil after finally getting the news and cutting his holiday short.

His surveillance team were still watching their targets in São Paulo and Maresias, waiting for the horse to fly home.

The listening team was listening.

And Jorge was in wintry Amsterdam, with a big, dark cloud looming over him.

In those cold, grey and windy days, I took a lot of coca, fuck a lot of prostitutes, so I forgot a little of those thoughts of persecution I was feeling in my bones.

– Jorge

Jorge met the horse, Sandra, for the first time at her hotel. She'd been recruited by her brother, Marc, the guy Cesar had anonymously surfed beside several weeks earlier. Jorge grabbed the bag of blow she'd brought and left. They'd catch up later for a drink, though she was definitely not his type for a fling.

Back in the huge apartment, he still felt a keen sense of aloneness. He opened the bag, took out the two kilos and helped himself to ten grams. He then jumped on a tram into the city to find his buyer, Mohid, a millionaire coffee shop owner with blow clients all over Europe. Jorge wasn't using mobiles, but Mohid was at the coffee shop and drove Jorge back to the apartment, picked up the 1.99 kilos, paying for half now with the rest due in a week.

Jorge then went to his suppliers to buy skunk, hashish, ecstasy and MDMA powder for Sandra's sweet return. This was all routine, but peculiar dark vibes persisted. He couldn't shake his anxiety or sleep at night. 'Thoughts of tragedy and dread were stronger than ever.' In emails to Martino, Jorge warned, 'Be careful man, I'm having creepy premonitions.' Martino blew it off, joking about Jorge's 'crazy run' from Hotel Unique with no foreboding of his own demise, or sense of the eyes and ears all over him.

Ignoring his sixth sense, Jorge packed the drugs into a sleeping bag, then a sports bag, and took it to Sandra's hotel. He gave her cash for the trip and wished her good luck. She was calm, and seemed fearless as he left her to go to the Red Light District, as much for his enduring superstition as to dilute his undying anxiety.

Sandra took the train to Schiphol airport, checked in the bag and boarded to go back to Brazil.

Cesar's team was on alert. They knew the tactic of buying a horse a new ticket only hours before departure. So, like Caieron, the agents were going to the airport twice a day to check the arrivals of international flights from Paris and Amsterdam. From the wire-taps, they knew she had a return ticket, which they'd confirmed with Air France. If she used it, she was flying straight into their hands, and their fireworks show.

Sandra's flight landed in São Paulo on a Monday night. She cleared immigration, took her bag, breezed through customs and walked out. She got a cab and left, untouched. She'd done it. No cops, no customs busting her – she was free. She'd made her first return run a big success. Without telling the partners in Brazil, Jorge had bought her a new ticket on TAP Air hours before the flight – standard practice. She'd left a day earlier than the original Air France booking, blindsiding everyone to stay safe.

The listening team only learnt she'd slipped through their fingers when she called Rocco. 'I didn't know, my friend, that you would arrive so early,' he said. Rocco then called Martino, saying 'the girl orgasmed'. It was a blow to Cesar's agents, but thinking on their feet was part of the job. They needed a Plan B fast. They knew that Sandra was staying overnight in São Paulo, and were keeping eyes on Tocci at the Blue Tree hotel, and Martino, who was at his girlfriend's house.

Cesar flew in from Santiago at 2 am Tuesday, was at the office by 7.30 am, talking to his agents and his top boss in São Paulo. Tocci was still in room 609 at the Blue Tree hotel. At 8 am, they heard Martino call Tocci. 'It's time to wake up. We have work to do.' Martino dropped in to see Tocci and a couple of other guys at the Blue Tree. Cesar and his boss were debating whether to take them down now. Then the listening team sent news: Sandra was booked to fly to Brasília at 7.45 pm that night on GOL Flight 1782. From deciphering the cryptic phone chats, the agents were sure she was taking part of the package on the final leg. The plan now was to let Sandra fly to Brasília, see who she met and then arrest her. Cesar would be there waiting, finishing the job he'd invested his soul into for the past six months. Then, he would trigger the rest of the busts across Brazil.

Almost at the same time, on the other side of the Atlantic, Jorge was walking over to his good friend Antonio's apartment near Leidseplein, just behind the three-star Quentin Hotel he'd used a lifetime ago as a horse. Antonio had good news: a surprise guest, Dimitrius the Greek, on a six-hour transit stop from Bali to Brazil. They chatted about Bali and the furniture Dimitrius was importing to Brazil. Jorge revealed the recent dark turn of events, from his Unique run to his creepy premonitions.

I said, 'Dimitrius, things are not right. They don't feel good, I feel something wrong.' I told him about the phone call at the party, my escape run and my strong concerns about our freedom. I explained to him everything that was going on in Brazil, said it was very strange. I advised him not to go back because everything is bad and hot, something wrong was floating through the air.

– Jorge

Cabelo said to me, 'Federal police want to arrest everybody because this Bali thing is fucked up. Don't go to Brazil, man, you're going to be arrested.' I say, 'No, I'll stay in São Paulo, I'll stay in my mum's house. No problem.'

– Dimitrius

Scared for his friend, Jorge pushed harder.

I look at him and tell him to wait a few days, trying to convince him to stay with me in the apartment, to don't go back. But he didn't hear me, he didn't listen or believe me. He told me that I was paranoiac, obsessed and I had run in vain, because since my run, nothing really had happened. He was very secure of himself. 'No, I'll be fine, I'm a businessman. Nothing is going to happen, no one can stop me.' He was looking at me while closing the zip of his North Face jacket. It was kind of synchronised as he said, 'See you later,' and zipped it up, and he left the apartment in Amsterdam, and boarded back to Brazil.

– Jorge

In São Paulo, Caieron decided to take Tuesday night off from his airport run. It was a long and traffic-congested drive and he'd been doing it now for eight days straight, morning and night. Traipsing to the airline desks, spending at least 30 minutes at each one, had yielded nothing so far. He needed a break. He'd stay at the federal police bureau and send his agent, Cintra, with São Paulo cop Druziani. Caieron was also expecting a call from Cesar's agents later on, as once they'd busted Sandra in Brasília at 9.30 pm, they'd take Martino down in São Paulo. Caieron wanted to be there to question him, particularly about Jorge.

A couple of hours later, Caieron's ears pricked up. Druziani was back and singing in the corridor. 'Dimi is on the plane, Dimi is on the plane.' He and Cintra walked in, smiling. 'What the fuck?' Caieron asked. Druziani sang, 'Tomorrow, Dimi will be arrested, Dimi will be arrested tomorrow.' Caieron's pulse flew. 'What? How?' 'It's confirmed, boss,' Cintra chimed in. 'He's checked in and he's on the Air France flight. Here's the number. He'll be in São Paulo first thing in the morning.' Caieron was ecstatic. It was finally happening. 'I can't believe it. I can't believe it. Really?' 'Yes, it's 100 percent.' The atmosphere was electric. They started laughing, cracking jokes at Dimi's expense.

'Boss, there's one way he can escape.' 'How?' 'Well, if the plane crashes – then he's going to be free,' Cintra said, and they laughed.

Caieron called Jair in Florianópolis, alerting him that he needed to mobilise the teams for Timi, Rufino and Zeta's busts. Dimi was on the plane: it was time.

Then we went out to celebrate, to have a good dinner after the news because everything is done. It's just a matter of time, just sit and relax, he's coming, he's on the airplane.

– Chief Caieron

Caieron was also expecting the call later about Martino's bust. It had been a very good day – so far.

CHAPTER FORTY-TWO

SPEAR FISHING

Cesar stood a little apart from the bustling group waiting for their bags at the luggage carousel in Brasília International Airport. He was disguised, dressed in a dark suit and tie, pushing an airport trolley, looking like a suave businessman, not a horse-hunting cop. He was scanning the crowd for Sandra without really knowing what she looked like – he'd only seen old ID photos. He knew she was no stunner; he'd heard the playboys discussing her on the phone. They'd been worried she wasn't one of their usual babes who could beguile their way through airports. 'She's not pretty, not a beauty, but she's cool,' one had said to the other. Cesar was using this as a guide. 'I start to look for a "not beautiful but cool" girl.'

He didn't have any doubts she was here. The agents at São Paulo airport had called him, saying, 'She's on board, carrying drugs, and wearing blue jeans and a white shirt.' As yet, he hadn't seen anyone who fit that description.

Suddenly, a girl caught his eye. She was wearing a very heavy winter coat – odd, in midsummer. He looked closer, glanced down at the old ID shot, then up again. It was her, no doubt: long dark hair, big coat and a plastic-wrapped sports bag, but no blue jeans or white shirt. She'd changed on the flight. Smart, Cesar thought. She'd done her job flawlessly, a perfect drug runner whose only mistake was picking a marked run.

Cesar watched her calmly but purposefully pushing a trolley towards the exit. Strong, steady strides, seconds from the door, she no doubt felt she'd made it. A federal border control agent assisting Cesar walked right behind her, pushing a trolley too. Cesar hung back a bit, making a quick call to alert his agents outside. 'She's coming.'

Cesar was excited but totally cool. He knew how to hunt – he'd learned by fishing. He'd spent years as a spear fisherman, starting as an eight year old and almost turning pro as an adult. Living in landlocked Brasília, he didn't do it anymore, but used his prowess in the crime game. 'For me, it's like spear fishing; you have to stay cool. If you don't, you won't catch the fish.'

The agents outside were acting casual, masking their state of red alert, waiting and watching to see who was picking her up. Cesar came out, wheeling his trolley quickly, not wanting to miss the action. Sandra was at the taxi rank. It was time. The agents moved in.

'How are you, Sandra?' one quietly asked.

'I'm fine, but who are you?' she replied calmly, with dawning recognition as the agents encircled her.

'Sandra, we are the police. You are under arrest.' She would claim later that they beat her up during the arrest, but it was all recorded on CCTV cameras at Cesar's request, to protect his team. It was no Hollywood-style bust: no aggression, no hysteria, no handcuffs. It was a stealthy kill, like spearing a fish.

Sandra stayed outwardly cool as they hung by the kerb for a moment. Cesar paced back and forth, a little hyper now as he made quick calls to trigger the busts across Brazil. A couple of minutes later, he grabbed Sandra's plastic-wrapped sports bag and put it on his trolley. Then, with his perfectly straight posture, he led the straggling corralled horse and agents back inside the terminal. Cesar looked into the distance and a grin spread across his face – he couldn't help it.

> *I am very happy with the job. I think, 'It's all worth it, all the time I spent out of my house, my vacation I ended. It's all worth it.'*
> – Chief Cesar

Sandra was traipsing behind, uncuffed but loosely surrounded by five agents. She couldn't see Cesar's glee, but her own look was an extreme contrast – her arms wrapped protectively around herself, her face reflecting abject misery.

She wasn't alone. Agents across the country were making many people miserable tonight. Two of Cesar's agents had been waiting in a hotel in Florianópolis for Cesar's call. As soon as it had come, they met with ten of Caieron's men then burst into the 'Big Brother house' on the lake, brandishing M16 military rifles and pistols. They arrested seven people including their target, Augustus. They found him lying on a bed, listening to loud music and smoking a joint. He took the bust calmly, as did the others in the house.

> *The first reaction of these people is 'Where is the warrant?' It's the first reaction every time we go into a house with guns here in Brazil.*
> – Brasília agent

Cesar's agents also arrested three guys in Brasília, including one of their top targets, Rocco. Martino was taken down at his girlfriend's house in São Paulo. Caieron had got the call and was soon sitting with him, asking questions about Jorge – the one who got away. Despite Caieron's clever mind powers, Martino refused point-blank to say anything about his friend.

Sandra was packed off to the police station. Cesar left Brasília airport and was now in a deadly high-speed car chase, flying down the highway at 190 kilometres an hour, wondering if he was going to live to see tomorrow.

It was the only time I think I could die doing my job – it was a dangerous chase. I've arrested people doing bank robberies with M16s and pistols, but never imagined that I could die. But this night, I thought I might not arrive home.

– Chief Cesar

Cesar didn't ask his agent to slow down. They were chasing their big target, Tocci, the catalyst for the whole operation. The baron of ecstasy, who'd mocked cops for being unable to catch him, always with a rat in the force to keep him safe – until now. It was a matter of honour to catch this badass. Cesar wanted to show that good, straight cops had the ability to bust anyone, even arrogant, well-connected drug dealers like Tocci, and he wouldn't let a potential deadly car crash get in his way.

It had gone wrong a little earlier. They knew Tocci was driving 1000 kilometres from São Paulo to Brasília and would arrive in the early morning hours. He wouldn't go home – Cesar knew his MO now, he always slept elsewhere the night of a drug delivery. By morning, he'd know about the busts and try to escape, so they had to catch him on the road tonight.

Cesar had told the agents to wait at a sharp bend, where Tocci's Mitsubishi Pajero would have to slow down enough for them to see if he was inside. The spot was 130 kilometres from Brasília, far enough to allay any suspicions.

But the agents went rogue. They parked at a petrol station 30 kilometres from the Brasília highway checkpoint. By chance, Tocci stopped there, jumping out and making a quick call on the public phone. He got back into the Pajero and sped off, like he'd seen a ghost. Cesar was sure he'd spotted the unmarked Renault Logan and realised it was a police car, as they'd bought a fleet of these recently.

By the time the agents called Cesar with the news, he was at the Brasília highway checkpoint, and alerted the cops to pull up the Mitsubishi Pajero coming at breakneck speed.

Cesar and his agent then started cruising down the highway, looking for the Pajero. It flew past. Cesar and his agent did a u-turn and started driving back. Tocci's Pajero flew towards them again. They were going in circles. Cesar's agent was again forced to find a place to u-turn then tore off after Tocci at 190 kilometres an hour. They had to catch the Pajero before it vanished.

It came into view up ahead, stopped on the side of the highway. 'We realised something was wrong.' They pulled up next to it and saw a guy, Leandro, one of the smaller targets, at the wheel. Tocci was gone, fleeing from the car into the dark bush.

Cesar had no choice but to call off the chase tonight. The police chopper wasn't equipped for night searches, and running after Tocci in the dark was futile. Cesar was pissed off. He'd just lost the trophy of Operation Connection Netherlands into the blackness of night.

Back at his office, he started writing reports. Red-handed busts without arrest warrants were deemed illegal if the official paperwork was not lodged within 24 hours. Cesar wasn't planning on getting any sleep tonight. Tomorrow, they'd look for Tocci. They also had to bust Sandra's brother, Marc, who was on an island off the north coast, watching a surf comp. His fireworks show wasn't over.

Back at the São Paulo federal police bureau, Caieron wasn't sleeping either. Dimi was in the air on his way to São Paulo. Tuesday had been Operation Connection Netherlands' big day, Wednesday was Operation Playboy's turn. And Caieron was terrified of sleeping through the alarm and missing his 50 percent.

> *I almost didn't get to sleep because every time I took a nap, I was dreaming I lose my time, that I didn't get to the airport. Then I look at my watch, it's like 2 am, 3.30 am – it was insane.*
>
> – Chief Caieron

In Amsterdam, three hours ahead of Brazil, Jorge was in bed, having nightmares again. Alone in his huge apartment, the feeling of dread was overwhelming him.

CHAPTER FORTY-THREE

THE LION AND THE BUFFALO

He woke with a ninja at the foot of his bed pointing a gun at his head, shouting, 'Don't move – or I'll shoot you.'

> *It's like a movie. The first seconds I was confused . . . I thought he was a thief, the guy in black, the face mask. I thought he wanted to kill me. I took some seconds to wake up properly, to understand. And then, I saw the dog's coat, a uniform with PF [Polícia Federal].*
>
> – Timi

Moments earlier, his girlfriend had crawled out of bed to investigate the sound of a dog and knocking on the door. It was 6 am, still dark outside, and Timi was sleeping. She opened the door to a nightmare: federal cops with pistols pushed past her, one asking, 'Where's Timi?' 'In bed, asleep,' she managed to say. He put a finger to his lips, instructing her to be silent, then skulked inside with the others.

They dispersed through the rooms with a sniffer dog, opening drawers and cupboards, rifling and searching. Two cops and a dog were now with the target in the bedroom. Timi was lying half-naked, shocked and shaken but unsurprised. In his soul, he'd known this day was coming, just not when. Now, he knew that too. 'Come on, come on. Wake up, get up, get dressed. Let's go, let's go,' the cop shouted, waving his gun, warning, 'No sudden moves, or I'll shoot you.' Timi had no plans to do a Tocci. He felt sure they would shoot him given half an excuse. 'Come on, you are under arrest. Come with us now.'

'Why, what have I done?' he asked, the old cliché.

'Oh, okay, you haven't heard of Rodrigo Gularte in jail in Indonesia?' Another cop came into the room shouting, 'Where are your drugs? Where are you hiding your drugs?' 'I don't have any drugs,' Timi answered truthfully. 'Come on, get your shoes on. Let's go, let's go, let's go,' the gun-waving cop ordered.

Minutes later, Timi was cuffed and staring out the window of a police car, watching his girlfriend sobbing her heart out in the early dawn. It was déjà vu of four years ago in Paris, but so much worse. The siren started screaming as the car tore off, his girlfriend and life fading in the distance. His reality was now the nightmare inside this car, and the cops, jeering and joking at his expense, clearly relishing the moment.

'Hey Timi, you drive very fast, you drive like crazy. We see you, we follow you. You must drive slowly,' they laughed. 'He won't need a car where he's going.' They'd just confirmed one thing for Timi: it hadn't just been paranoia when he'd sensed a tail. It had been happening often lately, prompting him to suddenly floor it, zigzagging in and out of lanes at high speed, circling and u-turning to lose any cops. In the end, the reckless driving had been futile.

Two weeks earlier, he'd been brought in for questioning and released, but he'd been hearing whispers about a police investigation for a while.

After Rodrigo busted, I was feeling scared. I finished my activities, I was out – I didn't have drugs. I was six months stopped but I already left the trace, the trail of shit was there. And I always feel like police follow me. I was living in fear; people saying to me that police will take action . . . that police know about us – people alert me. And me and these guys, we are with paranoia, scared of police. We knew that after Rodrigo, after Cafiero, the big cases, that police gave a lot of importance. We were sure it will reflect here with police, on us. We knew that one day, we will get the justice consequences. Everybody was waiting for the tsunami.

– Timi

Inside the federal police offices, Timi spotted Rufino – he'd just got the same shocking wake-up call at his dentist dad's expensive high-rise apartment on the waterfront, less than two kilometres away. Timi wasn't relieved to see his old school friend. He was pissed off. Rufino had failed to pay what he owed, despite Timi chasing him for months. It had taken this dire scenario to get face to face with him. Now, Timi needed cash to pay a good lawyer and try to extricate himself from this mess.

Up in São Paulo, Caieron was at the airport waiting for Dimi. It didn't matter that the Florianópolis busts went first. Dimi was on the flight and, unless he had a parachute, there was only one way out – along the walkway, straight into Caieron's clutches.

But as Caieron stood waiting with two agents in the corner of the air bridge, watching passengers stream out, he couldn't see Dimi. He only knew him from an old photo, and didn't know what he'd look like today. Caieron's eyes were working like a laser scanner, locking on every face for a split second, looking, checking, then rejecting; look, check, no – look, check, no – look, check, no. He was so in the zone, so focused, so intent on catching Dimi, that he automatically said out loud, 'I know her,' when he locked on the familiar face of a star TV host. She heard him, and turned to look at this curious guy standing in the corner of the air bridge, watching passengers. Even the agents did a double-take at the boss.

For Caieron, this was surreal. This was the moment he'd been waiting for. He'd lost Jorge. He could not lose Dimi. Look, no, look, no, look, no. Caieron's mind was racing with thoughts. Where is he? Where is Dimi? He was flying at the pointy end, he should be here by now.

'Man, a lot of people already left the aircraft. Let's go to immigration?' an agent suggested.

Caieron's heart was pounding. 'No, no. Stay here, he's here. He didn't leave the aircraft yet, stay here, man.'

'Maybe we've missed him, boss. He went past and we didn't see?'

'No, we didn't. He's coming, he's coming,' Caieron said, feeling increasingly anxious.

It was at least two, three minutes of people getting out, it was a long wait, because at that time, every second is an eternity. I got nervous because it's impossible I miss him. I know he is in the plane, but we're not seeing him. I start to have second thoughts: Did I miss him? Is it for real? Was he actually on the plane?

– Chief Caieron

More passengers flowed past – 30, 40, 50. Suddenly, Caieron froze. He had no more doubts. It was the Greek, the drug baron, lord of the playboys. Caieron's prime target was coming towards him through the throng.

> *It's like freeze, you freeze; everything freezes. In the first second, you don't believe you are actually seeing that guy. And one second later, that's the guy. It's insane, it's insane the things you feel, it's hard to put in words how excited, the kind of emotion, you are 200 percent satisfied. I mean, you are completely satisfied, completely. It's an overdose of excitement.*
>
> *It's a glory moment, the guy is coming to me. He never suspects, he is kind of relaxed and I am enjoying these small seconds, savouring the moments from when he walked out the door. I'm seeing him, like a lion when he is lying down and the buffalo comes into his view, you just have to wait. It was like a movie running through my head. That's the guy – that's the guy – everything else doesn't matter anymore, because that's the guy who sent the other guys to the death penalty.*
>
> – Chief Caieron

'Dimitrius Christopoulos,' Caieron called as Dimi came close in the tide of passengers. Dimi turned and looked up, unsuspecting. It took only a split second for realisation to hit; Jorge had been right.

'Federal police. You're under arrest,' Caieron said, then took him by the arms, and snapped on handcuffs.

'Why are you doing this? What did I do?' Dimi asked on cue, craning his neck around to look Caieron in the eye.

'Think it over, my friend,' Caieron said. Dimi looked down at the floor, then back up.

'We pay for what we do,' he mumbled.

'That's right, man,' Caieron smiled, flashing the arrest warrant. 'This is why you're arrested. There is a warrant against you.'

'Hey, Chief, look at me,' one of the agents called. Caieron turned, the agent clicked, taking a celebratory photo of the lion and his buffalo: a hunting trophy.

I was kind of savouring the victory. It's finished, we did it all perfect.
– Chief Caieron

For Dimi, the photo captured the moment when life as he knew it died. In seconds, he took a nosedive from heaven to hell – one he'd been blithely confident he'd never take. Caieron noticed Dimi was very cool and seemingly keeping it together – only the large sweat patch growing around his neck gave any hint of his distress.

The federal police were waiting for me at the door. Fernando Caieron says, 'You're under arrest.' I say, 'Why?' 'Because you are a leader of a gang of drug traffickers.' So he took me to jail, and says many things to me. He says, 'I arrest many people already, everybody tells me you're the boss. Your friend Andre is in jail. He already gave you up.' I say, 'I don't know Andre.'

– Dimitrius

Back at São Paulo police headquarters, Caieron was considering whether or not to offer 'the benefits' to get Dimitrius to talk.

I was interested in giving him the benefits, then I wait for his lawyer. When I went to enquire, 'No, I prefer to remain silent.' Okay, that's it. I told myself it's better because the guy's a murderer. He sent Rodrigo to death, that's a fact. For sure, a lot of guys were arrested by his hands, I mean a lot of families suffer because of this. Sometimes you see what happens in a family when a son or daughter is arrested. I mean, it's hard. I'm not saying what Rodrigo Gularte did was good – it was wrong – but I don't think Dimitrius deserves any kind of benefits.

– Chief Caieron

Further north, on the island Fernando de Noronha, police were now chasing Sandra's brother Marc who was there to watch a Hang Loose surfing competition. They found him hiding in a forest near Cacimba do Padre beach. The hotel manager had dropped him there earlier, and obligingly showed police the spot.

The two Fernandos now had most of their targets in the bag. Cesar put an alert out for Tocci at border checkpoints, particularly airports, thinking he might flee to Italy. Caieron was sure Jorge was still in Europe and he wouldn't stop hunting him, but right now he had another headliner, Dimitrius, and was about to use him as the star pin-up in his Operation Playboy media blitz.

I made a call to my boss in Brasília. I guess it was in this moment, he said, 'Very good job, very good work, don't talk to anyone. I'm going to give your number to a journalist and she's going to give you a call, then you can tell her everything. It's huge, man. We have to put this at national level, not state level.'

– Chief Caieron

CHAPTER FORTY-FOUR

SCOOPED

The story of Operation Playboy broke in one of Brazil's biggest national newspapers, *O Globo*.

> *The federal police yesterday dismantled a gang that enticed upper-middle class youth, surfers, gliders and other extreme sports practitioners, to transport cocaine to countries in Europe and Asia and on return bring to the country synthetic drugs like ecstasy, LSD and skunk. The chief of the gang, Dimitrius Christopoulos, was arrested on landing in São Paulo from Paris.*
>
> *. . . According to the federal police, it was the gang of Dimitrius Christopoulos that sent to Indonesia the Brazilian, Rodrigo Gularte, 32, recently sentenced to death by a court in Indonesia for drug trafficking . . . The group is also responsible for enticing other young people who have been arrested in recent months in Frankfurt, Paris, Amsterdam and Lisbon. Named 'Playboy', the operation of the federal police was coordinated by the delegate Fernando Amaro de Moraes Caieron . . .*
>
> *– O Globo*

The playboys were a media hit. The story was picked up by TV news bulletins and photos of them splashed across screens. The busts of both operations – Playboy and Netherlands – were merged into the one story, with Playboy taking the glory. That night, Caieron went out for a celebratory dinner in São Paulo with his sister and her husband, who by chance were in town. 'They were so proud, they had the newspaper from Rio – "Man, look at your name".'

> *I got arrested in the morning . . . the next night, all the television channels* [say] *'arrest the big boss of Brazil'. I'm not a good guy, but they say I'm the big one and I'm not the big one.*
>
> – Dimitrius

The next day, Caieron was flying back to Florianópolis with his playboy star. Dimi was taken from the cells, handcuffed, put in a flak jacket and escorted by men with M16 military rifles. As the plane lifted off, Dimitrius watched São Paulo, and his life, disappear behind the clouds. Sitting next to him was the cop who'd just made him famous. Caieron suddenly turned, truly curious, asking, 'Why did you send those guys to Indonesia?' Dimitrius kept silent. He had no inclination to talk to this cop, especially not about Rodrigo. Caieron took it as a further sign of his guilt – innocent men protested.

The flight took about an hour, then it was showtime.

Looking cool with his dark shades, shaggy dark hair, jeans and white t-shirt with *Polícia Federal* slashed across the back, Caieron walked Dimitrius out to the top of the aeroplane stairs. On the tarmac below were two marked police cars, camera crews and, further back, journalists, all waiting for the gangster drug boss to descend. They stood for a moment while another cop checked his handcuffs. Dimi wasn't exactly from central casting. With his boyish haircut, baby face squinting in the summer glare, wearing baggy blue tracksuit bottoms and a t-shirt partly covered by a flak jacket, he looked like the boy next door. But he was still the star of this show.

Caieron grabbed him by the upper arm and walked down the stairs close to him, shoulders touching. Many cops stood around, including some with M16s. As Dimi was loaded into the back of a police car, Caieron shook hands with a couple, then jumped in before they took off. Both were heavily marked black federal police vehicles, with a strip of seven sirens across their roofs flashing and screaming. An agent sitting in the front of the vehicle carrying Dimi held an assault rifle, clearly visible through the window. It made for dramatic television.

Fifteen minutes later, the cars pulled into federal police headquarters, where camera crews were already filming. Dimi's car stopped outside the undercover car park, giving the media the chance to get their shots. As the back door was swung open, Dimi could be seen crouching inside.

Caieron moved in, the withering look on his face belying his euphoria. He grabbed Dimi by the upper arm and led him out. Dimi squinted in the hot sun, looking around at the guns and cameras. His face remained neutral, showing, if anything, just a hint of sardonic disbelief. Caieron gripped his arm, walking him across to the elevator, accompanied by three police-men dressed in black, holding assault rifles, and followed by camera crews.

As they waited for the lift, a bright light blazed in Dimi's face – a cameraman trying to get a better shot in the darkened car park. Dimi, known for his mellow politeness, looked up at the guy with an expression of incredulity. Caieron pulled him into the small lift, followed by the three policemen, squeezing in one after the other. As the doors were about to close another policeman, a chief who regularly dealt with the media, jumped in too. The crews got their final shot of Dimi, looking slightly vulnerable, squished in the back of the lift with no chance of escape – handcuffed, in a flak jacket, surrounded. It all left Dimi with no doubt that he was Caieron's prize catch.

Once upstairs, Caieron did some quick paperwork, then went off to an office for a press conference he'd called from São Paulo. The Florianópolis journalists had all been badly scooped by *O Globo* breaking the story. They wanted a piece of it. Dimi's dramatic arrival was a good start. Caieron also gave them a photo of Zeta, who he advised was a local guy who was part of the Florianópolis cell. They'd intended to arrest him, but he was now in America. Caieron exposed the kingpin who got away – local surfer Jorge Break, now on the run in Europe. He gave journalists a photo of Jorge lounging back, smiling, on a beach chair – probably in Bali, Caieron thought.

Meanwhile, Dimi was taken down to the police cells. He walked in and saw Rufino and Timi. No one smiled. This was so far from their dreams and usual catch-ups in Bali or Europe, or when Dimi flew down to Florianópolis to pack a surfboard bag and they'd have a nice dinner afterwards. Right now, the future looked bleak, but Dimi felt sure it wasn't over. They just needed to stay strong, stick together and shut the hell up.

When I got to jail, I met everybody. I say, 'Please don't give me up, don't give me up because Fernando Caieron doesn't have any proof. He doesn't know each one do anything. He only knows Timi because you stayed in jail in France. He only knows that; he catch you with what? If you say nothing, nothing is going to happen because he doesn't know.'

– Dimitrius

But Timi was angry, consumed with resentful thoughts. He was sure if these guys had paid people what they promised and looked after busted horses, they probably wouldn't have snitched. If they'd paid Gaspar what they'd owed, he wouldn't have skimped on the carbon fibre cloth and made those bad blow boards, and Rodrigo wouldn't be facing a firing squad. Timi was upset and scared. He knew the feds had a lot of intel, he'd already seen the rumoured book of surveillance photos.

People alert me about, 'Eh, Caieron has a book of you there, you have more photos than a top model. You and your friends have a top model book in Polícia Federal.' And then I saw when I was there in the office, shots to identify me, on the beach, in board shorts, in wetsuit, driving the car. Caieron's team follow me for a long time – a team of many agents – all those agents know who is Timi, who is Dimi, who is Rufino, who is Break. The police know all about my life.

– Timi

Rufino and Timi had already turned on each other, shouting and screaming in a vicious blame game.

Yelling, day and night, day and night, about the horses that were not ready to do a run and they put us in jail, like Cafiero. Like the other horses they didn't pay, money they didn't pay me. The other prisoners say, 'You will give problems for us in here, Playboy Operation. You discuss when you go back on the streets – okay?'

– Timi

Timi felt upset with Dimitrius too. He'd helped all these guys get rich when he only ever got small cash, and even then he had to pester them for it. He was fuming he'd chased them for six months and still they'd failed to pay him the last $5000 they owed – a lot of cash to him, one night at Hotel Unique for them. It meant he didn't have cash protection now to buy an expensive lawyer with a bag of tricks.

They piss on me. They don't give a fuck about me at that time, you know? These guys who must pay me, they don't consider me. They had the money but they didn't pay me, you understand? Even I needed a lawyer, even I got busted. They should pay me. It's my money. They should pay me my part of the money. I confuse friendship with this, I helped them so much. I help them to get a lot of money and for my small part of the business, they must pay me, they didn't pay me. They sometimes didn't pay horses. Those who have part of Rodrigo's drugs, they never felt anything when something bad happen with somebody. For them, it's a statistic, a number, score 3–1. My team make three goals and lost one.

– Timi

His bitter anger, tangled with fear and paranoia, was instantly spotted by Caieron. He had Timi brought up to his office for an interview, starting his usual show, using all the cards to inflame his terror and rage. Timi was smart – he could see what Caieron was doing – but it was working anyway. Timi glanced at the statements of Cafiero, Conte, Olaf, Renato. Caieron warned that Dimi would probably talk too. He was cornering Timi. He told him that phone records showed he'd been calling Cafiero, the pale surfer, many times right up until his bust. 'Why?' 'Just friends talking,' Timi replied. 'And I'm Santa Claus. Think the judge will believe that?' Caieron said.

Aware there were always cash disputes between these play-boys, Caieron taunted, 'Did these guys pay you what they owe? Are they paying for your lawyer now?'

He also used his trump-card photos. As soon as Timi denied knowing Big House and Jorge, he slapped a photo down on the table. 'Ah yeah, but in this photo, you're together, you're smiling, joking. Very friendly.' Then he used his ace. 'If Rodrigo Gularte gets executed, you will be charged with his murder.' It had the terrorising effect he'd hoped for.

Caieron put homicide on the table, making me feel heavy culpability. I already felt very bad and he exploited that. I really don't know if he can do that, but I didn't know about the consequences we get. But my lawyer says, 'No, no, no, take it easy.' But Caieron, 'You will pay for that homicide and all your friends get homicide.' I was really terrified about that possibility.

– Timi

Timi had already heard from other cops that they'd seen images of his car outside Rodrigo's flat the day before his run from security cameras in the petrol station opposite. Timi believed them because he was indeed there, and they also knew he'd driven a different model car that day.

Back in the cells, the agents didn't stop the pressure, feeding his fears and guilt over Rodrigo.

The police were always talking, saying about the family of Rodrigo, 'Hey, Timi, they have money, the mother will pay to kill you in prison.' They joke too. 'Eh, if she pays me, I will kill him now,' they joke. Everybody jokes ... but using psychological torture. Caieron, he's a son of a bitch. Fernando Caieron, bastard. Lying a lot, and I don't know what's real, what is not, you know? I thought that in one moment that I really could be responsible for homicide.

My conscience in that time was very heavy. I was fragile, vulnerable, you know, that time after Rodrigo was imprisoned. I felt very culpable, those boards they show every time on television, the boards of Rodrigo . . . I gave those boards to him, you know. A great part of what they accuse me I recognise my acts, my culpability.

– Timi

Timi was a nervous guy. I guess I told those guys, 'Listen, man, you sent someone to the death penalty. The guy is going to be shot and you guys hired him to do this, and you know Indonesia is the death penalty, would you like to answer for homicide?'

– Chief Caieron

Timi was ready to talk. He felt he owed nothing to his old school mates and they'd screwed him first – he wasn't going to wait for them to do it again.

We had good times together, we enjoyed very good times, very funny times together. We were really good friends, but this relationship by the drugs makes that friendship go down. These guys just seeing the money – they got blind by the money. I always treat that in a friendship level. They don't care about friendship. For them, they just looking for money, money, money. They are very ambitious for money. They got much money putting drugs in Europe – spending a lot, big hotels, but they don't pay the people they must pay. They didn't give the smallest part of payment, pay the little money, they don't pay all the horse – but me, they must pay me my money. I couldn't accept that, impossible. I'm not ambitious like them. I make much money for

370

them, and they didn't pay me my little part. It's nothing for them. That's why all the shit happened, cos they don't pay. They lie – even people in jail don't talk if they pay . . . and that's why they make the wrong thing, the wrong way. They don't care, they don't give a fuck about anything. No friendship, nothing.

So I was not gonna wait for them to talk about me to police. Was very possible they were going to fuck me, the same as Conte, today get a benefit and fuck me.

– Timi

Caieron twisted the knife. 'These guys, they don't pay you. They're sons of bitches, man. You trust them, but they are with the best lawyers. Will you wait for them to come here and fuck you . . . or will you try to defend yourself?'

Timi was ready. He would confess what he'd done for the promise of only one year in jail and the rest in home detention. He would talk about himself, aware he'd be implicating Jorge, Dimitrius and Rufino, but he refused to snitch on others like his good friend Gaspar, even for the promise of less time.

When Timi came back to the cells, Dimi saw him and knew. He walked into the corner of the cell, standing out of view of the CCTV cameras with his back against the wall, and urged him, 'Please don't give me up, why you going to give me up? No, no.'

It didn't work. Timi was talking.

Dimitrius was later sent out of the police cells to jail, so he couldn't influence Timi's decision. Now, Dimi knew things were bad.

I always think about this – make a certain amount of money, and start a business, and then stop. But when you get inside, things flow . . .

playboy life. You never let this thing go, so you keep doing it until you get death or jail.

– Dimitrius

None of the other friends from the old Joaquina surf crowd were talking. As much as Timi had his reasons for snitching, to them it was the ultimate sin – a dance with the devil. This was a war against the cops and they wouldn't cooperate, no matter what. As much as Caieron wanted to find out where Jorge was, those who knew – Dimitrius, Martino and Rufino – refused point blank to say one word about their friend.

Now Jorge was number one on Caieron's hit list. He would soon request Interpol issue a Red Notice for him, the closest thing that exists to an international arrest warrant. Jorge would be a wanted man in 192 countries, with almost nowhere to hide.

CHAPTER FORTY-FIVE

THE ONE THAT GOT AWAY

In Amsterdam, Jorge felt completely alone.

I woke up with a knock on my door — it was a cold, snowing morning. Pietro came into my apartment in a rush. He was pale and his eyes were wide. He told me right away what he'd seen on the internet and all my people were arrested.

I went to a cyber café to check the news and there was the reality of the facts, the Operation Playboy was launched, many of my partners busted and my picture was in all the newspapers and internet sites. The main TV news was exposing my name and picture as a wanted man. I felt cold, numb, a thousand thoughts rushed through my mind, the image of my family and friends pass like a film and the idea of never seeing them again, the feeling of never going back to your loved ones, to your own land, is devastating and unbearable. I understood the dimension of what was happening and I went home fast. It was not safe to be on the streets anymore. I was numb, dizzy, intoxicated by all that information, that change my life forever.

Looking around that apartment, I felt alone, because from my group, I was the only one in Europe. Vulnerable, because my picture was all over the internet, scared by the dimension of the bust and shame for my family and friends. I knew then, I had lost everything I'd left behind in Brazil: cars, jewellery, cash and drugs. But the most important, my mum, my family, Ana my lovely girl, and my friends. I was sure I would never see them again. I was alone in this huge apartment, empty, cold, very depressing, because I was used to seeing a lot of movement in the apartment, all the guys, all the parties, my partners and I celebrating our victories, successful scams – and I was alone. All my friends in jail and I was sitting in Amsterdam in this huge apartment by myself – was weird. I felt sad and frightened about my fragile freedom.

– Jorge

Jorge thought about the deep sense of nostalgia he'd felt when walking across the Friendship Bridge to Paraguay a few weeks earlier, looking back at the twinkling lights of Brazil. It had been a strong feeling of sadness, and he now realised that in his soul he'd already known the true poignancy of that moment.

I didn't know then, but I was running to become one of the most wanted men in Brazil, member of Interpol Red Notice list. I knew something was not right, and my instinct was telling me to keep moving, but I was not imagining that an avalanche of events was approaching. I was escaping from a huge operation that would change me and my life forever. I was leaving to never return, and I was going to a sinister and unknowing direction, where solitude and fear rule. I was left alone in the world with €28,000 and my clothes.

– Jorge

He knew he had to disappear. So he did.

EPILOGUE

DARCY

I spent two years, six months, and five days without anything.

When Darcy flew home from Portugal, he was in great shape after getting mentally and physically fit behind bars.

I felt good, I felt like Superman cos I was doing exercise, 200, 400 pushups and pullups every single day, and I was meditating every morning, asking 'Please, please let me hug my dad and my mum before they die.' That was my goal in life. For the rest of it, I didn't give a shit.

Are you tempted to run again?

No way. No way, after all I went through and all the suffering I witnessed from my whole family.

Darcy considers his time as a trafficker and his bust as a path to enlightenment. He is no longer addicted to blow and now lives a simple life, teaching English and surfing at Joaquina.

I fully accept my destiny. I fully accept who I am, and I know I did wrong things, and I am clear about the life I had. I was an idiot, but that was the way it had to be. I had to learn the hardest way. I believe I've been blessed since day one to go through all that to become the man I am now.

I had an addiction, to coke, alcohol, and I was just partying. My life was dark. If you're addicted to that shit, you're in a dark hole. At the time, it was like a party, it seems amazing, great – it wasn't. I paid for everything I did.

I'll tell you what, the journey goes on. I'm fit, I surf, I feel good. I have a clean mind and I don't owe anything to anyone. Life became very simple.

ZETA

Two weeks after the arrests of Dimi, Timi and Rufino, Zeta returned home to Brazil to face the music. He knew Chief Caieron had his arrest warrant and that if he'd stayed in America he'd be a fugitive wanted by Interpol, so he turned himself in at the Florianópolis federal police headquarters.

He spent 30 days in the police cells, with his mum regularly bringing him food. He was then released to await trial. He was convicted and sentenced to four years and four months but granted freedom while he appealed. He didn't do another day. The conviction was quashed, and even Dimitrius shook his head at Brazilian justice.

Zeta was free but he is the guy who, after Luis Alberto Cafiero arrived in Bali, is supposed to go there on the plane, sell the drug, take the money, come back. He got free. The judge says he has nothing to do with that. But he's the operations manager! Zeta got released, 'No you're not guilty' – but he pay for that ticket.

Because in Brazil, the justice, you pay [for] *influence.*

But fuck Dimi, they [police] *want to fuck Dimi because Rodrigo Gularte, because involved with Marco Archer. They think we are a corporation, drug corporation. But like I told you, many people, even the drug dealers, got mad about this. It's not a corporation, it's just a freelancer.*

– Dimitrius

DIMITRIUS

Dimitrius was sentenced to 15 years prison. He served a total of about three and a half years and was eventually acquitted on appeal, despite openly telling me on the record that he was a trafficker and a 'little boss'. Dimitrius believes his biggest blunder was using his real name in the game. 'My mistake was "Dimi". Could [have been] Peter, Paulo – can be John! Change names, so easy. Never think professional.'

RUFINO

Rufino was sentenced to ten years and eight months jail, but was allowed to remain free while appealing. One conviction was dropped but after appeal by the prosecution, the court upheld the original conviction and ordered Rufino's arrest. Rufino heard the news and fled. Then one weekend the feds heard he was back at his father's waterfront apartment, just up the road from the federal police building, and went to nab him. It turned into a high-speed car chase before they caught him. However, Rufino won his appeal and was acquitted.

CHIEF FERNANDO CAIERON

For Chief Caieron, these acquittals were a symptom of the Brazilian justice system.

That's the kind of game we are playing here. Sometimes it doesn't matter which kind of proof, or quality of proof or how much proof you had. Doesn't matter.

I did the best I could. I send all the evidence to the judge, I can't do the investigation and then be the judge.

Despite the sacrifices on his personal life, working sometimes around the clock on cases, he was fully aware that ultimately, it could all go up in smoke.

I mean, there is a lot of bribes in Brazil too. We federal police already made some operations showing that some judges were selling sentences. Not only one judge, not only one state, it was much more than once we show this. I mean, picture this – in Brazil a judge has to work 35 years, and after that he's going to be retired and will receive his salary every single month. But if a judge gets convicted for crimes, even if he worked only 3,4,5 years, he's going to be dismissed of his judiciary power, they are going to say you are not a judge anymore but you are going to receive your paycheck every month.

They made this law for themselves. If one day, they rob, steal, do whatever they want, they are not going to work as a judge but they get paid. I mean, the way I see, it's almost an invitation to sell some sentences, to get money off some guys being accused. Give it a try, man. What's the worst can happen? You don't have to work for the next 30 years and you're going to receive pay as if you're working.

And the dirty judge goes on a paid holiday for life?

Yep, yep, receiving the money as if he was actually working as a judge.

Would he go to jail?

Very rarely. They don't give a shit. Understand. Most of judges in Brazil obey the law – straight guys, but we have 20,000 judges in Brazil.

A lot of times, we face these justice problems. You can imagine how hard it is to be a federal police or even civil police in Brazil.

Chief Caieron's Operation Playboy resulted in more than 50 busts, including those made in other parts of Brazil as a direct result of intel he passed on.

He became well known for his work, and laughed at a story he heard about surfers sitting around sharing a joint, saying, 'Come on, let it go Caieron, let it go,' when someone was taking too much time to pass it on; a testament to Caieron's tenacity. Chief Caieron keeps fighting the good fight, sure that every small win is a step in the right direction.

MICH TOCCI

Mich Tocci turned himself in about two weeks after fleeing from his car during the highway chase with Chief Cesar. He didn't stay locked up for long. About a week later, on a Saturday night, he applied for, and was granted, release. Chief Cesar saw it as a Tocci tactic. In the first stages of a case, the judges are appointed randomly, so you can't ever be sure of getting a pliable judge, but on the weekends, only one judge is rostered on. Tocci waited and chose the judge he wanted.

On the Monday, another judge followed suit and released all the others Chief Cesar had busted, including Martino, horse Sandra and her brother Marc.

The lawyer of the other defendants said, 'Look, you have to extend this freedom of Tocci to our clients, cos Tocci is pointed out by police as one of the ringleaders of this organisation, so you have to extend freedom for the rest of the group.' And the judge said, 'Yes, I will,' and put everyone out.
– Chief Cesar

The defendants were outside awaiting a trial, and kept finding ways to delay it. Eventually, they faced court. Martino, Sandra and Marc were convicted and sentenced to two years and two months' jail, but because of the delays to get the case to trial, the judge applied the statute of limitations and allowed them to walk. All others were acquitted. Tocci was convicted and jailed for another drug crime in the time it took for this one to be heard.

Chief Cesar is philosophical about the result – he had to be.

Sandra was caught with the drugs. All the wire-taps showed the drug belonged to the others. It was quite clear to us, but for the justice . . .

I heard a lawyer in Florianópolis gives a lot of 'presents' to the judges in Brasília?

Yes, it's quite common.

It must be frustrating?

I also cannot understand, but it's the only way you can change things; do your part of the job and try to do it correctly. Okay, it's difficult, let's try to make it difficult for them. I have two daughters. I do this to try to change things for a better future. I know that it's quite difficult because it's the whole system, but every operation I take part in, I do my best.

– Chief Cesar

TIMI

Timi spent about a year in jail, then moved to home detention at his mum's place. He missed one curfew, and was sent back to jail for a few months.

DIEGO

Caieron kept his end of the bargain and wrote to the judge, requesting Diego's release as soon as he'd busted Andre, citing Diego's confession as a vital source of information. A lawyer then publicly claimed Chief Caieron had forced Diego to sign that statement, in the dark of night, to implicate Andre. Chief Caieron sued her to preserve his reputation and was successful. Before the damages were decided, the lawyer was executed – shot dead at point-blank range when she arrived home in her car one night. The killer shot her twice through her windscreen and several times through the driver's window before fleeing in a car. No arrests were made. Caieron felt sure it was a result of the lawsuit, that she was perhaps threatening the drug dealer who'd hired her to pay the damages or she would reveal their name.

SOLANA STAR

The ship that launched Andre's drug career when he was a university student had a tragic end. It was seized and sold by the police. Its name was then changed twice – *Charles Henri* and *Tunamar*. On its maiden voyage, *Tunamar* sank off the coast of Rio, killing 11 crew, adding to the popular superstition that it's bad luck to rename a ship.

Songs and documentaries have since been made about the 'summer of the can'.

TIZZY

He was sentenced to 4.5 years for the highway blow bust.

> *I did 25 months, one week and ten hours. I know that because I counted every minute.*

LUCAS

Lucas, who had flown to Bali with drugs and had the fight over surfboards in Schiphol with Jorge, was a well-known horse and boss but never convicted. He is now a police officer in Brazil.

ANDRE

Andre didn't stay in jail for long. He gave his lawyer US $50,000 to go to Brasília and buy a deal. A judge granted his freedom

120 days after he'd first been banged up. Caieron kept him under surveillance, sure he'd get back to work. Nineteen weeks later, Andre was back in jail, when his talking horse was busted with 3 kilos of blow at Florianópolis airport.

Three months later, Andre escaped. Five months after that, he gave himself up on advice of his lawyer, sure he'd probably get a light sentence. He got a shock, and 37 years. Fourteen months later, he paid a couple of guards US $10,000 to leave a door unlocked for ten minutes. He fled on a false passport, making it to Bali, then trying to go Sweden. He was busted en route in Amsterdam, then extradited back to Brazil. He again escaped to live as a fugitive.

MARCO

Marco Archer Cardoso Moreira – Curumim – was shot dead on Nusakambangan Island in January 2015. He was the first westerner to be executed in Indonesia and the first Brazilian ever to be executed.

I can't believe they fucking shoot him.

– Rafael

RODRIGO

Three months later, Rodrigo Gularte was executed by firing squad, alongside seven others – including Australians Andrew Chan and Myuran Sukumaran.

Sometimes I feel like – I killed him, you know, when I remember giving him those boards. I feel like I have Rodrigo's blood on my hands . . . I give to his hands those boards – that's the last time I saw him, when I gave those boards to him. And that's the cause of his death. Those boards.

– Timi

Anadolu Agency / Getty Images

Rodrigo in his coffin after execution. His cousin, Angelita Muxfeldt, checks the condition of his body at the hospital morgue in Jakarta.

He was my friend. We were sharing the same roofs, the same trips, the same experience. He was moved by adventure instinct, and its fuel adrenalin. He knew what he was doing, and the risk he was taking, and he was very very brave. After his bust, I flew from Bali with a selfish feeling that he could snitch and not even a word he spoke.

As much as I think about it, the less I understand what led us to send Rodrigo – how irresponsible and insane we've been.

– Jorge

It's crazy to get killed for this . . . I mean, it's insane, insane. Those guys are psycho, psycho.

– Chief Caieron

RAFAEL

Rafael was approached by one of the playboys to do another blow run to Bali just after Rodrigo's execution. He said no.

JORGE

There's no ex drug dealers, no ex prostitutes . . . that doesn't exist. Once you're a prostitute, you're always going to be a prostitute, once you're a drug dealer, you're always going to be a drug dealer. Guaranteed. There's no way back. That's my opinion.

Jorge vanished without a trace. The rest of his story remains untold – for now.

ACKNOWLEDGEMENTS

Many people have helped me to make this book happen.

My heartfelt thanks to all those who trusted me with their stories. Particular mention goes to a few on both sides of the law. Extra special thanks to Chief Fernando Caieron for his series of interviews over several years which gave me the springboard for this book. His openness in giving details was crucial to putting together the jigsaw of Operation Playboy. To Chief Fernando Cesar for his time in Brasília, and federal agent Bernardo Girotto for his insights. On the playboy side: a huge thanks to Jorge for his stark honesty in untiring interviews and showing me inside his world, to Timi who laid himself bare sometimes getting very emotional reliving the still raw stories, to Andre, Darcy, Dimitirus, Rafael, Tizzy and the late Marco Archer for revealing some of their most poignant moments.

Deepest thanks to Sydney journalist Malcolm Holland, who's been a constant support and sounding board for the past five years, and for casting his sharp eye over chapters.

Big thanks to Melbourne journalist James Foster for his help with everything from giving his regular opinions, sometimes brutal and always helpful, to looking over the final pages.

Thanks to Rio journalist and blogger Hugo Cals for his keen and enthusiastic research and tenacity. A delight to work with. My gratitude also to Rio lawyer João Balthazar de Mattos, and to Portuguese translators Wanda Dall Agnola, Daniela Ortega and Tracy Blanchard.

Thanks to my mum Sue Bonella and sister Simone Bonella for being my test readers.

Finally, thanks to the Pan Macmillan team, especially Head of Non-fiction Ingrid Ohlsson for giving me the freedom and time to write this book and for her insightful opinions; to Senior Editor Georgia Douglas who has done a fantastic job in the final months with everything from gentle whip cracking to great editing advice; and editors Jo Jarrah and Libby Turner.

Thank you!

*

Chief Fernando Caieron wishes to acknowledge his core Operation Playboy team. 'They were an excellent hard-working team.' Jair, Cintra, Bernardo, Paulo Ricardo, Bona, Heitor, Villar, Pilguer, Oyama, Topor, Lagos, Gueller, Silvio, João Vieira, Mirapalheta, Copetti, Ortiz and Silnei and administrator Simas.